The Dollar-A-Year Principal

Miracle at Munson

The Dollar-A-Year Principal

Miracle at Munson

John Dunworth

Watersun Publishing Company, Inc.
Swampscott, Massachusetts

Library of Congress Catalog Card Number
00-130150

Copyright © 2000 by Watersun Publishing Company, Inc.
www.watersunpublishing.com

Interior design and typesetting by Maureen Dempsey; cover
design by Hannus Design Associates.

ISBN 0-9628917-4-6

5   4   3   2   1

Dedicated to

Richard Angus McKenzie

1948–1997

Nephew and Teacher

Loved by All Who Knew Him

Table of Contents

Table of Contents

Preface

In 1997, a public school in Northwest Florida was floundering so badly that it faced imminent closure. Closing the school would mean hardship for the children and families involved and the inevitable demise of the community itself. The situation seemed hopeless.

What would have to be done to turn the situation around?

Could a plan be devised to meet the challenge?

Could test scores be raised?

Could costs be contained?

Could faith be restored?

Could the school really be saved and could it be saved in time?

The answers to these questions and what happened to the children, teachers, principal and families as well as others involved with Munson Elementary School is what this book is about. It tells the story from different perspectives and it teaches many lessons.

The national focus on the performance of the nation's schools as well as the crisis in confidence facing America's teachers and educational institutions makes the message of Munson Elementary particularly timely. Today, many schools face devastating ultimatums, many politically motivated. *The Dollar-A-Year Principal: Miracle at Munson* is the response of one school to an ultimatum motivated by undeniable reality that was devastating in its finality.

I must warn you that this book is different, certainly for a current book about schools and schooling; it is positive, supportive and encouraging. Some say inspiring. If you permit, it will reach the inner recesses of your "heart and mind," perhaps even your soul. I did not intend for it to be this way, but I had a very special experience at Munson Elementary. We all did. I have described it as the best year of my life. *The Dollar-A-Year Principal* shares this experience and in the process shares the secrets of good schools and how you and your community can have the best schools in the nation. I only hope that experiencing this story through these pages enriches your life as much as living the story enriched ours.

Dr. John Dunworth

Acknowledgments

This is a story that had to be told and a book that had to be written. All of my friends and associates far and wide believed the story should be told. "It is a wonderful story," they would say. "It contains so many lessons." I agreed. Colleagues in The West Florida Literary Federation were particularly enthusiastic about my effort—and this group includes some fine writers. However, telling the story, I would quickly learn, would be easier said than done. Is it really possible to capture in words what happened in the hearts and souls of the wonderful people who *are* the Munson story? I wondered.

There are those who believed it possible and enthusiastically responded to my very first attempts. I think of Mrs. Mimi Schroeder, a superbly sensitive writer in her own right, whose subtle guidance and review of my early work inspired me to continue. I will be forever grateful to Mimi. Mrs. Gail Baxley at Munson would take weekends and painstakingly transcribe my early scribbles to the electronic version required in today's world. No easy task. Her work was invaluable. Mrs. Ruth Tempest, an author and serious literary critic, reviewed Part I and graciously provided many helpful suggestions for which I am most appreciative. They contributed greatly to the quality and clarity of the manuscript.

I owe a particular debt of gratitude to Mrs. Julie Cameron, a communications specialist and editor. Julie coordinated the entire effort, edited much of the copy, and provided the technical expertise to bring the work to fruition. I can't thank Julie enough for taking on this demanding assignment. To the publisher, Mr. Paul

Solaqua of Watersun Publishing Company, Inc., I owe much. His enthusiastic response to the draft manuscript and his faith in the author were a constant inspiration as the book was fine-tuned for publication.

My long-suffering wife, Lavona, deserves my unending gratitude. She supported me through the long "Munson year" and again through the equally long "year of the book." Without her love this story would not have been possible. For Lavona's support came in many forms—as a professional educator, as an author, as a helper, and as a loving partner. I will always be deeply grateful.

And of course, to our cats Molly and Polly I will be in debt forever. For they have advised me in no uncertain terms I have the rest of my life to make up for my absence and seeming disregard for their wishes and needs. Royalty expects to be treated royally. So be it.

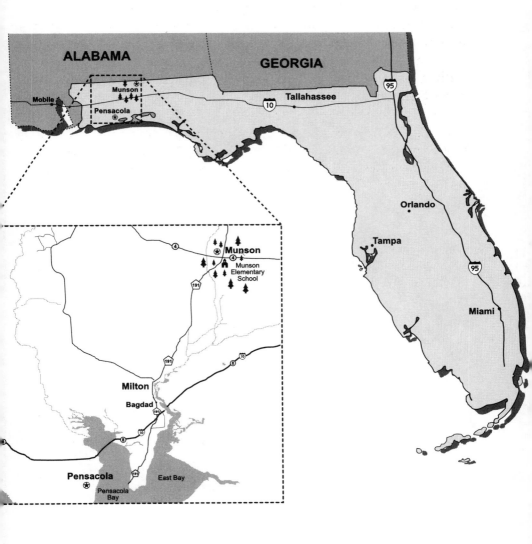

Munson, Florida

Author's Note

Names and stories directly related to children and parents
have been changed sufficiently to protect the identities and the
privacy of the children and the families involved. However, even
with modifications, every effort has been made to convey the real
meaning of the occasion. All other names and events are as accurate as my memory and notes allow, which according to a very
close member of my family, isn't saying too much!

Introduction

by Daniel A. Talany, Ed.D.

I remember the afternoon when I received the call. It is not that I haven't received the call before. From time to time Paul Solaqua of Watersun Publishing Company, Inc. has contacted me to ask if I would be interested in reading a manuscript. So, when my secretary indicated it was Paul, I knew he was probably calling about a manuscript. This time, however, there was something about the conversation that piqued my interest.

He said, "Dan, this one is different, like something I've never asked you to read before. This isn't a typical book. It's a story. I thought of you when it came to me. I think you're going to like the story. I hope you will agree to read it. I don't think you'll be disappointed."

In my previous experiences with Paul, he had never been as suggestive about a manuscript as he was on this day. What struck me most was that I felt he was working hard to hold back his enthusiasm. He talked about how this was a great story and he wanted to look at ways to make it work. He really did not need to talk very long when I interjected, "Absolutely, I'd love to read it." Our conversation briefly went over the basics I had come to anticipate, but it was how Paul continued to hint about the story and not what his words said that generated eagerness in me to read it. I know Paul realized I was keenly interested and so he didn't have to say much more. Paul knew what he had, and he knew that I sensed it. It was just a matter of Priority Mail.

Less than two days afterward, the U.S. Postal Service envelope arrived at my office and as soon as I had a spare moment I closed my door, sat at my desk, and opened it. I was excited in a strange kind of way but I didn't know why. I told myself that the heightened anticipation was likely unfounded. Let's face it. Paul had told me that the manuscript was a story about a school that was saved from closing as told by the principal. I said to myself, "Why am I tearing this open now when I should be doing important things?" The manuscript was a two-inch thick pile of double-spaced typed pages with a most intriguing title. I looked at my clock and gauged how much time I had and rolled back in my chair with the manuscript in my hands. I thought for a moment that there are probably some unique circumstances in the book that merit note and the story line seems quite appealing. But what could there be to justify this level of anticipation? Why was I compelled to start reading it now, when it could surely wait?

I looked down and I reread the title, *The Dollar-A-Year Principal*. Now that catches your eye, especially if you're a practicing school principal, as I am. I thought out loud to myself, tongue-in-cheek, "I hope this isn't an omen about my next annual review!" Obviously and thankfully, it would not be. As I really didn't have much time to read it then, I told myself that I'd make time later. But as I got up and put the papers off to the side in the pile of materials I have for "take-home," my curiosity got the better of me.

I was able to read the first chapter about the circumstances of the story and now I wanted to know about what had to be a "happy ending" for Munson Elementary School. Although I wanted to continue reading, I realized I had stolen too much time and I was late for a meeting. I re-bound the manuscript with a couple of rubber bands, placed it in my briefcase rather than in my "take-home," and went back to work. For the rest of the day, my mind returned to the story and that night after domestic routines and responsibilities afforded me discretionary time, I read it.

I read the entire manuscript in one sitting. I couldn't put it down.

The Dollar-A-Year Principal is a wonderful story about one man's experience with a school and a community filled with hope for its children and future. More than this, the story is **a *metaphor* for education**. It brings with it many lessons and reminds us of what education should be about.

I actually read the story twice more during the next three days. The story itself is wonderfully told in a style that relaxed me, yet compelled me to reflect on who I was and what I was all about. Reading it again and again was easy because with each reading a new connection, revelation, and insight emerged. I saw in this simple story implications for us as parents, for us as educators, and for us who make decisions about educating our children. Every episode carried with it a message about what we need to know, believe, and do to educate children. The lessons showcased what effective leadership can do.

There are lessons in this story for everyone who has a stake in education. Teachers and principals will surely recognize the lessons John Dunworth has so eloquently painted on the canvas of the Munson Elementary School story. Parents and communities, as well as policy makers who read the story can find much to consider about their attitudes, roles, and responsibilities. If education is about hope for the future, then the story of John Dunworth and Munson Elementary School is a living *metaphor* for that hope.

The manuscript I read so eagerly that day is now a full book with a mosaic of the author's experiences that prepared him for Munson Elementary; the teachers delightfully telling "how it really was" from their perspective and Dr. Rex Schmid addressing current issues of assessment and high stakes testing. The disturbing impact of these tests on schools and children gives cause to reconsider our dependency on such instruments for measuring children's success in learning. In addition, the book highlights the Dollar-A-Year Principal's Principles—the foundation of the author's beliefs about schools and schooling. These powerful statements are as easy to understand as they are to remember and are, in reality, the secrets of a good school. I recommend them to every school in the nation.

In the last section of the book, I have been invited to share with you some of the messages I received from this story, and the lessons I learned from it. These messages and lessons will be nothing more than one elementary school principal's reflection and insight about a story that moved him. I cannot assume nor expect that anyone else could feel or will feel the same way about the story as I do. The story of *The Dollar-A-Year Principal* reached out to me in a way that is unique to who I am and what I do. It will likely do the same for anyone who is interested in the education of our nation's children. It will mean different things to different individuals. Every reader will make different connections and come to different conclusions. But the lessons about responsibility, purpose, and commitment will be the same for everyone. The educational metaphors of this story are individual in their applications, but universal in their implications. That is what makes this a special story. That is why it was special to me and I believe it will be special to you.

Part I

The Story

Munson Elementary School

Chapter I

In the Beginning

The Call

It's a heavy, hot humid day. The shade of the trees, particularly the big oaks, suggests that the small building would be a haven from the sticky heat.

A mother approaches with her three little ones—all hot, all sweaty, all tired. The children are clean, but frayed edges and faded shirts go with the old pick-up truck and the housedress that has been washed too many times. The eyes are tired but the look is wistful, searching, hopeful. The smile is kind. The children, with their questioning eyes and clinging hands, are not sure. After all, it *is* a school.

As I look out at the little group approaching to register even before school has started, I am reminded that there is much poverty and disparity in America. But there is also hope and opportunity and the lessons that make us free.

The door opens.
I welcome the family warmly.
I work here.
I am the principal. They call me Dr. D.

I haven't always been the principal of this little school in rural Florida called Munson Elementary School. As a matter of fact, until a few weeks ago I was living the life of a retired educator in a neighboring county with my wife, Lavona, and our two cats, Molly and Polly. For five years I had served on the Board of Directors of the Pensacola Symphony Orchestra, chaired its development committee and generally kept busy with some professional involvement, travel, reading, writing, and the usual activities of retirement.

Lavona had just completed her term as president of a distinguished organization called Les Harlequins, and we were catching our breath between responsibilities. Perhaps we were vulnerable.

Then it happened. On June 26, 1997, the *Pensacola (Florida) News Journal* published the following story reporting the imminent decision of the Santa Rosa County Board of Education to officially close little Munson Elementary School:

> *Residents Fight to Save Their School*
>
> *The fate of an elementary school that has served generations of Munson families will be decided tonight following a public hearing.*
>
> *The Santa Rosa County School Board will vote on whether to close down Munson Elementary School, a school plagued by low test scores and enrollment, district officials said.*
>
> *"Munson residents won't let that happen without a fight," said Charles James, who plans to attend the hearing. "Ever since we found out about this, it's been the only thing on anybody's mind," said James, 36, who*

attended the school and has a daughter, Valerie, 10, who now goes there.

At the Munson Country Store, the time and date of the meeting is written on a marker board outside the front door. Fliers are posted at the store, asking people who aren't sending their children to the school to enroll them so student numbers will increase. If the school closes, the 80 or so current students will be sent to schools 20 or more miles away.

"We don't look forward to ever closing a neighborhood school," said Benny Russell, school superintendent. "But when it comes down to the basic facts, the enrollment is down and the test scores are the lowest in the county."

The school has averaged 87 students since 1990, but is projected to drop to 67 next year. Per student cost is $6,078 compared to the district average of $3,507. Munson residents counter this is just a down year for the school that has served their community for 73 years. And they worry what will happen to their community if the school, which serves as the area's only meeting place and social center, is no longer there. The community's high school was closed in 1983.

Lucy Quina, "Residents Fight to Save Their School," *Pensacola (Florida) News Journal*, 26 June 1997, reprinted with permission.

Phrases such as "close down," "will be decided tonight," "served the community for 73 years," and "students will be sent to schools 20 or more miles away" triggered an immediate response. The realities also initiated some very careful thought. Lowest test scores, high per pupil costs, and declining enrollment were sobering facts. But for some reason, almost in a blink of my glaucomatous eyes, I decided to try to help save little Munson

Elementary School from extinction. It was probably the easiest decision I had ever made. It was clear, unclouded, certain.

I have served in many roles in education including those of teacher, principal and even college president. Schools are my bread and butter. The same for Mrs. Dunworth. I had the time. I had the experience. I had the will and I was presumptuous enough to believe that I could turn the situation around. If my health would hold, I knew I should try.

My wife, a wise, insightful, wonderful person, said, "Go for it." It would, of course, change our lives, interrupt the golden years of retirement, put an end to travel and all the pleasant things couples do together when they finally have the time to really share life. We would be apart when we wanted and needed to be together. It would be hard.

My plan was to offer to serve as principal of Munson Elementary School for one school year at a salary of $1 per year.

I called the superintendent's office late the same afternoon. We knew each other professionally, but not well. Mr. Russell had left his office, but as a former superintendent of schools, I was certain he would be at home preparing for the fateful board meeting. I pressured his secretary, but she protected him well, as she should. I called a number that I was not even sure was for his home. A pleasant woman's voice answered with just the right amount of cordiality as well as reserve. Obviously, the superintendent's wife was in her helpful but protective mode. How many times had my own wife played this same part?

Mr. Russell came to the phone and I told him who I was and what I was proposing. At first there was silence, dead silence. Public officials receive quite a few strange calls. Then an incredulous, "Are you serious?"

I assured him that I was. We talked. His own ideas to cut budget, cut staff, cut buses and at the same time develop a strong instructional program paralleled my own. Of course, it would be easier to say than to do. He suggested we get together as soon as possible.

The board of education met that night. The public was heard. Recommendations were made, action was taken and the little school was to remain open for the 1997–98 school year. Munson

Elementary School received a one-year reprieve. The press referred to it as a "make-or-break year."

A few days later, Benny (we were on a first-name basis now) called it a miracle. The school desperately needed on-site leadership. It was the right decision, and somehow I knew it. It was also a daunting undertaking, however, given the time and the task.

On July 10, the board of education met and took action on my appointment as principal at a salary of $1 per year with some reimbursement for gasoline. (Our home was almost 40 miles from the school.) A three-page contract followed, generally outlining the benefits I would *not* receive.

Naturally, I would be subject to all the rules and regulations of the board of education and the superintendent of schools. The $1 meant that I would be accountable. It was official.

Only two weeks had passed since the *News Journal* article and the telephone call that would change the lives of so many people, as well as two cats. I told the board that night that I was honored to become a part of the Santa Rosa County School District. I explained that our focus would be on basic skills, hard work, and a renewed partnership with parents and the community—that we would try to become the kind of school to which they would want to send their sons and daughters and a school they would want to attend. I pointed out that rural America had been hit hard in this century, that too many small schools had been closed, and that in education bigger is not necessarily better. I stressed that in some situations, smaller can be much better and at the same time economically viable. I said I believed Munson Elementary School could be a fine school and still operate at a reasonable cost, and I pledged everything in my power to make it so, and soon. Then I went home. But I did not sleep.

Lavona and I had traveled to Munson on the previous Sunday afternoon. We stood there together, looked at the beautiful forest and the empty little school and wondered silently, "Could it be done?" We held hands and we prayed.

The Bureaucracy

"Through that door," the uniformed voice orders in a tone that is accustomed to being obeyed. The heavy odor of human bodies, of sweat and fear and disinfectant confirm that I am in the right place, and that this really is the County Jail.

Fingers are inked, rolled, soaped, and wiped.

"Five dollars," the hard voice intones.

It doesn't smile. I don't linger. It feels like a hard slap across the face with a wet towel. It is the bureaucracy.

One of the first official actions I have to take is to file for appropriate state certification to become a principal in Florida. This requires transcripts back to my undergraduate days following WWII, an application form and a $56 fee.

At $1 a year, I will need to work for more than 56 years to recoup just that one expense. Transcripts aren't free either. Added to that is $40 for a security check, which I fully endorse, as well as the $5 for fingerprinting at the local jail. I now have to work over 100 years just to break even!

Given that I hold a doctorate in educational administration, served as president of George Peabody College for Teachers in Nashville, Tennessee, was dean of education and professor of educational administration at the University of West Florida, and am fully and currently certified as a principal (and almost everything else) in the state of California, it all seems rather redundant. But redundancy is what bureaucracy is all about. As they say in the Far East, "Bend with the bamboo." It is a helpful saying, and I use it several times while getting through the process. I also use some other words. They really help.

Meetings are immediately scheduled with Benny and his staff to clarify issues, responsibilities, and goals. Although it is not stated quite this way, flexibility is graciously built into the schedule to accommodate the aging principal. However, eleven-hour days will not provide much opportunity for "flex" time.

It is at these meetings that I learn that Munson Elementary has not had a full-time principal since 1993. The principal of Central High School, 22 miles from Munson, held the title and stopped by the little school a couple of times a week for relatively short periods. Being principal of a high school, even a small high school, is a full-time responsibility. The same goes for an elementary school. I also learn that most of the teachers have taught at Munson for many years but in anticipation of the school being closed are now in new assignments throughout the system.

Serious attention is given to the eventual transition of leadership when the "make-or-break year" reaches a successful conclusion. No one discusses what will happen if it is not successful; there is just a brief silence and downcast eyes. We all know that if we are successful, Munson will not need an abrupt change in leadership at the close of the year. The school will be an emerging new entity, somewhat fragile, in need of nurturing and not the buffeting winds of change.

To provide continuity in leadership, the superintendent appoints a teacher/assistant principal. His name is David Johnson. It is a wise decision; David Johnson will be a key player in the drama of Munson Elementary School.

The "must do" list is endless. New teachers have to be employed. We are authorized four teachers, including David—one less than last year. Our teacher assistants were reduced from three to two, and our buses were cut from five to three (later changed to four). Fiscal reality is a hard taskmaster, but a necessary one.

For now, there will be no physical education teacher, no media specialist for our library and computer lab, and no guidance counselor. Teachers will have to be multi-talented. In addition, there will be little help for our special students, and I understand there are a bunch of them. I wonder why?

In some ways, we are returning to the "four-room school" of yesteryear. But our plumbing is much better. Many children received a superb education in those little schools. Some children, regretfully, did not. We can learn much from the past.

Mr. Johnson

I think about David Johnson, the newly appointed teacher/ assistant principal. David has the reputation of being an absolutely outstanding elementary school teacher. He is also very well grounded in computer technology and its application in the educational setting. This will be important at Munson. In addition, he has completed his master's degree in educational leadership and is ready to begin the shift from the classroom to a principalship. Most importantly, he is willing to take the professional risks that are involved in saving Munson Elementary School.

We meet for the first time, his thick hair and groomed beard contrasting with my balding head. He is the father of three, and is married to a very fine teacher. They worked in the same school. They will miss each other in his new role. I wonder what it feels like for this modest, highly competent man to be working with a principal old enough to be his father.

What can he learn from me? The wisdom of the sages? Ha, would that it were so. To be principal, he will learn:

the application of judgment,

the time to compromise and the time to stand,

the time to reward and the time to punish,

the time to spend and the time to save.

He will learn to live with one foot in the present and the other in the future.

I hope he will learn not to overthrow first base; not to make a federal case of every disturbing incident; when to let the water roll off his back.

He will learn:

when to listen and when to speak,

when to cry and when to laugh,

when to wait and when to act,

and when to dare.

He will know failure and he will know success. He will learn about "administrivia" until he is nauseated. As a teacher, he knows most of these things now, but he will learn to apply them in new situations: with employees, patrons, bullies and bosses. But the goal is the same—the success of the children for whom he is responsible. He will learn to measure every decision in terms of its contribution to children. He will be uncompromising in this. He will be fully absorbed. He will experience fear, sadness and frustration, but also great joy. He will succeed and he will be fulfilled. It will be his life.

Being an administrator means that you carry the responsibility— there is no one else. It also means that you make the decisions, fast and under pressure. They had better be good ones, for there is no time to change.

We plan, we set specific objectives, and we go to work. I rise daily before 5 a.m., leave by 6 a.m. and arrive a little before 7 a.m. depending on traffic and weather. The cats don't like it.

Most days are a blur. There are not many days left until the opening of school and at the present time, there are no teachers except David, few supplies, a paucity of appropriate textbooks and a shortage of current instructional materials. Instructional television is on the horizon but not operational. The school has yet to be wired for ITV. Some computers function, some do not. Software is in disarray. Almost everything is in disarray. Deferred maintenance is everywhere. And although there are actually eight available classrooms, they are very small. Several are not used. Classrooms have no windows except for a small transom over one door. Lights are dim. It could be a pretty school, but looks remarkably like an ugly school—something akin to a prison cellblock. In fact, the rumor was that it was to become a prison.

A walk down the hall suggests a rural town that has been hit by a big super store with every other store closed and boarded up. The feeling is that the place is going out of business, the same feeling that is projected from our dark empty classrooms. Teachers need instructional space and our town needs to use its "boarded up stores." Down comes a wall. Two small classrooms become one beautiful classroom. This must happen three more times in the next ten days.

Can we beat the clock and the calendar? We must. The minute hand used to move at what seemed like 120 minutes to the hour. The pace was slow and time had a heavy liquid feel about it. Life, on most days, was languid. Not now. Now each minute is fleeting, like a wisp to be grasped. So much to do but not enough of these precious units. Oh, to slow the minute hand. But it refuses. If anything, it is increasing its speed. I can feel it.

Where We Live

In some measure, we all live in enclaves of compatible conspirators. Or at least we try to. Overstated, we are for social reform or against social reform. We might be for reasonable taxation or against taxes, for choice or against choice. We like being with others who view the world as we do, whose God is the same as our

God, whose tastes are the same as our tastes, whose traditions are
the same as our traditions, and whose causes are the same as our
causes. We accept diversity in small doses. Sometimes we do not
accept it at all. If you want to break out of that mold, you relocate
to urban America—except you don't break out; you merely join a
new enclave. If you want to preserve the mold, consciously or
unconsciously, you may live in rural America and try to protect that
world. The changes of modern times make it difficult but you try.
You don't usually join an enclave in rural America; you are born
into one or you may marry into one. It is a stable world. The little
school is in rural America. More specifically, it is in the rural
South.

Place, Past, Partners

When traveling north from Milton, you approach the gentle
rise on Munson Highway and see the small yellow sign showing
two children; you know you soon will arrive at the little school. A
clearing in the trees, the sign "Munson Elementary School," the
long and somewhat stately approach to the parking area, and the
low profile building nestled in the trees tells you this is the place.
A small, attractive courtyard with shrubs and grass neatly frames
the flagpole with the flags of state and country fluttering gently in
the light breeze. Several other buildings suggest older times and
past service. Crossing the courtyard, you reach the entrance to the
"main building," our four-room school in the Blackwater River
State Forest. It is said to be the smallest public school in the state
of Florida and it is located in its largest forest.

We say "four rooms" because there will be four classrooms
and four teachers. There are other rooms and a small office, but it
is really a four-room school, albeit a modern four-room school.

In my mind's eye, I occasionally see a glimpse of a rural school
of old—wood frame, steps up to the door, a wisp of smoke slowly
curling upward. The pot-bellied stove is glowing on this cold
morning. The lessons are hard.

The ancestors of our little school go back to those days as do
some of our families. In a real sense, Munson Elementary School

has been part of this community since the very beginning. Classes were first held in the company commissary owned by Bagdad Land and Lumber when the company built a logging community, known as Munson, in 1912.

More than a decade later, in 1924, a fine two-story brick school was completed, serving young people through twelve grades. It was called "Munson Consolidated Agricultural School" and graduated its first class in 1930. An impressive framed old photograph of the school hangs in my office along with a print of Winslow Homer's famous "Snap the Whip: A Memorable Image of Childhood in Rural America." I note that this school was founded in 1924, and I was founded in 1924—no doubt coincidence. I would like to believe that we both have a future.

Other buildings were added over the years: a cafeteria in 1952, a vocational/agricultural shop in 1953, a library in 1957 and a gymnasium in 1962. The small cafeteria still stands and is used extensively. The library is now a so-called multi-purpose room with termites, and the vocational/agricultural shops have been allowed to deteriorate and only serve for storage. The gymnasium stands proudly, showing the ravages of age on the outside but still strong on the inside. How many roaring victories has she witnessed? How many sad defeats? What stories might she tell?

Only a day or so ago, a graduate of Munson visited in my office. He was big, burly and strong—a man of the forest. "I can't tell you how many times as a boy I had to bend over that desk because I wore the wrong shoes on the gym floor!" He smiled, recalling what nostalgically seemed like pleasant rather than unpleasant memories. "That floor is pretty special; still is." He added, "And our kids had better take good care of it." I thought there might be an implied message for the principal and I smiled too. It is a beautiful floor and a fine gym and I share his pride.

On Sunday, January 14, 1973, the fine two-story brick school was completely destroyed by fire along with all the school records. It was a day of despair; but not for long.

These were fiercely determined people and, as their forefathers before them, showed this aspect of their character in time of tragedy. Our country became great because of the strength, determination, backbreaking hard work and the resourcefulness of the men and women of rural America. Although poor, they took sustenance from the land. There was heartache, fear, sickness and death and yet they prevailed. They were weary but they had faith. They helped one another. They were family.

Therefore, it wasn't too surprising that one week after the disastrous fire in 1973, the school reopened. Temporary walls were installed in the gymnasium to create classrooms and the "school" emerged. In 1975, a new facility, the school that is here today, opened. Everyone was very proud. It had carpet throughout and central heating and cooling. The compressors and other parts have since been replaced but the carpet is here today after almost 22 years of dedicated service. Although worn in places and patched in others, it still looks bright and inviting.

In a budget-cutting move in 1983, older students were sent to a neighboring high school and the little school officially became Munson Elementary School.

Munson itself consists of one church, the offices of the Blackwater River State Forest, a volunteer fire department, the Country Store and the little school. There is no city or town or shopping area—except for the Country Store. It's the kind of place that offers fried okra. Loyalty to "Munson" primarily represents the long years of identification with Munson High and later Munson Elementary, not to a town or village. There are several churches in our attendance area but only one elementary school. The attendance zone for Munson Elementary is more than twenty-five miles long and ten miles wide and its legal boundaries read like the field notes of a wilderness explorer:

> *Begin at the point where Dixon Creek crosses the Ala-*
> *bama-Florida state line (Section 25, T6N, R28W); fol-*
> *low the meandering of said creek in a southerly direc-*
> *tion until the intersection with Coldwater Creek (Section*
> *32, T5N, R27W); follow the meandering of Coldwater*
> *Creek in a southerly direction to the intersection with*
> *Blackwater River (Section 17, T2N, R27W); follow*
> *Blackwater in a northeasterly direction to intersection*
> *with the east boundary line of Santa Rosa County; fol-*
> *low east boundary line of Santa Rosa County in a*

northerly direction to the Alabama-Florida state line;
follow the state line in a westerly direction to the point
of beginning.

There are reported to be 2,500 people who live in this 250-square-mile area, ten folks to a square mile. Fifteen hundred are registered voters. As with the rest of the country, not many vote. Sixty-seven families have children currently attending Munson Elementary. When Munson children go home after school, they may not see another child until they return to school. Those who have a brother or sister are fortunate.

Housing is generally sparse and modest. There are a few homesteads with working farms but not many. There are also some new modern homes, even a few pools. There are no two-story homes that I have been able to identify but there are many homes with wheels. It seems that mobile homes are the most popular form of housing.

For the old families who attended Munson High School and for their children and extended families, there is no question that the little school is in many ways a community center. The gym is used by the local sports association. If you are married near here, your reception in all probability will be held in the multi-purpose room or the cafeteria. If you enjoy clogging, a class is available in the evening at the little school. And if you like great food, you will visit around Thanksgiving and Christmas time when the cafeteria offers, at a reasonable cost, a home-cooked turkey dinner for about a hundred people. As a meeting place, recreation center, adult learning center or social center, the little school plays an important part in the life of the area.

There is clearly a partnership with the past. And when you look into the faces of little children, there is just as clearly a partnership with the future. In a way, the little school is a fragile link. So many of those links have been broken in America; we pray this one will remain strong.

The Dream Team

Forty teachers apply to teach specifically at Munson Elementary School. Santa Rosa County Schools are highly respected, and recruiting well-prepared teachers is not a problem. But 40 candidates are willing to take on such a horrendous task. The challenge, the opportunity to be part of saving this little school, the desire to be where they are desperately needed, must have been motivating factors.

The interview team will be Nancy Welch, the director of elementary schools, David Johnson, and myself. Preliminary screening is conducted and the interviews scheduled. We all know that the decisions we make here will be the determining factor in the success or failure of the undertaking.

Nancy Welch is a precise and penetrating interviewer—very skillful and very thorough. David, with his 19 years in the classroom, knows exactly the areas to explore, the skills that must be evident and particularly the technical knowledge that will be essential given the realities at the little school. My task is to probe in all areas, to synthesize responses and to see the "person" as well as the "professional." Experience is an invaluable aid in both this process and in making the final decision that will match the competencies and qualities of each candidate with the very special needs of Munson Elementary School. While I draw on the expertise of both Nancy and David, I am mindful of the fact that the final decision and responsibility are mine and mine alone. They are tough interviews—demanding on the applicants and demanding on the interviewers. And so it should be, for not only is much at stake, everything is at stake.

Interviews are completed, decisions made, and the Dream Team established. And what a team. When we succeed—and we will—it will be the teachers who, with parents, volunteers, and the children themselves, will deserve the credit. Many other dedicated and concerned people will work very hard and long to assist; but the knowledge, the skill, the creativity, the perseverance and the courage, as well as the stamina, the sacrifice and the love and caring of these teachers will determine the final outcome. They are Mrs. Davina Sanders, Mrs. Elizabeth Coogle, Mrs.

Alisa Rogaliner, and of course, Mr. David Johnson. They will be in God's Hall of Fame.

The Meeting

The superintendent requests that a community meeting be called one evening soon to review the school board's decision and to introduce the new dollar-a-year principal to the local community. I ask the school secretary, Virginia "Judy" Lindsey, how such a meeting would be announced; how would they get the word out?

"Why, the Country Store, of course," she says. In this area, news, all kinds of news, travels fast even when you don't want it to. In fact, that kind of information travels the fastest. Posters are put up in the Country Store, the word is passed, and signs are placed on the schoolhouse door. We are "fixin" to have us a meeting, and we do.

The superintendent, three members of the county board of education, several other dignitaries, and David Johnson and I, along with a host of folks from the community and a few children, make up the group. We meet in the cafeteria and the room is full.

It helps to remember that the superintendent of schools is an elected official. Benny Russell is a fine educator, highly trained and experienced with a deep concern for children and youth. He is also a very successful and adroit politician. In fact, he was born and raised in these parts and is proud of it. That pride shows and is a warm message to an audience in Munson. Of course, back in the early 1980s, he presided over the closing of Munson High School, so there are some old wounds that may never fully heal. But on balance, he is highly respected and well liked.

Mr. Russell's comments are open and honest. He makes the point that we are not about the business of placing blame. There were just too many factors that pointed in the direction of the possible closing of Munson Elementary that could not be ignored. When the board of education decided to maintain the school for one more year, there had to be conditions—and those conditions were harsh.

The cost of the operation has to be reduced, there has to be a significant turn-around in the quality of the educational program, and there has to be some indication that enrollment would at least stabilize. If these conditions are met, if it is a good school operating on a reasonable budget and providing sound programs for children, its future will be bright. If not, its future is bleak. It has one year. No more. Could it be done? Mr. Russell believes it can, the board of education believes it might be possible, and one other person *knows* it can be done. He backs his optimism by offering to serve as Munson's principal for the critical school year at a salary of one dollar. I am that person.

It is a great introduction and it earns me a standing ovation before I even speak. My thoughts are, "Quit right now, while you're ahead," but that doesn't seem the responsible thing to do. The other thought that flashes through my mind is, "Yes, you have been a teacher, principal and superintendent of schools as well as professor, dean and college president, but that principalship was a long time ago." Yet I can still ride a bicycle and my bicycle riding days were also long ago. Anyway, it is too late now. As to the nuts and the bolts of the job, this school will not benefit from a pencil-pushing, form-filling, record-keeping administrivia automaton. It will just have to muddle through on that score. What the school needs is leadership and that I know I can provide, in spades. I enjoy being with the folks tonight.

I tell them of my plan to have the very best instructional program anywhere. I feel particularly encouraged, as we are just finishing the teacher interviews and I know we are going to have a tremendous team. I stress that we will be on a tight budget and that it will be absolutely essential that we live within our means. Not a bad rule for anyone and well received by the frugal and realistic people who make up the Munson community. I stress that we will have to work together if we want our children to succeed. We will need volunteers to help, parents to follow through at home with discipline and lessons, and the willingness to have their children read to them *every* day and hopefully vice versa.

I ask them not to believe everything their children tell them about what happens at school and in return, I will not believe everything their children tell us about what happens at home! Children have great imaginations. They laugh. I conclude that we can't do it alone and in spite of the fact that this is a state institution, I ask them to join with me in a moment of silent prayer for our children and for help in saving this little school. I meet some wonderful people tonight and I know we can succeed.

The Count Down

We are really on the count down now. School starts August 18. It is hustle, hustle for everyone who works at the place—secretary, custodians, teachers, and staff in building maintenance and other support personnel—not to mention the principal.

A measure of the commitment of the superintendent of schools and the board of education is their willingness to cut the red tape and authorize the absolutely essential work that will help this school to come alive. We must revitalize this place—with people, paint, lights, supplies, equipment and all the things that say "we believe in the future." In a way, the superintendent is saying, "If you are willing to invest your lives in Munson Elementary School and its children, we will match you with the essential elements you need to get the job done."

Today, Director of Elementary Schools Nancy Welch visited little Munson to help. We found old files, requisitions never processed, shelves without books, big plans, big reports, and buried skeletons. There are remnants of a rear guard fight for survival, and the flotsam and jetsam of abandonment. The crew tried but the winds of time and the sea of reality were almost too powerful. Who was at fault? Everyone and no one. Direction was lost. The end was in sight. The pall of closing was apparently in its final stages of being draped over this little place.

Nancy is worried about me. I don't think she is used to working with a septuagenarian.

"You look pale," she says. "You're perspiring. We don't want you having a heart attack." The implication could be "At least not now." I tell her she doesn't look so hot herself, although actually she is a very attractive woman and is always immaculately groomed. Her mind is immaculately groomed, too. There has been no time for a break or for food or water and it is late afternoon. I know she means well.

Disaster struck today. Virginia Lindsey, or "Mrs. Judy," is Munson's school secretary and she is ill. I first met Judy over the telephone. I was coming out to the school for the first time as principal early one Monday morning. I thought I should let her know, not surprise her, so I called her at home that Sunday afternoon. Her voice was very hoarse; it concerned me.

Judy has worked at Munson Elementary for 29 years. She knows every child, every parent, every policy, every file, and every secret. The school secretary is the nerve center of any school and is vital to its operation. In view of the fact that the principal is new, the assistant principal is new, and all the teachers are new to the school, her importance is magnified even more, if that is possible.

Judy is diagnosed with pneumonia and although valiantly tried to carry on, is eventually hospitalized.

I visit Judy in the hospital. She is doing well but the doctor wants more tests. The tests indicate lung cancer. It may have spread. She takes the news bravely and prepares for the biggest battle of her life. We are all deeply concerned.

At school, we "muddle through," as the British might say. Temporary help comes to the rescue and we manage to get by. We all miss Judy. We look forward to her return but we are not optimistic. What else could happen to this little school? What would happen to Judy?

Since the beginning, the local press has followed the Munson drama closely. There was the story in the *Pensacola News Journal* on June 26, 1997, with the headline "Residents Fight To Save Their School" and then a follow-up article on June 27, "Munson Receives Reprieve." On July 12, the story receives top billing on the front page of the *Pensacola News Journal* with the paper's banner reading in large print "BARGAIN PRICE FOR PRINCIPAL: $1 A YEAR" with the sub heading "Ex-UWF Dean Offers to Lead Munson School." The story even displaces the U.S. Navy's Blue Angels flight demonstration team from top spot, which in this part of the world is unthinkable, especially on a day when this fine group of aviators is to perform!

The *Press Gazette* in nearby Milton, Florida, runs a comprehensive story on July 14 under the headline, "Dunworth, Johnson to Head Munson School." It is read widely throughout the local area.

On July 17 the *Pensacola News Journal* gives strong editorial support to the project saying, "John Dunworth's noble offering...may well translate as the ultimate in...volunteerism."

Following this there are letters to the editor of support and appreciation. The "little school," as many now refer to Munson Elementary, is becoming a household word and I am quickly becoming known as the "dollar-a-year principal." The deep concern for the fate of the school and the children it serves, coupled with the genuine feelings of appreciation for the "noble" action of the dollar-a-year man, brings tears to the eyes of many. Everywhere, people ask, "Can it really be done?" "What will you do?" "Why did you take this on?"

I try to answer, I smile and I worry. A large audience is watching this drama unfold: watching, waiting, listening. Is this attention only the overture, the tinkling bells before the crashing cymbals that are poised and ready? I wonder.

Thoughts That Wiggle in My Mind (On Learning)

Learning is a process of making connections. New information connecting with old information. New ideas connecting with earlier ideas. New words and their meanings connecting with old words and their meanings. Earlier experiences connecting with current experiences.

Teaching is the process by which we help learners make these connections. However, it is the learner who makes the connection, not the teacher. No one can do it for you. If the learner does not make the connection, learning is not taking place.

We are not an empty glass into which we pour information and then call it learning. It starts on the inside.

Remember the little child who said to the sculptor, "Who told you there was a horse in that rock?"

Remember the exclamation, "I've got it!" I've got it." That's learning. It is an individual process.

Making connections can take place in a group. It can, and it does. But it is usually difficult, and the larger the group, the more difficult it becomes. There are exceptions but that's the general rule.

We frequently need help in the process. We go just so far, and then things become murky. We need clarification or an additional piece of information, or perhaps just encouragement. We turn to the teacher. A hand goes up. Many hands go up. We need the help right now or the process of making the connection will be derailed.

Too many hands are up. The teacher can't get to you fast enough. The connection starts to fade for lack of the missing link or clarification. The teachable moment is lost. How sad, and what a waste. It is not only time that is lost, but also enthusiasm and the joy that comes with learning...making the next attempt just a little more difficult.

Everyone is different. Everybody knows that. Why do we put children together in a classroom and act as though they are the same? We order books by grade level. We compare children, we grade them, we even fail them because they are not the same. Intelligences, experience, environment, health, learning style, speed of learning, readiness for learning and on and on, are a reflection of our uniqueness as individual human beings. We should cherish that uniqueness, not try to bury it.

And this business of time...

The important thing is that children learn, that they make the connections that in turn will make the new fact, or procedure, or concept an integral and meaningful part of that child's being. That is the process. That is learning. Because each of us is unique, it happens at different speeds. And the process never ends. It continues for life.

So why do we fail children when they do not reach some arbitrary time goal? Oh, I know the answers we give. But do they make any sense, given the givens?

Learning is not a time race.

Business as usual will not get the job done at this little school. Also, we can't change the structure of schooling in the United States and in the State of Florida, at least not in one school year. However, we *will* have to move some mountains.

We will have classes and grades and grade levels. We'll compare students as required by law. We may even "fail" students, but they won't know it.

We'll think of classrooms, not as a grade, or even as two grades, for a grade implies that we are all at the same place, and we are not, but as 20 or 30 individual learners on 20 or 30 individual learning tracks. Good teaching will help each child take his or her next step on the track as efficiently as possible, and make the connections that say, "I am learning. Really learning." Children will not and should not be at the same place in this process if we do it right. The important thing is that each is moving on his or her road to mastery and is experiencing the joy that goes with that accomplishment, each step of the way.

This isn't a revolution. *It is a change in attitude.* Because we are small, we have a chance. Because we have fabulous teachers, we even have a better chance.

How will this play out on standardized test scores? I'm betting my professional life and the future of this school on the answer. But I do worry. It will not be easy.

The Plan

There are only 180 instructional days in the school year. The year is longer than that, but there are planning days, legal holidays, and the traditional breaks in December, spring, and of course, summer. This is a long-standing pattern in American education and is built around the reality that an agrarian society required all hands to help with the planting, caring, harvesting and other needs of the farm during a portion of the year. We are no longer an agrarian society and eventually the pattern will change due to forces that have nothing to do with planting or summer or agriculture, but much to do with technology, teaching and learning. However, it will take time.

Although I do not share this publicly, I approach the task of saving Munson Elementary School as a war being fought on three fronts. To win, we have to be successful on each front. I list them in my mind: the instructional front, the fiscal front and the demographic front.

On the instructional front, it is clear that too many children have not achieved as well as they might have at this little school. There are probably a thousand reasons, but at the moment, they are irrelevant. According to data I have been studying long into each night, it appears that some children have done well, but many others have not. As with a good physician, we will work hard at diagnosing needs, targeting deficiencies, and encouraging gains, while at the same time providing a rich academic diet for all children. This means diverse instructional materials; individualized attention; intensive tutoring; computers; and intellectually stimulating, challenging and demanding lessons.

Expectations must be high. We have the kinds of teachers who carry this load and are highly motivated to do it. My job is to support them, encourage them, have faith in them, and to put it bluntly, get out of their way. And support must mean tangible support: materials, equipment, time, computers and software.

As with any principal, my daily concern and support will convey an important message to teachers. There will be down days and up days. I know they will need encouragement, recognition and understanding. They may even need a gentle reminder now and then, but they must know that I believe in them and am fully aware of the tremendous load they carry. If I do not convey this, I seriously jeopardize the teachers' and students' success and the ultimate quality of the total instructional program. Due to society's frustration, we regrettably send a different, more threatening message to teachers with predictable results. However, *the easiest way to begin improving education in America is to re-invest our faith and confidence in America's teachers and show it!* That alone will not address all of our problems (or their problems), but it is an essential ingredient in any effort to improve American education. It is what we practice in the little school.

As I stress repeatedly in the community, *parents must be partners in the instructional process.* They must value learning. They must ensure that their children follow through on homework and lessons. And there will be homework, good homework. We ask that they listen to their children read to them at least 15 minutes each day; they must demonstrate that reading is important by reading to their children each day. Some will serve as volunteers at school and will help tutor children and support teachers in this area. These are very important lessons too. But of greatest importance, parents must love their children and show it. As hard as a teacher may try, no teacher can compensate for the void of love in a child's heart.

"Fiscal reality," I frequently say, "is a hard taskmaster." Most publicly supported agencies are not threatened with extinction if they are not cost effective. Perhaps they should be. On the fiscal front, the little school has no choice. We *must* operate in a financially responsible manner.

One can realistically argue that small schools are particularly expensive to operate. Obviously, it costs about as much to heat and light a classroom of 30 children occupying the space as it does with 20 children. But that is not where the problem lies. As in most businesses, labor costs drive budgets. All employees must be assigned wisely and thoughtfully. And that applies in large businesses as well as small ones. If two people can accomplish the task assigned to three, reductions must be made. Income in public schools comes primarily from state and local taxes and the public deserves to have their tax dollars used carefully and efficiently. Indeed, they demand it.

Last year's budget for the little school has been cut dramatically, and it is my job to make it work. So far, we are right on target. Although unforeseen problems could cause concern, fiscal affairs are the least of our worries as long as we keep focused and do not waver from our objective.

On the demographic front, the situation is discouraging. Clearly, we have many more children in the sixth grade (who will leave us in June) than we now expect to enter kindergarten. Of course, that can change. If it does not, enrollment for the 1998–99 school year will be marginal at best.

We do know that there was growing disaffection for Munson Elementary. However, there is much love and deep long-standing support for the little school. Will the latter prevail? As programs improve and parents assume "ownership," will the disaffection turn to affection? Will an exemplary program bring parents seeking the best for their children? Will our small size and individual attention be attractive to others?

We do not see real estate development on the immediate horizon or any significant migration into the area, But we are still confident. "Is it just wishful thinking?" we ask. We think not. We have the germ of a plan.

A startling thought just struck me. We will not have 180 schools days to "win" our battles. The Competency Based Test of Basic Skills (CTBS) is administered over a three-day period in March! Test data influences the decision about the future of the little school; this means we have only 138 days to win on the instructional front. I am amazed at my own audacity to take on this task. We will just have to work harder. Much harder. Just 138 days.

Final Preparations

What a flurry of activity. Although the teachers are not due to report to work until Monday, a week before the children arrive, they are already at school working almost around the clock.

Grubbies are the dress of the day. Painters, plumbers, electricians, carpenters and locksmiths are winding up their work. Things look great. Our next task is to make this building a place of learning. And that means books, computers, maps, globes, paintings, tests, pencils, crayons, paste, paper and seemingly a thousand items to help create an environment that is stimulating and challenging. One teacher brings her daughter to assist, another her friends, one her husband. Although cheerful, their actions now are deliberate, thoughtful and professional. For this is when the teacher comes face to face with reality; what the teacher does here can shape a child's entire life. In a few days, the rooms will be full of young faces, looking to the teachers to guide them, challenge them, discipline them, and teach them. The responsibility is theirs and theirs alone.

Teachers should be among the highest paid professionals in our society. If they do their jobs right, they combine knowledge, wisdom, creativity and caring in a delicate blend that meets the exact needs of each child. A teacher is a partner in the process of building human beings. It is a staggering responsibility. At this busy time, and before the children arrive, these thoughts and feelings slip through the cracks between confidence and fear, reminding every teacher that what they do here is eternal. In their private thoughts, most ask reverently for God's help.

Because of its size and the distribution of children by grade level, classes at the little school will be as follows:

Mrs. Sanders	Grades K–1
Mrs. Coogle	Grades 2–3
Mr. Johnson	Grades 4–5
Mrs. Rogaliner	Grades 5–6

Given our economic constraints, there really are no other viable alternatives. There are advantages and disadvantages in this organization. It encourages the teacher out of necessity to look at students as individuals rather than as a group, each moving on his or her own learning track, moving forward as smoothly and efficiently as teaching materials and time permit. That is an advantage. Some of our classes will be quite small. This helps. Other factors being equal, small classes, at least where we are today in teaching and learning, mean better education. They also mean more expensive education. Realistically, we teach in groups because of time, resources and reality. Our smaller classes in the little school, at least in the all-important primary level, will be a tremendous boon to good teaching. In large groups, combination classes just compound the teacher's problem no matter how hard he or she tries to individualize work for students. That is a disadvantage. Perhaps we make it too complicated. A graduate of earlier times told me just today that he was *twice* as smart as anyone else because all through school he had been in classes with two grades in every class. It made sense to him.

Ideally, we would have no grades at all. Mastery would define success, and each child would move up the scale of mastery at different rates of speed and ease. Children would not be compared. Groupings for the application and internalization of knowledge would be based on several factors but not on the artificial designation currently referred to as first grade, fourth grade, and so on. In time, the term "grade" might disappear from the lexicon of learning.

I get to know Larry and Patricia. Larry Gill and Patricia Davis are our two full-time custodians. Larry has been here for years, and Patricia attended this little school. I have never seen anyone work as hard as Patricia. No wasted movements, just go, go, go.

Patricia's daughter attends school here and is a delightful girl. Patricia's sister is in charge of our cafeteria. I believe I used the wrong term when I referred to us as a team. We're a family.

Patricia has a profound hearing loss but is such a remarkable person that you quickly forget about the hearing problem.

Larry is a methodical man, methodically groomed, methodical in his movements, methodical in his thinking. He is quite a philosopher too. You never see Larry rush yet he always seems to be where he is needed. Larry puts in long hours but his schedule is unfathomable. There was a little tension at first. I told Larry I didn't mind what time he reported to work as long as he had the flag at the top of the flagpole by 7 a.m. each morning. We understood each other.

Larry is from the old school that says, "Repair it, not replace it." He has kept some equipment going for a very long time, much to the consternation of the people "downtown." Their motto: "Old stuff should be replaced." I'm not sure I like that idea! Larry has kept some equipment operational for so long that it has more value as an antique than a piece of equipment. Actually, some *are* antiques.

I like Larry. There was talk that Larry was going to be transferred to another school. No way! Larry and Patricia are essential to this school's operation. They work hard, very hard, spat occasionally, and care about kids, safety and the things that really matter. I appreciate them both very much. Do they know? "Don't wait, tell them now," I say to myself. And I do.

The board of education's department of transportation has an office "downtown" in Milton, about 20 miles south of Munson, that is responsible for maintaining the 260 buses and planning bus routes for the entire county. As far as specific routes go, it is actually the drivers who work most of it out and make it go. At least that's what the drivers tell me.

Good school bus drivers are special people, very special. Patient, skilled, wise and cautious, they emphasize safety for the charges in their care. In the hot months, and there are many, the heat can be stifling. It is in the high 90s today with humidity to match. No air-conditioned buses here! Driving a 7-ton, 35-foot, 65-passenger vehicle over the winding country roads and dirt lanes of the rural South takes a *real* driver. Dealing with children of all ages for the long trips twice each day takes the patience of Job, the wisdom of Solomon, and the love and understanding of a saint. Indeed, Becky Cabaniss, Sheila Watts, Betty Grice and Michele Dozier are all saints. Each is also boss, enforcer and captain of her school bus and "Don't you forget it." I don't.

We are counting on these ladies to get our children here and home again. We will take it from there.

I am amazed at the quantity of paper, reports, data and documentation it takes to operate this little school. Much of it seems to pertain to compliance. It really is staggering. Two computers just to handle the flow. Unbelievable. Of course, it is equally as bad in every school and every business in the country, from what I understand. It is just more noticeable here. Our little school has only four classrooms and four teachers!

I don't believe it is the fault of the superintendent of schools or board of education, although procedures can and should always be reviewed for relevancy and importance. I remember the signs in World War II (my war) that said, "Is this trip necessary?" Perhaps some signs that say, "Is this report necessary?" should be posted in the main offices of every school system and business in America. Unfortunately, most of the "requests" begin with or are based on the following:

The State requires . . .

The auditors require . . .

The federal government requires . . .

In compliance with . . .

Although not stated, the fear of litigation and its consequences seem to be omnipresent. I'll learn more about this but I can see it is going to be a problem. I *can't* let it detract from our main mission. Correction. I *won't* let it detract. I wonder if I will go to jail. This is going to be a tough lesson. I thank the little school for making it so clear.

It is Thursday, August 14, 1997. The *Press Gazette* publishes a fine article and photograph of our faculty under the headline "Munson Elementary has a New Teaching Staff." The superintendent calls a meeting of administrators and teachers who are new to the Santa Rosa County Schools. Referred to as "New Faculty Orientation," this is one of those command performances where everyone is expected to attend and everyone does. Although we all dislike being taken away from the critical work of preparing for the big task ahead, it is a sharp reminder that school starts on Monday and that time is almost up! Tomorrow night is really the deadline, for we have scheduled an open house for parents and children to meet their new teachers, visit classrooms, discuss standards and goals, as well as policies and procedures. The business of schooling is about to begin.

Over 150 new teachers attend the meeting in Milton High School's cafeteria this morning as well as school administrators, the superintendent of schools, the board of education and other dignitaries. Refreshments and speeches and introductions are followed by more introductions. I am asked to come to the podium to introduce the little Munson group—the smallest group in the room. Benny (Superintendent Benny Russell) also invites me to make a few comments. I tell everyone about our "Dream Team" and what we are about and why. As I am wont to do, I am respectful but a little irreverent. I don't defer much to people in high places having been there too long. Fresh from the barrage of recent bureaucratic incursions into the professional time and lives of our little team, I say, "One of my functions at the little school will be to protect you," as I turn to our little four-teacher team, "from you," as I turn back and stab the air with my finger, pointing to the senior administrators about the room, the superintendent and the board of education. I smile, they understand, and we all laugh. The teachers applaud with great enthusiasm.

Back at school, there are a thousand last minute details including finalizing the Student/Parent Handbook and the Teacher's Handbook that covers the major policies and procedures of the board of education and little Munson Elementary School. Gail Baxley is helping.

I first met Mrs. Baxley when her laughter rippled through the office; it was a pleasant sound. Gail, as the staff calls her, is a senior teacher assistant. In fact, she is our only teacher assistant, the other TA being in the "family way" and at home considering the pros and cons of being a working mother. I believe she will devote full time to being a mom.

Mrs. Baxley had only been back a few days from summer recess, being on the same calendar as teachers, when I realized this lady could do almost anything. A very intelligent, modest person with an infectious sense of humor, she has the unique ability to juggle several activities at the same time and never drop one! When we were revising one handbook, she would be at the computer producing the second. As a teacher assistant, she moves effortlessly between roles in the office and the classroom. In the cafeteria, she serves as cashier and the monitor of Title I meals and, as I would soon learn, also serves as mother of the little ones and tyrant, when necessary, over the larger ones. She seems to know every parent and every child but never divulges a confidence. Being from the rural South, she has the speech patterns and the expressions to match and reminds me now and then, when I comment on some colloquialism, "Don't worry, we're fixin' to get you talking like us before too long." She also reflects the values of honesty, hard work, and directness that characterize the good folk of this region.

I once said, "Gail, you would make a good principal."

She answered shyly but without much hesitation, "Yes, I would." And then she was off to three more tasks leaving her lilting laughter lingering over the pleasant thought.

Chapter II

School Days

Counting Schedules

Some people count sheep when they are unable to sleep. Tonight I am counting schedules, for tomorrow is the first day of school. Schools run on schedules: bus schedules, bell schedules, class schedules, library schedules, faculty schedules, duty schedules, breakfast schedules, lunch schedules, fire drill schedules, bus schedules. I am repeating myself! We expect a good day tomorrow. If it is not, it will not be the fault of the schedules: bus schedules, bell schedules, alarm schedules. Alarm schedules? No. Alarm clock! It is time.

The First Day

The first day of school has finally arrived, and what a glorious day it is! The schedules are working (with one exception), the planning has covered almost every foreseeable problem and there are no tears in the kindergarten—the ultimate test!

The look of expectation on the faces of these children is a clarion bell to do our very best, and more if possible. We have high expectations for each one of these children and are reminded that they all have high expectations for each of us. We are all eager, enthusiastic, focused. One of my responsibilities will be to maintain that high level of enthusiasm and commitment. This is not just any school year; it is the most important year ever in the long life of this little school.

There is one problem, however, and it is a major one. The bus schedule is flawed. "Transportation" was trying to get by with three buses where formerly there had been five. It wasn't working. It may have looked good on paper, but not driving down a dirt lane at 5 a.m. Some children were on the bus more than two hours *each way*! That is not acceptable. Tommy's mother and several other parents called the "transportation department" and also spoke with the bus drivers personally but without success. It is a credit to all these concerned people that the conversations are reasonably civil. I marveled. The bus drivers know what is causing the problem but do not have the authority to make the necessary changes. The last resort is the principal. I listen carefully. Bus routes are not "my thing," but before the end of the week I am an expert.

Tommy's mother says, "All Tommy can do after more than two hours on that sweltering bus is to run for water."

He says, "Mommy, I am burning up it is so hot."

Our mandate this year is clear, and in plain language means, "Get it done for less." But all the time I think of Tommy and all the other little ones in big hot buses. It doesn't escape my notice that I am sitting in an air-conditioned office, not a sweaty, sweltering, smelly, yellow box with a big diesel engine grinding out noise and more heat and more heat and... Am I the sadistic commandant of some horrible prisoner of war camp? Back to reality.

It is easy to throw money at problems but I have to be sure we explore every other alternative first. To compound the matter, we not only transport our own children but also carry high school students to specific transfer points where the older students leave the bus, board another, and are on their way. Working your way around or through the largest forest in the state is no simple matter.

We are able to avoid expanding to the original five buses but we have to add one additional bus, making it a total of four instead of three. Each driver is paid for four hours per day. We can accommodate this increase but will have to economize elsewhere. Now, Tommy gets home in about an hour, which is not unusual in these parts. In fact, one of our local residents pointed out, "Travel and rural living go hand in hand. When my children want an ice cream cone or a visit to the mall, we face a long drive each way," she added. "We're used to it."

Since the school buses arrive at 7 a.m. each morning, I try to be at school no later than 6:45 a.m. The "dawn patrol," as we affectionately refer to it, is the schedule that requires one of our four teachers to be on supervision duty at 7 a.m. every morning. That "duty" rotates every week but it seems advisable for the principal to be available and visible. Mr. Johnson is on hand too and is of invaluable assistance in setting and maintaining pupil behavior. In fact, I jokingly refer to Mr. Johnson on occasion as "Show me a line" Johnson. We believe children should be orderly and respectful. No running or loud talking in hallways and certainly no boisterous behavior indoors at any time. To help achieve these goals, we started off the first day of school by forming the children into lines when moving groups from one place to another. Children do not leave a classroom until excused. They then proceed in an orderly line to the cafeteria or library or computer lab as the case may be.

Primary grade children are a delight. In learning this behavior they may be seen following their teacher quietly down the hall with a finger lifted to their lips in the traditional "quiet sign" that every child knows so well. If a class of older children does not follow the rule, the children are asked, quietly, to repeat the exercise until they have learned. And Mr. Johnson's firm but quiet voice can be heard, "Show me a line, please." And it works. Discipline means standards and consistency.

I took an action when I first visited Munson Elementary School that perhaps set the tone in the area of student discipline. I discarded the rather heavy paddle that was used to force compliance. In my almost fifty years in education, I have never struck a child. I am not going to start now. I strongly support firm discipline and appropriate and respectful behavior, but violence is not the way to teach the lesson of responsibility. Viewpoints differ on this but I am the principal and at this school, that is the way it is going to be. Sometimes, it is really fun being a principal. It is not quite like that at home!

The press visits the little school to cover the events of the first day of the new year and notes that the school superintendent was a lunch guest. *Pensacola News Journal* staff reporter Heidi Nieland wrote a great story about "Munson's Fight for Survival..." Her lead said, "John Dunworth's salary went into the red on his first day of school. He treated the superintendent to a $2 cafeteria lunch." The story was accompanied by a fine photograph by *News Journal* photographer Michael Spooneybarger. My bald head was prominent as I was talking with a fifth-grader in the cafeteria. Also visible was the "laminated watermelon slice" around my neck identifying me as "Dr. Dunworth, principal." The Associated Press wire service picked up the story, giving it wide visibility. And, to paraphrase Shakespeare, thereby hangs an almost unbelievable tale, at least for all of us involved with the little "four-room" school in a big forest in the deep South in a place called Munson, Florida. The tale would begin in 24 hours.

The first day of school very forcefully brought home that many of our families are not rich. Over 60 percent of all the students at Munson Elementary are on the free or reduced lunch program provided through the auspices of the federal government. Although "government" in general is not particularly well liked in these parts, this program guarantees that children will have two nutritious meals a day at school. Some eat breakfast before they arrive and some bring their lunches but most of our students eat both breakfast and lunch at school.

The primary children sometimes need assistance and older students are enlisted to help open milk cartons and take care of similar important duties. "I can't cut my waffle" may be a reflection of the limited strength and dexterity of the kindergarten child or possibly the culinary skills of the cook. But Edith Wolfe is one wonderful cook, so I know it is the former.

Edith is our only cafeteria employee and regularly prepares and serves about 130–140 meals a day. Edith's grandmother did the same work for 40 years in Munson School, so it is certainly in the family. As a matter of fact, Edith would be hard put to do all this work if her family and friends didn't pitch in and help almost every day. Although I appreciate it deeply, I am disturbed that the system makes such demands on people. As with Tommy on the sweltering bus, this matter too must be addressed.

If this school were to close, "It would be like losing part of my soul," says Edith.

"It won't close and Edith won't always have to carry this impossible load," I say to myself. But I do worry as the calendar inexorably counts the days remaining until the bell rings or tolls.

Mirror, Mirror

Media and mirrors have much in common. Both distort, both can be fun, and both can be addictive. One by-product of media attention is fame. Fame is ephemeral and is often gone in minutes. The media report their stories to inform, to entertain, and to produce profit. The order may be different and often is, but these are basically the rules. It is an honorable profession. When involved with the media, however, it is wise to remember the rules, the by-products, and the mirrors.

Media Blitz

The crashing cymbals of the media startle all of us on Tuesday, August 19. It is the second day of school and substitute secretary Kathy Turner accepts a telephone call from a radio station in Salt Lake City. Station personnel had just heard about Munson Elementary School and want to conduct a live interview with the principal, by telephone, for their early evening audience—the commuters on their way home from work. I ask myself, as I asked myself many times in the days to follow, "Is this appropriate? Will it help the school?" It seems to me that to have a group of informed people rooting for Munson Elementary could only help, be they local or national. The tone of the query is supportive. They are "pulling" for the little school based on the AP story. I say, "Yes, I will be pleased to be available." They call a few hours later at my home, due to the time difference, and we go directly on the air between the commercial and the helicopter traffic report. I suspect we have a good audience and many people outside the Panhandle of Florida are becoming aware of the plight of the "little school."

Before the day is over, WKRG-TV, the CBS affiliate in Mobile, Alabama, calls to schedule a visit to Munson the next morning for an on-camera interview, a tour of the classrooms and even the surrounding country. "Channel 5," as it is referred to locally, has a wide viewing audience from Mississippi to Florida and is highly regarded.

While this takes place on Wednesday, CBS "This Morning" calls from New York and requests a live interview via satellite with Mark McEwen, the show's host. Following several calls, it is scheduled for early Friday morning, just before school. That means I will really have to be up early!

Telephone conversations are now going back and forth between New York and Munson—between producer and principal—between the big city and the little community. It all seems somewhat ironic, that the big folk are coming to the little folk to get a story about a little school.

Television producers, I learned, are very sharp people. Our initial conversations are long and thoughtful, their questions penetrating and insightful; they want facts and much more. I am impressed and I cooperate as best I can. If they think this story is worth telling, then I will do everything possible to help facilitate their work. Munson is going to be on the map in big letters and it would soon have even more friends far and wide. I chuckle a little; it might be difficult to close a national icon!

On Friday morning, I arrive very early to find the big mobile satellite truck with dish in place and cables already running to the classroom selected for the live CBS "This Morning" broadcast. Although I have participated in remote broadcasts, this is my first live remote interview on national television. No notes, no tele-prompter, just you, the unseen ear plug providing the connection, the camera and crew and a few million viewers! And no editing. You do not see the person to whom you are speaking, so there are no clues or facial expressions we often rely on in normal conversation. Just before air time, the voice of producer Beatrice Gruber came through the ear piece from New York to offer reassuring words: "Things look great," "You sound fine," and similar ministrations of comfort before I hear the cheery words of the host saying, "Good morning, Dr. Dunworth."

The camera crew had worked with every U.S. President of recent times as well as many major figures in world affairs, entertainment, and numerous other fields. I urge them to remain "set up" in the classroom and present a lesson to the fourth- and fifth-grade class on this fantastic technology. They are gracious and do a superb job. Not surprisingly, the boys and girls are polite when presidents and politicians are mentioned but really come to life when the personal anecdotes about country music stars and other entertainers are discussed. It is quite an experience for all of us.

A little later that morning the big truck with the big dish leaves for other assignments. It is a first for Munson Elementary. Would it be the last?

The next week the ABC affiliate in Pensacola, WEAR-TV, visits the little school. More interviews. In addition, there are calls from Harry Smith of "CBS Evening News," from "NBC Nightly News," and from Fox-TV. Fox explores the idea of my coming to New York for an appearance on a morning talk show. I am tempted but decline. Tom Brokaw's "NBC Nightly News" people are really serious. They propose sending a team of four people—cameraman, soundman, network correspondent, and producer—to visit for three days. "CBS Evening News," although interested, had a breaking story to cover. Little Munson Elementary School is becoming well known locally and even nationally, and it is only the second week of school.

I am a bit concerned. Although interested in all aspects of the story, reporters are clearly stressing the "dollar-a-year" angle. Conversations with producers suggests their full awareness of the implications and other aspects of what is occurring at Munson Elementary. Bigger is not necessarily better in education, we agree. What is happening here could help prove that point, if we are successful, and have a significant impact on America's schools. The traditions and strengths of a small community, its values and continuity would clearly influence the quality of education provided to its children. Money is not the primary issue. Using what is available would enable us to have an excellent school and operate it for less.

It seems to me that this is the real story. The fact that a former college president is trying to help out for $1 a year is nice and appreciated but is it that important? Evidently so, for it has been the lead in *every* report of the story about Munson Elementary School. People who are in the world of writing for a business usually mean business. And they are good at it. I console myself with the thought that an in-depth academic story, never read, is not going to influence anyone. Indeed, it is one of the problems in the field of education. We should be effective communicators and we are not. Skip the jargon, skip the long sentences. Speak to the concerns of the listener—not the speaker. Get real. Talk real. Be real. We underestimate people. They are smarter than we think. If the dollar-a-year angle captures attention, the other ideas will come through. Every teacher knows you have to gain a child's attention first if you are going to teach anything. I feel better.

The NBC team arrives September 3 and will be with us until Friday afternoon, September 5. What an intense time. Network waiver forms had already been distributed to each family stating the following:

> *I hereby give permission to videotape my child for this report and to use the videotape and my child's name and information about him/her to publicize and advertise the report. I understand that the videotape may be edited and that you and others may re-use the report on television and in other media anywhere in the world...*

Almost every form was returned signed. There are visits to classrooms, interviews with Edith in the cafeteria, discussions with teachers, bus drivers, parents, grandparents and even a visit to the Country Store. They are very professional and very thorough. My problem is that I am trying to run a school and be available at the same time. On Thursday the Pensacola Symphony Orchestra Guild launches its 1997–98 Music in Education series in the primary grades of Munson Elementary. It is fortuitous that the symphony group is at the school the same time NBC is covering the Munson story. It provides some excellent shots that found their way into the final story including a little boy with his fingers in his ears!

Friday is Grandparents Day; grandparents of all of our students are invited to school for lunch (here we refer to it as dinner) with their grandson or granddaughter. Even some great-grandparents attend. One woman had been in the first graduating class in 1930 and many had attended the little school over the years as had their sons and daughters and the sons and daughters after them. It is a very beautiful and touching moment and, of course, NBC is there.

It is a little hard to say "Good bye" to Bob Dotson, Laurie Singer, and the crew; they head off down the long Munson Highway, back to the big city and the seemingly glamorous world of network television. One fifth-grader whispers our ambivalent feelings as he works hard on an arithmetic lesson with camera, sound boom and correspondent hovering nearby. "When," he says to me in a soft voice, "are all of these nice people going home?" The time has come.

That weekend, Lady Diana the Princess of Wales was killed in Paris and a little later Mother Teresa also died. It would be three weeks before "NBC Nightly News" would air the Munson Story under the caption "The American Spirit." They tell me it was a long segment as national TV goes. It lasted 2 minutes and 45 seconds.

The media blitz is over. The cymbals are still.

There are responses to the publicity from both the mighty and not-so-mighty. Their words of personal appreciation are particularly kind. Some send money to the little school. In a very personal way, many share part of their souls, to use Edith's expression. If for no other reason, and whether we succeed or fail, those words of caring are worth an entire year of work! I am humbled. And although we received beautiful letters from Tipper

Gore, from the Secretary of Education, and from legislators and leaders and neighbors and friends, one of the most touching was from a little family in the Midwest. Actually, it was from a mother and her little baby and included a matching gift of appreciation from the child with the wish that there would be someone like me to "care for her education" in the years ahead. It was a sincere, sweet gesture.

I wrote and said I would "treasure the gift as a reminder of all the little children whose lives and futures we hold in trust." The matching gift, of course, was in the amount of $1.

It reminded me in some ways of the story of the Widow's Mite.

The Warehouse

"Dr. D, the warehouse just called," says Kathy, the substitute secretary. That is good news.

Old, used, and mostly unusable furniture and equipment are sold for salvage according to state law. However, the school district's purchasing office in Milton, which handles all of this, knows the budget problems we face, and helps us out. They alert us when discards come in and before they are collected for public sale. I'm sure they notify the other schools too, but perhaps not quite as quickly.

At any rate, I am soon climbing over broken and discarded equipment that has served well for years and should be replaced. I don't want our children to have too many hand-me-downs, but living within one's means is essential.

Minutes in a metal warehouse standing in the blazing sun and you feel as though you are cooking. Clothes cling, sweat runs and handkerchiefs become wet rags. Sometimes the trip is futile; the equipment is in such terrible shape. Other times it is possible to salvage a piece here or there. Even a few extra chairs will come in handy when tutors are working with individual children. We need those chairs.

I was raised on the old adage, "A penny saved is a penny earned." The warehouse is one way to save quite a few pennies. There are other ways, too, and Munson teachers take advantage of every one of them. If a grant is offered, our people compete and win the award. If a competition awards a computer, we compete aggressively and add a fine piece of equipment to the school's inventory.

I do think some of the faculty went a little too far when they started "shaking down" textbook vendors and other suppliers of educational materials. Of course, this is not acceptable practice in most schools but our folks were desperate. With our new fame from the media blitz, the teachers suggested that if we are successful, wouldn't it be nice to have an instructional product associated with our little school? Now is the time, so please consider sending this or that book series for all of our children, without charge of course.

It didn't work. Publishers are undoubtedly not as sanguine regarding the outcome of our enterprise as we are. Businessmen are sharp people. We evidently aren't a very good investment; it is a sobering lesson.

Solomon

It is the second week of school, and Mrs. Rogaliner appears at my office door with two of the largest boys in school—each hot, sweaty, flushed and one with a bloody nose that is not helping his clean, ironed shirt. I imagine he will hear from his mom about that. Red soil suggests that part of this altercation ended on the ground, which was, I learned, the point at which Mrs. Rogaliner had efficiently and authoritatively intervened.

"Dr. Dunworth," she states in a serious and formal tone, "I believe your immediate intervention is required with Jamie and Harold." Mrs. Rogaliner has a great command of the language and often uses phrases and terms that reflect her academic background and professional sophistication. She is a superb teacher.

The boys stand sullenly with heads bowed while Mrs. Rogaliner explains how the fighting had come about. She leaves to meet her class that is scheduled to begin in moments, and I am left with the boys. What would Solomon do, I ponder.

The boys, it seems, are good friends. However, occasionally when one would push too hard on the other, physically or figuratively, a flair-up of fisticuffs would spontaneously erupt. Several children exhibited similar behavior. Indeed, we are a little perplexed by the behavior of the older youngsters at Munson. Many seem strangely deficient in social skills. Hitting, shoving and verbal outbursts are common responses to the most minor frustration. The concept of taking one's turn, even in conversation, seems foreign. How much is related to culture, to environment, to isolation, to poor teaching, or to bad habits from the past is uncertain. I am getting the nagging and disturbing thought that some of these children have been together for too long. Some as long as five or six years, moving from classroom to classroom to classroom, year after year after year. It is repetitive just to say it, never mind to live it. Deep friendships have been established, but also deep animosities—animosities between families as well as between children. Sometimes these flare up and cause problems with little apparent provocation. This may be an argument against a school being *too* small, or at any rate, too isolated, too insulated, without the leavening influence of different children with different backgrounds, different experiences and different personalities. Clearly, in education, "bigger" can be too big. Can "smaller" be too small? This will take study.

I meet with each of Mrs. Rogaliner's two boys individually. We talk, we discuss alternative avenues to cope with their feelings, and I stress the newly adopted policy that would guide all such behavior in the future at Munson: "Zero tolerance for fighting." Any student involved in a fight was guilty by definition. "He hit me first" did not excuse a participant. This means that students would have to find other ways to cope with anger rather than violence or they could no longer remain at school.

Each is denied privileges for a week, and I call each boy's father to reinforce the lesson at home. Parents are supportive, but not without reservation. Or as expressed locally, "I tell my boy if anyone bothers him, he's to whop 'em and to whop 'em good."

But it does not end there. The school district's guidance office has some wonderful resource people and we begin immediately with excellent instruction in helping youngsters to "Stop, think, and consider options and consequences before acting impetuously."

It takes great skill on the part of Mrs. Rogaliner, not to mention determination, consistency, high standards and unbelievable patience and respect for every child. All of us marvel at her fortitude in working with this difficult group. It is a masterful demonstration of professionalism of the highest order. And it works.

It also takes time, several more bloody noses as well as the relocation of one or two specific children. But before the year would be over, little Munson School would end using fighting and violence as a solution to personal problems between children. This would be accomplished without the use of the old paddle I had discarded before the first day of school. To all of us, it is a tremendous achievement and means so much in the lives and futures of these youngsters. "Whop 'em" is out.

I like to believe Solomon would have been pleased.

Taking Stock

School has now been in session for six weeks and it is time to take stock. The bus problem has long been resolved. I had my first experience with the Civil Service Board and was able to employ a teacher assistant to replace the former TA who resigned to raise her family. Mrs. Sanders helped with the interviewing process, as the TA's primary assignment is with K-1 children.

Mrs. Debbie Marmont was selected and reported to work immediately. That seems like ages ago. Time is moving so quickly. As with all of our key staff, she is computer literate as well as exceptionally well suited for the role of teacher assistant; and that is interesting in view of the fact that her recent experience has been primarily in a stock brokerage firm. Perhaps coping with the crises in the market is good training for dealing with crises in the kindergarten. At any rate, she is an outstanding teacher assistant.

Things are going remarkably well in spite of our problems. Physical plant issues still take a considerable amount of time but are being addressed: compressor breakdowns in the air conditioning unit, holes in the blacktop, lines on the playground, a safety violation in a kitchen electrical outlet, and persistent termites in our multi-purpose room! Large book orders, which should have been placed last year but were not, have yet to arrive. However, teachers are improvising very effectively. Our library computer is "down" and the inventory is in disarray. This will be corrected soon, but much of it is out of our hands. Technical personnel are in short supply in most school systems, and we are no exception in Santa Rosa County.

We are on target as far as our strategy to reach children with individualized instruction and support. But it will take more people, more computers, and more helpers if we are going to do it right. As is the practice in rural areas, we look to our neighbors for assistance.

We didn't have to look far. I now know how the superintendent, Benny Russell, felt when I called back in June, for I received a very similar call from Dr. Bill Evans, professor and chairman of the teacher education division at UWF's College of Education. The call seemed like a miracle, because Dr. Evans, on behalf of the college, was volunteering to help Munson in any way the College could. That is, individual faculty members, graduate students, and undergraduate students offered to give freely of their time to help these children and this little school. It was a magnanimous offer.

In addition to the University of West Florida, Munson is blessed with another prestigious neighbor—the United States Navy. "Why," one might ask, "would the Navy be a neighbor, considering the fact that Munson Elementary is situated in a very large forest?" The answer is quite simple. The Naval installation that neighbors Munson is an aviation training command. Where better to teach new pilots strategic flight maneuvers than a large forested area where training would not conflict with civilian communities? Hence, U.S. Naval Air Station, Whiting Field is our illustrious neighbor.

Whiting Field is only about 15 miles away (just a stone's throw) and is said to be the most active air base in the world. The base is credited with approximately 2.5 million take-offs and landings every year. It provides primary and intermediate level training in fixed wing aircraft (VT) for Navy, Marine Corps, Coast Guard and even international students. It is also responsible for helicopter training (HT) in these branches of the service as well. With over 2,000 employees and five training squadrons, it is a great neighbor.

A special part of Whiting Field for us is Aviation Training Squadron SIX (or VT-6 as they are locally referred to). They play an integral part in Whiting Field's daily operations, but they also have close personal ties to our little school; Mrs. Rogaliner's husband, Lt. Cdr. Jeff Rogaliner, USN, is a VT-6 flight instructor. Through their initial requests, the squadron becomes an active part of our school. VT-6 Commanding Officer, Lt. Col. John Mills, USMC, and his wife Barbara are deeply committed to this community and its education, as well. They not only wish to help but take time themselves to do so.

With the word spreading, other members become involved and soon the wife of the squadron's Executive Officer, Mrs. Roxanne Lumme, is also donating her many and varied talents. Under her tutelage, the sixth-grade class creates its own newspaper and budding journalists emerge. As a result of many caring individuals, an entire squadron takes Munson Elementary School under its wing, so to speak. It is a very special relationship. A formal partnership is arranged and sharp, young military personnel are now tutoring boys and girls, teaching lessons on patriotism and helping out in important ways. The presence of so many well mannered, well groomed, well spoken men and women of diverse backgrounds and races greatly enriches the lives of the children and indeed all of us at Munson. The significant male presence, sometimes missing in an elementary school, provides fine role models for the boys and special tutors and helpers for all of the children. Sixth-grade girls and aspiring young pilots in our student body in particular think this is cool! And it is.

Others help too. The Escambia River Electric Cooperative, Inc. has aided Munson Elementary through "thick and thin." Cellular One provides free cellular phone service. Merchants and charitable organizations pitch in where needed, including Wal-Mart in Milton, Emmitt Smith Charities, Inc. in Pensacola, and the Benevolent Association of Santa Rosa County. The State Division of Forestry is always helpful, as well as the local Munson Volunteer Fire Department with their superb safety programs for children, the VT-6 Officers' Wives Club and innumerable concerned citizens and friends. When a school is in trouble, everyone needs to help.

As is the case in many schools in Santa Rosa County, parent volunteers continue to offer invaluable and indefatigable assistance in so many classrooms and in so many ways. As we seek help from others, we must always remember that parents have a deep-vested interest in seeing this school succeed. The lives and futures of their children are on the line and it shows in their commitment and hard work. Equally as important, we want them to be partners with teachers; serving as a parent volunteer can help. Although we respect each other's roles, this school belongs to the people—not to me, not to the employees, not even to the children—but to all those who have come before, who are here now, and hopefully will be here in the future.

A school belongs to families, taxpayers, grandparents, all citizens, and yes, children. It belongs to what we call the "community." It is one of our most precious possessions whether we have children or not. We should guard it. Protect it. Nourish it. Parents are reassured to again see a fine school under the big oaks at Munson. "We have our school back," said one father with tears in the corner of his eye. "It's good."

I am frequently asked why I volunteered to serve as principal for a year—and for $1. Part of the answer is so I could be part of giving this school—a good school—back to its rightful "owners." It would be devastating to fail.

Judy, the secretary, is on sick leave and is now considering retirement. Kathy Turner, the substitute secretary, continues to give fine, loyal service on a daily basis. Gail Baxley provides the continuity in procedures and is the glue that holds the place together. Everyone is working very hard. It is going well.

Tonight, report cards go home, marking the end of our first reporting period. I see some apprehensive faces in the hallway. Perhaps that is not all bad; school is serious business.

What I Learned at School Today

I finally learn about camouflage flu! Children show up at school in camouflage outfits and are very proud of their clothes. At first I am a little worried; are these the offspring of some activated militia group? Could be. But then the light dawns. It's hunting season.

As a matter of fact, it has been hunting season for some time, but I haven't heard very much about game, just about dogs—except they don't pronounce it that way, more like "dawgs." Sometimes they refer to hounds and also foxes. The hounds are very special and require much care and training. It is quite a "science" and very competitive. I am amazed at the interest and the enthusiasm. We will have to capitalize on this in our lessons or we will miss a great opportunity. Sometimes I believe I am learning more than the kids at Munson. It's nice to know that old "dawgs" can still learn!

It won't be too long before our unexcused absences will increase, thanks to an outbreak of this unique flu—or maybe they will be excused absences. I am sure that spending the day in the woods with your daddy and your "dawgs" teaches some pretty important lessons too. Don't want to get too carried away with all this book stuff. Is this the principal talking? I can't believe it. I wonder how I would look in one of those camouflage suits...

Oh, yes, I learned something else recently. I learned about head lice! I am sure that was a problem in other schools in my past experience, but I was pretty far removed from the business of checking scalps for lice.

They are impossible little critters and spread like wildfire. Once identified, a child with head lice must be sent home from school and cannot return until either the Health Department or a physician has certified that the youngster has been treated for *pediculosis* and is free of head lice and / or nits.

So I don rubber gloves and oh so cautiously explore a little scalp. There haven't been too many cases but it doesn't take many. My eyesight, I claim, isn't all that good so I delegate the task to Mrs. Sanders, the K-1 teacher. All kindergarten teachers are experts in this field. Mrs. Sanders, of course, delegates it to the teacher assistant—who, being a sharp lady, often comes back to me and says, "I'm not sure." When we are all sure, we call home and give mom the great news—except mom isn't home but at work, so she calls her boyfriend who is currently out of work and graciously comes over to school and takes over. And you guessed it—in his camouflage suit!

Eventually, the little one gets back to school with a clean bill of health. But of course, there are the brothers and sisters.

Some days are a joy. A little girl tells me over her breakfast in the cafeteria that her mother wants to know if I remember the days when people rode in a horse and buggy. Do I seem that old to parents? I remember the famous observation that anyone who is 15 years older than I am is old. I must seem ancient to these children. Well, why not? I am ancient.

For the first time, it is a little cooler, justifying a sweater. At least six different children tell me how much they like my sweater. My day is made! It reminds me to comment more often on their pretty clothes. My job is to make their day, not the other way around. They are an absolute joy to be around. Each is so unique, so ready to learn, so full of life, so vulnerable. I have a feeling that most of the "bad" things we see in children, we teach them.

Schools are just full of wonderful stories. Today, I was hugged. If this were a big city, you might think I had said, "Mugged." But no, I said hugged—as in throwing out one's arms and wrapping them around the object of your affection. Reciprocity is expected. If you don't hug back, it always seems to me to be the ultimate rejection. Of course, policy frowns on all this.

The little children love to hug their teachers, teacher assistants, and volunteers—the people in their daily lives—the people they have come to trust. But I am not quite prepared for such demonstrative behavior. Here I am the "principal" on cafeteria duty, moving between tables to help out and to ensure proper behavior. A little kindergartener jumps up and looks directly into my face with the most angelic (although partially toothless) smile and a look of expectation and unconditional love, and throws her little arms wide and envelopes me! Before lunch is over, several others follow suit. By that time, I have become quite skillful in handling the situation with propriety. I think they like my fuzzy sweater.

Occasionally, this happens in the hall too, when a primary group is going to or from class. I'll be standing in the hallway, outside the principal's office no less and one child will step out of line with arms wide and that beautiful, sometimes wistful smile, and we have a brief little hug. And then the little child is back in line with a wide smile in place, happily on the way to the business of learning. I step into my office with a big smile on my soul. It lasts all day, perhaps forever.

On the issue of policy, I will just have to leave the matter to a higher court. I don't know one good principal who doesn't bend one bad rule at least once each day.

There will be a temptation when this year has passed and the die cast to study Munson Elementary School under a microscope. Why did it fail or why did it succeed? What did they do or not do? What had the greatest impact or the least? It is doubtful if many of these exercises will be particularly enlightening or helpful; other factors are at work.

This school wasn't in danger of closing; it was, in effect, closed. The formal action was only hours away—literally. Hope was abandoned.

In my youth, I spent some time at sea. I visualize a lifeboat with volunteers to take a precious cargo through rough seas to a safe haven. Will it make it? Can it make it? Who are these people who risk so much for so little? None are offered rewards or promises. Why?

Every teacher working in this school is here by his or her own choice. All competed to get the posts they hold. And there was no assurance, succeed or fail, as to what would happen in the future. They wanted to make this "voyage." The same with the principal. Some people believe we are all here because of divine intervention. Many times I believe it myself.

When I see these teachers at work every day—at such hard work—I marvel. Some "chemistry" is going on between us that is producing great results. It will defy the researchers—but not the believers. Faith can move mountains and it will be faith that will make this school well. If we lose faith, we die. I am certain. But our faith is firm. I marvel at that too.

The Academic Connection in Action

I never ceased to be amazed. The white van marked "University of West Florida" pulls up sharply, directly in front of the little school. A young UWF faculty member, Angela Martin, is driving and the van is full. She waves and nimbly alights with her bevy of graduate students as well as undergraduates, all dressed very professionally and well prepared to tutor and teach. All report to respective classrooms and are soon hard at work. They meet with individual children and with small groups on very specific tasks. Our plan is working. The children are delighted to see them and the time is utilized to the fullest. There are other lessons too.

"Will you talk to us in Chinese?" said one little group of third graders to their Asian tutor. Diversity is not our strong suit in Munson, although with our VT-6 volunteers and these fine UWF students we are improving. It would go on like this month after month, several days each week.

Our own teachers are very demanding, as they should be. It reminds me of medical interns working alongside busy physicians. Their focus is on the patient. Our focus is on the student. Angela Martin and these wonderful young people make a tremendous contribution to the progress of our pupils; it is appreciated more than they can ever know.

Munson's early emphasis on meeting individualized learning needs received another great boost in addition to the tremendous cadre of volunteer tutors and teachers in training.

It was late in the afternoon, a little before dismissal time, that I first got to know Professor Rex Schmid. Rex is the top specialist in UWF's College of Education on student assessment, tests, and evaluation.

One of our older pupils stops me in the hall to say, "Dr. D, there is a strange man way out on the South Forty." We call everything on the periphery of the playground the South Forty. I thank him and immediately go to investigate. Larry already had an eye on the man in the distance, as did one of the teachers. No one is allowed to loiter around schools.

But he is not actually loitering. He is hitting practice chip shots with his sand wedge, dressed in a fine business suit as well as white shirt and tie. All that is missing is the briefcase and sure enough, there it is, over by his car in the parking lot.

"Hi! I'm Dr. Schmid," he shouts and heads my way. "We met last month. You were in a meeting just now so I thought I would use the time to advantage. I certainly need the practice." We shake hands and laugh.

The long and short of it that fall afternoon was that Dr. Schmid and his team were offering to conduct a diagnostic analysis of the specific academic needs of each child in Munson Elementary grades 1–6. All gratis, of course.

It was an absolutely magnificent offer, for it is a very time-consuming process requiring special materials and knowledge. Each child is tested individually, one on one, in several basic skill areas.

The result is an analysis of the child's specific strengths and weaknesses in those areas. There is no grade in this process; the child does not pass or fail. It tells the teacher exactly where the child needs help. With that kind of detailed diagnostic data in hand, a teacher, with sufficient help, can attack each child's problems with ensuing success that can be quite remarkable.

I think of it as an academic MRI, if there were such technology available for learners as well as for patients. Dr. Schmid would also help us in innumerable other ways, particularly preparing for the dreaded standardized tests to be taken in late March. He would build our own confidence that the course we were embarked on was the right course for these children and that it would succeed. To this day, I do not know if he based his optimism on hard data or on faith. I'll probably never know.

One of my former colleagues refers to Munson's academic connection with UWF as a "master stroke." The letters "UWF" will appear again and again, as we continue the struggle to save Munson Elementary.

Discovery

There is an old rusted tetherball pole near the big oaks that appears to have been idle for years. There are weeds at the base; rust is everywhere; it is leaning and bent. It reminds me of the principal!

Tetherball is a great game. It doesn't require a Ph.D. in psychology to recognize that hitting that ball hanging on a rope and propelled by an opponent student, and hitting it with all your might and fury, is some kind of release. Middle and upper elementary youngsters love it. Few at Munson have ever played; I am amazed.

Chasing snakes, obliterating "killer" ants, playing king of the mountain, boys teasing girls and vice versa seems to have been the main recreation. All hazardous sports. New tetherball poles go up tomorrow.

An Unbeatable Team

Sometimes things are as clear as spring water. It is obvious that all of the children at Munson need to learn to play by the rules, all need to learn the importance of teamwork, and all need a planned program of exercise and physical development. That means the school needs to provide a first-rate program of physical education. And that means recruiting an outstanding teacher of physical education.

Ms. Cindy Cadenhead, the new P.E. teacher, is a find! With her shorts, her whistle and her no-nonsense yet warm rapport with students, we have ourselves a real "coach"! More than that, Ms. Cadenhead is an outstanding teacher. The top physical education student for the year in 1996–97 at UWF, she brings with her an earlier background in computers, maturity through raising a family, and recency of training of the highest order.

The program is launched during the second month of school and every child starts to learn seriously about rules, teamwork, sports, exercise, physical development, the discipline it takes to win and more. Ms. Cadenhead, or "Ms. C" as she likes to be called, designed recreation programs to help during the lunch period, allowed herself to be dunked at the Fall Festival, organized the Turkey Trot at Thanksgiving and a host of other activities as the year progressed.

The Turkey Trot was a one-mile foot race (walk for the little ones) with a prize of a real turkey for the winner of the girls' division and the boys' division for each grade level. Aviators from the training squadron volunteered to help supervise the races. It was serious business. Ms. C obtained donations of 14 frozen turkeys from merchants and made the local press. Some of the turkeys seemed almost as big as the kindergarten children as they proudly struggled to carry their prize turkey to their beaming parents. We all loved it!

Although only a half-time position, one by-product of the physical education program is the flexibility it provides in the schedule for all teachers. Classroom teachers have an almost impossible schedule beginning at 7:15 a.m., earlier if one has "dawn patrol" and must meet the buses and supervise children. Students are in class at 7:30 a.m. Lunch for teachers is 30 minutes when not interrupted by telephone calls, concerned parents or some similar "emergency." Unfortunately, these interruptions are the norm, not the exception.

The rest of the time, until the buses depart, teachers are again in intense interaction with children. No wonder one of the long established qualifications for this profession is a healthy bladder. Although it sounds somewhat crude, that's the reality. A daily 30-minute period of physical education for each class would help the children and at the same time give each classroom teacher a little planning time during the day. It was a must. We found the resources for the half-time position. The big task was to find just the right teacher. It wasn't easy, but it happened. The Dream Team was complete! One more wonderful teacher will be added to God's Hall of Fame.

Ms. C is proud of Munson Elementary, the fine old gym, being part of the team and the tough job ahead. And we're proud of Ms. C. Divine intervention? The evidence continues to mount.

Of course, new staff means some type of office space, furniture—just the basics. With hard work, cleaning, some paint and an aggressive approach against the termites, we are in business. Presto! An office emerges from a storage closet! For furniture, we have an old chair but need a desk. Thanks to frugal Larry, we have an ancient metal desk that had been badly smashed in the center by vandals many years before. Never know when you are going to need a bashed-in desk, so it was saved. With hammer and cleaner, Larry and Patricia soon have it looking fine. I contribute spackle and putty knife for "body work" and Ms. C adds the final touches. With blotter in place it works, and Ms. C has one of the best desks in the little school! Larry's foresight has paid off and I know he is proud that the old desk is once again back in use.

Other team changes came about during the first months of school. Judy Lindsey, the school secretary, decides to retire. She is coming along remarkably well although still under intensive treatment for cancer. In the "well" periods, she seems to enjoy her new leisure.

Gail Baxley, with her extensive experience and superb skills, moved into the position of school secretary and Kathy Turner, the substitute who was pinch hitting for Judy since the first days of school, was appointed teacher assistant. Now, we have two TAs, Kathy and Debbie. Roles didn't actually change too much.

Gail is now officially responsible for most of the office activity including budget, purchasing, records, attendance, accounting, breakfast and lunch monies and seemingly a thousand other important functions. We have no person available to be assigned to the library, so Gail, Kathy and Debbie have taken it upon themselves to inventory and computer catalog the entire collection of 2,727 volumes.

All are self-starters. They see what has to be done, and they do it. Kathy serves as receptionist while handling paperwork for teachers, running the complex and temperamental copier, answering the telephone, administering medicine and first aid to children, supervising the cafeteria, checking in visitors, receiving deliveries, sorting mail and helping teachers in a dozen ways. The two teacher assistants and the school secretary are a great team. Munson wouldn't last a week without them. The principal wouldn't make it through the day without their constant attention to the detail that it takes to help teachers stay on task teaching children. With this group, our Dream Team of teachers, Edith in the cafeteria, Larry and Patricia in custodial services and our four fearless bus drivers, we truly are a real team. Add our great volunteers and we're an unbeatable team.

Whenever I list our full complement of team members, it seems like a large group to educate 82 children. But hold on. We not only teach these children, we transport them thousands of miles, and hence the buses, the drivers and the thousand gallons of diesel fuel every month. In addition, we're in the restaurant business serving close to 3,000 meals a month. And of course, we are in the parenting business, closely supervising children every minute from the moment they arrive until they leave in the afternoon. We water them, feed them, bed the kindergartners, nurse them when they are ill, counsel them, medicate them, and, oh, yes, teach them to read and write and numerous other skills. In addition, we are also in the compliance business, the legal business, the accounting business, the maintenance business, the book business, the computer business and the public relations business. Schools are complex organizations; in this context, the team doesn't look large at all.

Fog and Forest

Wide ribbons of mist meander mindlessly through the forest trees this morning. They dip sharply over byways and highways, then rise high to the tips of the towering pines. They are beautiful until they tangle and become a soft, white snare, level with the hard, black surface of Munson Highway. Pure fear. The forest is quiet.

Children and school buses are out in this cloying killer. It is dangerous today. I trust God is with these little ones and the faithful and skillful drivers in whose hands He has placed their lives. We take much for granted. I worry. The buses arrive safely. The last one is delayed. It finally arrives and school begins. Lessons are learned. Life is good. Each, in his own way, gives thanks.

In God's Hands

As far as weather goes, this has been a wild year. Dense fog is not uncommon. Yesterday, the school went on tornado alert for the second time in just a few months. Today, there was a school bus crash. Our children were not involved and no youngsters were injured, but the car and driver that collided with the bus were not so fortunate. Our little ones had made the transfer to another bus just minutes before the accident. It was a scary way to begin the day.

In this part of the world we take tornadoes very seriously. When the warning sounds from the Santa Rosa County Emergency Operations Center, we act immediately. The system screeches its warning over the office monitor and all schools in the affected area are directed to "take cover." It reminds me of air raids in England during World War II. Children and staff are directed to go to assigned inside areas that engineers have identified as the strongest structurally. All children are on the floor facing walls with heads down at the baseboards. Some of the smaller children cry. Some try not to, but do. All are frightened. This is not a simulated drill; it is for real. A tornado has been sighted in this area and it is coming this way. Teachers and aides are on the floor beside the children, consoling, reassuring, ministering to their fears. One child will gently place an arm around the shoulder of another, perhaps a brother or sister or friend. Some hold hands. They are brave little boys and girls.

In time, the children change position and a teacher reads a story as we wait patiently for the "all clear" or for the ominous sounds of impending disaster. Many say a silent prayer. The principal prays too.

The Substitute

"I've told you for the last time, sit down!" When a substitute teacher reaches this point in a classroom, he or she has "lost it."

Substitutes are brave souls. The pay is a pittance and the demands are many. On call at a "minute's notice" to fill the gap when a teacher is not able to report for duty, substitutes must be very capable, resourceful and flexible people.

Children like to test substitute teachers. They always have, and probably always will. Excellent lesson plans from the regular teacher are essential but there can still be problems. I know the feeling.

It is 7:00 a.m. The buses are arriving and there is a full day ahead. Mrs. Rogaliner, Munson's fifth-/sixth-grade teacher, calls to tell me that her youngest child is ill and she has been trying, without success, for almost an hour to secure a substitute teacher so she can take her little girl to the doctor. I am concerned for her child, for the distraught mother, and for the crisis it is causing at school. She can get class started but that is all.

A small school has few options in a situation like this. That is one disadvantage of being small. All of our teachers have a full load. The only viable option is for me to teach the class. After all, I am qualified so let's get on with it. But what a class! These are our oldest youngsters and are noted for being a very difficult group to teach. I know some of them well, from frequent visits to "the principal's office."

"It will all end here," I say to myself.

Mrs. Rogaliner stops by on her way to the doctor, sick child in tow, and I tell her not to worry, I will take the class. I hope my terror is not too obvious.

It has been over 40 years since I had been a classroom teacher. I call my wife at home, a superb master teacher, but also years ago. She gives me some excellent advice and very specific invaluable suggestions. I have 15 minutes in which to plan. Professional substitute teachers have a "bag of tricks" for moments like these, differentiated teaching materials for every level and for all basic subjects. It's a must. In the brief time available, I build a series of lessons to augment Mrs. Rogaliner's fine plans and for several hours I teach school.

It is a successful morning. I am pleased. My wife's advice had worked; my own training and experience also worked. And the title of principal didn't do any harm. I could still walk the high wire with grace, but I am reminded ever so forcefully that teaching, if it is done right, is one of the most demanding jobs in the world. Again, I marvel at the energy and skill of our Dream Team.

Mrs. Rogaliner returns. Her child will soon be well with care and her husband, Lt. Commander Rogaliner, is off duty and at home serving as nurse.

The muffled sounds of children at play and at work say the school has returned to normal. It is a good feeling.

Thoughts That Wiggle in My Mind (On Teaching and Teachers)

Few scholars, observers, or students of schooling have the unique opportunity to be inside the process that is going on every minute in this special place. The intensity of the experience, the depth of relationships, the constant, continuing struggle for minds and insight are all consuming and seem magnified many times in such close quarters and under such relentless pressure. You can see it in expressions and motions. You can hear it in the tone of voice or laughter. You can feel it in the tension or joy in the air. You can measure it in the results. Every second of every day is an intense drama between human beings striving for the expansion of minds, bodies, and souls. Few of us ever experience such gripping struggles that impact the lives of others, forever. These are strong words but daily realities in every school and in every classroom.

These matters are not impersonal or abstract. They are not the actions of politicians or edicts of governments. They are the actions of one human being interacting with one other human being, perhaps a small, vulnerable child or a gangling, challenging adolescent, multiplied many, many times. A good teacher is the best of all of us in one helping many of us. Teachers must see and hear and feel everything—the look in the young person's eyes, the movements of body, the quavering voice, the shy laughter, the sullen response to a question, or the anger and hostility in an action. These and a thousand other signs speak volumes. They must be seen and felt and experienced and processed. And it is not only between teacher and student, it is between child and child, parent and youngster, parent and teacher, and on and on.

The process is perpetual. There is no respite, no rest, and no relief from the constant subtle innuendoes or the shouting signals of personal triumph or tribulation in the process of learning and growing.

Good teachers see it all, experience it, feel it, internalize it, know it, and use it in helping children. They are keenly perceptive and are patience personified. In other words, it is love translated into action, en masse.

It is the life of a caring mother or father, multiplied many times.

It is the career of a dedicated teacher.

And it is almost impossible for it is the job description of a God, an angel, or a saint. I say almost, for some wonderful teachers are in some ways divine beings, I am convinced. But that is a personal conviction. To build a system of education whose success depends primarily upon angels and saints is unrealistic. That it works as well as it does says much about teachers, parents and young people. The caring people are what are right about today's schooling and they must not be tarred with the same brush that too often is used indiscriminately to criticize and condemn. Few Americans wish to trade places with their child's teacher.

Every caring teacher, at the end of the day in a moment of exhausted reflection, experiences despair and disappointment at not being able to reach all of the youngsters that need them most.

Some, after too many days and months and years of despair and disappointment, give up. They may stay in the classroom, but their dreams and passion for teaching and learning and for young people are gone. The fire of commitment has been consumed. And we allow it to happen. It is so very sad, for I am absolutely convinced it does not have to be this way.

Mrs. D's Little Boy

The creaking of joints and the muffled groans said it was "Lap Sit" time. Yes, that is what it is called. Sitting on the classroom floor with a child on your lap is quite an experience, but getting down and up again—that's the real challenge!

Several times during the year Mrs. Sanders has a "Lap Sit" for the kindergarten children. What a joy! She has found that when children are held on their mother's laps and the child has the opportunity to tell about what he or she has learned, some wonderful things happen to the child and to the parent. The child's pride and the parent's pride join with love and respect in exquisite moments of shared affection. Joy in accomplishment, joy in knowing that the other knows, and joy in sharing are all beautiful to see and to experience.

Mrs. Sanders says, "These are moments that every child needs and should have regularly. They can change a child's life."

Unfortunately, some parents can't be present and substitute laps are enlisted for service. Mrs. D and also a dear friend, Mrs. Kathy Snyder, serve in that capacity. The floor, of course, is carpeted, but so-o-o hard.

Children's work and materials are everywhere. Mrs. Sanders reads a story and the children participate, showing off their new reading skills. Stories are told, skits are performed, songs are sung and a tear or two of love is shed.

Toward the end, Mrs. D's little boy wants to take her home. Failing that, he looked up and asked, "Can I go home with you? I love you." And with his little hand he reached up and caressed her cheek for just a moment and then his eyes slowly closed in rest. And he smiled gently.

From then on, he never fails to ask after Mrs. D. "Tell Mrs. D I love her," he always adds quite seriously. He's a wonderful little fellow, Mrs. D's Little Boy.

Pause

For over half the school year, children and teachers have been at the hard, hard work of teaching and learning, of lessons, homework study and tests. Learning is very hard work. The joy is reaching your next goal but the process is focused, demanding work.

There has been much progress and it shows. Children are proud of their accomplishments and parents and teachers are proud of their children. Can we keep up the pace? We must.

Today's Horses

Ten feet from the front door of our townhouse is a parking area, very convenient but no garage. When I look out, I see images of horses standing patiently in front of shops and other establishments, waiting quietly for their masters of past times. Now the horses are sleek metal and plastic and the hay costs more. They withstand heat, cold, rain, wind, storms and the sands of time. We expect them to "giddy-up" at a moment's notice, and they usually do. Sometimes they are sick and sometimes they die but they are really remarkable animals, today's horses with the big rubber shoes.

The Drive

There are five stop signs and two stoplights between my home and Munson. There are also several creeks, rivers, Escambia Bay, and in the rainy season, innumerable bodies of water that are not where they are supposed to be. U.S. Highway 191, Munson Highway, is an almost straight ribbon of two-lane highway gently undulating through the tall pines of the Blackwater River Forest. Creeks do overflow their banks, fog frequently threatens, and navigating the narrow road is sometimes a death-defying act as the blinding headlights and rain or fog obscure everything but the margin line demarking the very edge of the road. There is no paved shoulder. I am sure all drivers pray that the other person is holding a true course on his or her side of the road. Sometimes only a foot or two separate us from sudden death or worse. And some think flying is dangerous!

It is bad in the early morning because of the darkness and the traffic. In the late afternoon, it is bad because of fatigue and the concentration factor. I am sure all commuters face these potential killers regularly. Falling asleep is not something I like to admit, but so far it has happened three times, causing the car to momentarily cross the centerline. By God's grace, there were no oncoming cars at the moment—but that may not always be the case. Now I drink coffee before the long trip and stop if I feel too fatigued. The concentration factor is almost as bad, but I now have that under control and really concentrate just on driving.

On balance, as many commuters would agree, a commute can be enjoyable in many ways. But there is no question that it is dangerous. Eternity sounds like another place far away. I would rather be safe at home. My wife agrees. I remember that every time I take the reins and head out.

The long drive also takes me through Bagdad, a quaint old area of gracious white antebellum homes surrounded by ancient oaks draped with Spanish moss. The oaks spread their giant limbs over the road and form an arch to the past. The lights before dawn shine softly through heavy curtains almost like the oil lamps of old. The white picket fences, the verandas and lawns suggest another way of life.

Few people know what has been referred to as "the other Florida." It is quiet, peaceful, so very different in fact and perception from much of the Florida peninsula. Here, there are trees, seasons, cotton and country. There are farmers and loggers, rural communities and dirt roads, game and hunters. There is little glitz in rural Florida. It is real. The communities have been here from the earliest times and the history is rich and stirring. Some find the region out of touch with the modern world. Some feel it is the other way around.

The cock crows. The day is waking. The little school begins to stir. Edith is at the cook stove—there will be fresh biscuits this morning. Teachers and aides begin to arrive. Today's wonderful horses with the big rubber shoes rest after the long trek. They deserve a rest. Children with bags and books are waiting for buses in dirt lanes and byways, in front of houses, or by the big pines.

They will soon be arriving. It is another day in the country school. It will be a good day.

Angel in Uniform

Tony Chamberlin is on full-time, active duty in the United States Navy. He is also a part-time student at the University preparing to be a teacher when his twenty-year Navy hitch comes to a close. In between these demanding responsibilities, Tony donates his time and talent to Munson Elementary School; a lot of time and a lot of talent. Tony transplants "brains." He is a computer surgeon and a brilliant one. Although always in civilian dress, at Munson we see him as an angel in uniform.

There is no question that every teacher can use assistance in working with individual children on specific instructional needs. Our greatest potential helper is the computer—with the right power, the right software, and the right availability. It is not by accident that the little school has a higher ratio of computers to children than any school in Santa Rosa County and possibly in the entire state of Florida. We would double it tomorrow if we could.

We started with our little computer lab and a unit or so in each classroom. Most were attractive units but with very limited memory. Most could not accommodate the fine new software that is appearing in the marketplace. As the "techies" might say, "Nice boxes but not many brains."

Enter Tony Chamberlin. This gentleman can transplant "brains" and other components from one unit to another. We all become scavengers. Surplus computers come a dozen at a time from the Air Force, the Navy and a variety of sources. Unfortunately, not all of them work. No matter. Tony cannibalizes these units and literally builds several new, powerful computers that are a terrific asset to the little school. They quickly find their way into classrooms where new drops, including the Internet, have them online in no time.

In the future, I expect to see them lining classroom walls and hallways as well as one in the home of each of our pupils.

Computers and new technologies will not replace teachers. They are tools, helpers, sophisticated individual tutors, and they make a tremendous difference. Indeed, they can make all the difference for they may become the mechanism by which teachers can help negate the devastating structure we have imposed on them for so long.

To employ a much-used saying, Tony is a "God send" to Munson Elementary. I now know that God has a special hand in the future of this little place.

"Hey Tony," I joke as he passes the office carrying a newly salvaged "brain." "How about implanting that in the principal?"

He comes back fast and with a straight face, "I would love to Doc, but it would take two or three to get you up to speed! Can't spare them."

God works in wondrous ways.

Hope

Mother is here to take little Hope out of school. "The home environment is just not good for the children," mother said quietly, on the verge of tears. Much is implied. How very sad. Hope loves this little school and we all love Hope. She is a beautiful child with dark hair and lovely dark eyes contrasting with her wan face and simple dress and sweater. Sometimes I feel the school is the only stable place there is in the broken lives of too many of these little ones. Are we so presumptuous to believe we can fill the void in these children's hearts? We may provide physical nutrition and challenging lessons, but can we compensate for the lack of love and stability in their fragile young lives? We can only do our best.

The school secretary helps mother with the withdrawal form. I leave to get Hope and enter her classroom. There is a pause. She knows. Slowly, she reaches for her few little belongings, a worn pencil, an old notebook with a torn corner, and her folder with lessons. She rises slowly, clutching her possessions and a partly finished picture. Will it ever be completed? She softly touches her pretty new desk and tears drop silently on the polished surface. They seem alone and sad. Her teacher hugs her and holds her. Little friends gather for a tearful good bye. I take her hand gently and lead her down the lonely hall to the office—and to another place far away.

The Dilemma

In the world of classrooms and children it is an article of faith that all human beings have equal worth. Policies and practices often belie this fundamental belief but it is nevertheless basic in the lives of most parents and most teachers and indeed, I believe, in most Americans. Of course, we recognize achievement and accomplishment in our culture (more in some areas than others) and are critical of failure. However, most of us feel diminished in some way when we condemn, reject and discriminate against an individual for the innate characteristics over which that person has no control. Color, intelligence, physical characteristics, primary language, and even one's parents are part of the original equipment. So be it.

Every parent hopes for a healthy, "normal" child, but all children deserve our support and love. And it is this way, or should be, in every classroom. Hence, the many programs for children with special needs and the programs such as desegregation that are ultimately based on this article of faith. But do these efforts in themselves discriminate? Who should attend school and who should not? An unthinkable question. In other words, who should receive the costly attention? The gifted? The handicapped? The emotionally disturbed? Should we have small classes for "special" children and large classes for everyone else? More able students might "advance" quickly while "slower" students might fail. Should these be removed from the rolls as in earlier times? Obviously not.

As with any dilemma implementing our belief in the equal value of human beings, this requires tough, hard decisions.

Danger

The early morning sun silhouettes the pines, the oaks, and the little cluster of buildings that wait peacefully for the voices and laughter of children. Like a new day, a good school is a place full of hope and unlimited possibilities. However, sometimes it can be a place of danger.

Although the millions of children in the classrooms of America are in the safest environment devised, and it really is very safe, the instances of violence in schools are shattering and deeply disturbing. It is absolutely clear that lethal violence is an avenue of behavior for disturbed young people that was rarely considered in earlier times. And while the extreme mayhem of some gains national attention and poses a serious threat, the daily but less dramatic behavior of many others poses a greater threat. For in classrooms across the nation, teachers and counselors report a significant increase in the number of very disturbed children who by their actions deny other children, millions of other children, their right to an education.

The causes are not difficult to identify. Some occur before birth, many after. Alcohol, drugs, inadequate nutrition, attention or affection, as well as abuse, abandonment, and a steady diet of violence, all play their parts. The list is almost endless. Our priorities are wrong. Even when parents try very hard, and most do, they can make terrible mistakes. The demands on their time, energies and resources leave little for the complex responsibility of raising children. But these children end up in the classrooms we call safe. Some funds are available to help disturbed children but not nearly enough. An even larger concern is the fact that many parents refuse to admit the problem. Court actions and legal maneuvers almost paralyze schools in their efforts to properly address the issues.

At little Munson Elementary, I think of Jake, George, Sally and Don, to name only a few. These are sick children. The most devastating description of a child I have ever heard was from one of our most insightful teachers who said, "When I look into Jake's eyes, they seem empty. I don't believe he has a soul." Although perhaps as poetic as it is professional, such observations by people who live and work with these children every day must be heard. In the classroom, on the school bus, at home, or at any activity, these children are a constant problem. Soon they will be driving cars and having babies.

Their attention span is nil, their respect for authority equally so. Many strive constantly for attention, disturbing everyone in the process. Throwing, hitting, tripping, talking, hurting and shoving as well as committing all types of vandalism are common behavioral patterns.

Punishment is meaningless; expulsion from school is a reward. These children need professional help and a far different environment than a full, busy classroom.

This morning, I met with Jake's guardians and the school psychologist in one of the innumerable meetings required by law when considering a child for alternative placement. It was an endless meeting filled with the guardians expressing denial and hostility toward everyone. The best the boy can expect from home is a beating. It may take court action to move the child to a school with special teachers and facilities to better help Jake.

There are also other behavior patterns that concern us deeply. Through gestures and innuendo, Jake threatens suicide. Whatever the obstacles, Jake will be placed in an appropriate environment with trained help. It is a promise I make to myself.

But there is still George, Sally and Don, and a dozen additional students who are classified as having a learning disability. Some of these children, because of their serious behavior problems or other needs, will jeopardize the quality of the education the classroom teacher can deliver to all children. Jake and others like him not only need special help but also their impossible demands on the classroom teacher form a present and rapidly growing danger to every child.

Collectively, as a society, we must address what we are doing to our children. It is not enough to attempt to place blame. Violence as a diet for children must end. Support in every form must be more available to parents. Early childhood education must be implemented and available to all families and to all children. The role of the family and the community must be enhanced in supporting and nurturing children. The problems are not insurmountable—they only seem insurmountable.

Jake not only *has* a problem; he *is* a problem and affects every child in this school. I cannot let his problem cause this school to fail and at the same time, I cannot fail Jake. He will be helped and so will Munson Elementary.

Breakfast Time

It is early morning and the little cluster of buildings waits peacefully for the voices and laughter of children. Today, as with every school day, light shines through the windows of the cafeteria as I approach from Munson Highway. Edith is busy preparing breakfast for our hungry little ones. Some eat breakfast at home but most eat at school. School buses have been on the road for an hour, so it won't be long.

On the drive here, I always wave or tap my horn to send a "Hi" to lone children who wait patiently for the big lumbering bus that will bring them to this place of warmth and learning. As they wave back and shout "Hi," their breath tells me it is a very crisp morning. We establish quite a bond with our little "hellos." I miss the children when they are not there. I think they miss me too when my schedule changes. We sort of check on each other.

"I saw you coming to school this morning, Dr. D," one announces later with a big smile.

"I saw you too, Tommy. Where is your little brother?"

Everything at school is ready. The teacher on "dawn patrol"— which rotates weekly—the teacher assistant, and the principal stand ready on this cold winter morning. Inside, Edith is completing her last-minute preparations. Her daughter is helping. Gail has arrived moments before and has the cashier's and record keeping table organized and waiting. As with her bookkeeping, her timing is precise—never a minute early and never a minute late—she is a remarkable lady. Records are essential because many of these children are on federal programs and the accounting requirements are stringent.

Almost on cue the buses arrive. As each bus reaches the assigned drop-off location, children pour out and head up the walk to the assembling area before entering the building itself. Once a line is formed, we wait briefly and then the little ones enter first, followed by the older youngsters. They sit by class at the long fold-down tables with seats attached that have no backs. Book bags usually end up under seats or in assigned areas. Those who have had breakfast at home head for the tables marked "STUDY." When my wife and I made signs for each table the weekend before school opened, we were reminded of our earlier days as teachers.

As the children head up that walk from their buses, I greet them with a cheery "Good morning." It seems a good way to start the day. Well, not to the children, for in very few cases is there ever a response. Just a determined stride to the line with book bags and assorted articles for class in tow. I have tried everything. It hasn't worked. So much for the "beloved Dr. D myth," I think. And then it strikes me. Not only are the poor kids half asleep, they are hungry. They had been up before dawn. After dressing, most had gone directly outside to wait for the bus. Some fell asleep on the ride in; most wanted to.

A few were mischief-makers and required special attention on arriving. I referred those to Mr. Johnson with his assistant principal hat. I know all about the business of delegation. Anyway, I rationalize that it is good training. Mr. Johnson really does have a way with wayward youngsters and we all admire and respect his skills. You don't forget a lecture from Mr. Johnson, that's for sure.

The teachers are clearly more perceptive than I. They don't need to use greetings. Their presence is reassuring enough. Unnecessary words seem intrusive although special words are eagerly received. Staff members are quick to notice everything. "That's a beautiful new dress, Sugar," says one to a shy young girl. It doesn't require a response but the slight turn of her head, the lowered eyes and the beautiful smile that played around the lips say more than words could possibly say. It says that the comment had been heard and dearly appreciated and would make that little girl's day. It is nice to know that others notice and care.

A few parents bring their children to school on their way to work. It is nice. We are part of their family sharing in the raising of their son or daughter. I never cease to be touched by the moment—the parting smile or gesture between parent and little child and the welcoming gesture by the teacher or teacher assistant. Sometimes a handshake between principal and father follows. We have a common bond. Trust is reaffirmed.

Of course, for the older children grappling with their emerging identities, parents are best not seen or heard. "Just drop me off here, Mom," is the way it is usually expressed. "Here," is usually way out there, but everyone understands. Even then, a warm wave between teacher and parent says much, including "Don't worry, we'll take good care of him."

Breakfast goes smoothly. The primary grade children work their way through the serving line, proudly clutching their plastic trays. Today is scrambled eggs, sausage, toast, fruit and milk.

There are other choices too, as required by policy, but the eggs are the most popular today. If I am lucky, Edith may have a sausage or two remaining that I can gobble on my way back to the office. They smell so good, and my 5:30 a.m. breakfast at home now seems like a distant memory. Other classes follow in order, one group at a time, until all are served. Older girls help by opening milk cartons for the little ones when necessary. All of us are on hand to supervise and assist.

Occasionally, there is a spill. Patricia leaves a big mop and bucket handy and tries to be available, although her schedule is very demanding. In an emergency, I pinch-hit and wield the mop. At this point, one of the children invariably comes forward to take over. "I'll do it, Dr. D." I concede. It is a big mop for small youngsters but they do quite well and we all manage fine. They are always proud of their efforts and so are we.

Breakfast time is a happy time, albeit sometimes a noisy time. So many of these children have not seen another boy or girl their age since they left school yesterday. There is a lot of catching up to do. Stories about new purchases, family doings, a hunting adventure or a visit to grandma, all have to be related. And of course, the usual gossip about classmates as well as the girl talk, the boy talk, the gun talk, ad infinitum. To deal with the noise, Mr. Johnson instituted Story Time. It was a great success.

About half way through the meal, the PA system is activated and one of us reads a story to the entire group. Usually, it is a continuing children's story from an appropriate level book with a good story line, including suspense and excitement. The one I remember most is about the adventures of a boy and his dog. It was very well received. If any child gets too obstreperous, he or she is quietly reminded of the rules, and on occasion is isolated from his peers. It would be spring before the reminders would not be necessary. By then, at least for most of the students, the lessons had been learned.

At 7:30 a.m. sharp, the class bell rings and teachers appear to escort their respective groups to class. "Show me a line, please" is Mr. Johnson's favorite expression in this situation. Sometimes it has to be repeated for emphasis, but it always works. Mr. Johnson is kind but firm and very consistent. Children know it. He is an excellent example for all of us.

Mrs. Rogaliner's warm but regal presence is sufficient to convey to her older group the message "Time to line up." This is invariably reinforced with her favorite expression, "Excuse me?" in a thousand variations. One variation says, "Shape up, now!" Most do, in their typical pre-teen style and are off to a day of serious study that will stretch the margins of their minds—forever.

Mrs. Sanders and Mrs. Marmount nudge, herd and smile their little charges into line. Then off they go joyfully, fingers to lips and in perfect order, to the exciting world of learning. They are a delight to watch.

Mrs. Coogle and her creative bunch are off on some wonderful tour to the house of stories and books and numbers. They excitedly try to behave, and usually do as they follow their petite pied piper to another grand adventure of discovery. School is fun!

The distant sounds of children pledging their allegiance to flag and country say that classes are underway and that Breakfast Time is over. Well, not exactly. Edith and her volunteer helpers are resting and enjoying a cup of well-earned tea or coffee. As for me, I haven't forgotten. As they say in Munson, "That sausage is gonna taste re-e-eal good." And it does! Breakfast Time is over.

Winter Morning

I miss the magnificent sunrise each day shrouded gracefully in the morning mist and softly silhouetting the beautiful pines, pastures and winding roads to other worlds. It is from these worlds that children come to our little school in the big forest. Their dogs sometimes trot alongside the big yellow buses to wish their masters well and to let them know they will be missed. Parting is difficult. If they trot too far, the bus driver kindly stops and, unofficially of course, adds an additional "student" to our rolls that day. I miss those mornings.

Now it is dark in the morning—very dark. But these mornings bring their special beauty, too. On the shores of Escambia Bay, lights twinkle with warmth and the beginning of another busy day. Like life at sea, harbor lights with the promise of safety and life.

Morning is promise in color and lights. I like that.

Mrs. Coogle's Trojan Horse

Some classrooms are quite formal and structured. Others are less so. And then there is Mrs. Coogle's class. Here, second- and third-grade pupils live and learn in another world—literally. Oh, there is a structured area with desks and special circular reading tables and study centers as well as books and more books galore. There are computers and there are maps and globes and materials and chalkboards and all the rest. But what makes her classroom different is that she likes to have children actually experience the world they study. Most teachers do this to a degree, but Mrs. Coogle is an expert.

In science, they raise chickens and make real volcanoes—not only read about them. When they study space, they actually go there. And when they study history and geography, they are literally transported in time to the environment of that period. To the casual visitor, the classroom might appear almost chaotic. But not to these children and their creative teacher. Each child can take you on a real trip to a real place and explain exactly what they are learning and what it is all about. The enthusiasm and excitement make learning real and lasting.

Of course, all of this can lead to minor practical problems.

A little before dawn about three weeks ago, I saw Mrs. Coogle struggling out of her car with books and materials thrust under one arm and a horse under the other. I ran to help. Of course, it wasn't a real horse but a wire net frame of a good-sized creature, that with enough paper-mâché and the artistic talents of her little ones would become a respectable diminutive horse, actually, a Trojan horse! They were studying the Trojan War of Greek legend, so naturally…

Monday morning about two weeks later Larry reports that the school had had a "break-in" on Saturday night. The security alarm had been triggered in the middle of the night, the police summoned, and Larry called to respond. Larry lives a considerable distance from Munson, so such a call is hardly appreciated. After much checking, the culprit was finally discovered: Mrs. Coogle's Trojan horse. The wire frame, which was not very strong, had collapsed and the horse had toppled over, causing sufficient disturbance to activate the room's motion detector.

This incident prompted me to write the following memorandum which Mrs. Coogle and her children enjoyed so much it found its way into the homes of the entire class.

> *MEMORANDUM*
>
> *To: Teachers and Teacher Assistants*
>
> *From: Dr. D*
>
> *Subject: The Trojan Horse*
>
> *Mrs. Coogle's Trojan Horse died Saturday! Well, at least it fell over. What this will do to the course of world history, I am not sure. Her pupils will no doubt be involved in writing about the experience (which is great) and we will all be watching the drama closely. I bring it to your attention because in the process of falling, it triggered the security alarm, necessitating a trip for Larry from home to Munson and return, brought the police from their lair, and will no doubt require reports in 15 copies to someone.*
>
> *The moral of the story: make sure all moving things like horses will not move after you leave your classroom.*
>
> *The good news is that the motion detectors really work!*

I suspect those children will never forget the story of the Trojan Horse. I know Larry won't.

Flag and Country

It is a very cold morning. Children shiver as they stand smartly at attention with eyes lifted and hands over hearts and form a border of brave little citizens with their teachers, showing respect for flag and country. In the center of the small courtyard that forms the entrance to Munson Elementary School, the sixth-grade color guard raises the flags of country and state with dignity and military precision.

Mrs. Rogaliner is proud of her sixth graders and has played a key role in emphasizing patriotism at the little school. The martial refrains of the National Anthem and the voices of children ring out clearly through the crisp morning air and tell the world that this is America and that we are proud and that we are free. Every Friday at 7:30 a.m. sharp, except in storms, we share this experience.

All schools teach patriotism and love of country. But we have an advantage. Thanks to the volunteers from the Naval Air Station at Whiting Field, young men and women in military uniforms grace our halls and classrooms on a regular basis. Children know; they know that these young adults put their lives at risk every day for America and for the freedoms we cherish and share. The words and lessons become very real. They also learn that responsibility, discipline and freedom go hand in hand.

I recall a young officer drilling our youthful color guard of boys and girls. His orders were firm. He was a Marine. Lessons that day were on appropriate dress: dark pants or skirts, white tops and no jewelry. The next day at practice one of the boys appeared wearing his earring. The officer, in an unbelievably deft slight of hand, quietly and quickly removed the jewelry and handed it ever so subtly to our young surprised student. Jewelry did not appear again during any of our ceremonies.

Military cooperation was phenomenal. On one occasion, the superintendent of schools, the senior commander from NAS Whiting Field, the Navy choir from NAS Pensacola, and a representative of our local Congressman all graced our little square.

The military personnel were in their finest uniforms and it was very early. It was a splendid occasion for the 82 boys and girls and their teachers and staff. Patriotism comes in many forms.

Schools teach democracy in increments—increments of responsibility, freedom, knowledge, human understanding and respect. They teach the value of work, the necessity of self-discipline and the skills and insights to better appreciate our past, to function effectively in the present and to challenge the future. Our little ones must learn these lessons well. The world depends on it.

Randy and Mrs. Sanders

"Dr. D, do you have a minute?" It is 10:35 a.m. and Mrs. Sanders' class is at P.E. for 30 minutes. "I need to talk to you about Randy."

"Sure." I motion to one of the chairs in front of my desk while I take the other. I really dislike talking across a desk. It gets in the way.

"You remember when Randy enrolled about three weeks ago? Well, he's a real terror in the classroom. I've tried everything."

I certainly do remember. His mother was constantly admonishing him to absolutely no avail. Talk about Dennis the Menace. I thought then, "Poor Sanders."

"Well, I have discovered," she continues in her lilting, melodic, Southern accent, "that he has always been punished for bad behavior but never consistently rewarded for good behavior. I'm turning this around and I need your help." She has my attention. "For each day of especially good behavior, I will give Randy a 'smiley face' and I want him to bring it to you at the end of the day—just before he goes home on the bus. His reward will be a smiley face sticker, with much praise from you."

She gives me a sheet of colorful stickers that would excite any six-year-old. "After five days of smiley faces, he can then have his choice of any toy in this big pickle jar," which she also presents to me to keep just for Randy. Of course I agree to cooperate. Mrs. Sanders flashes her wonderful smile and leaves, saying as she rounds the corner, "I think it will work."

Since then, Randy has been to my office so many times we're pals. He calls me "coach." "Coach, I got a smiley face today," he proudly announces with a big grin. I congratulate him with great enthusiasm and we go through the ritual of getting out the big sheet and he proceeds to select the colorful award.

Sometimes he puts it on the back of his hand to show his mother when he gets home. Other times, he'll put it on my telephone to announce his accomplishment to the world! After five days, Randy is allowed to reach into the pickle jar and make his toy selection. What a joy!

This has gone on for about a month with tremendous success. Randy isn't perfect, but he is now a leader in his class and is often a model of responsible behavior. He comes by now and then, but is sort of nonchalant about it. He doesn't seem to need that "kid stuff" anymore! Being "good" evidently brings other rewards that make it all worthwhile.

I muse, how can Sanders be so wise for her age? She is without a doubt the best K–1 teacher I have ever worked with. Parents love her, children love and respect her, and the entire school is a brighter place because of her delightful laughter, her warmth and her deep concern for children. She glows with love for every child and they flourish.

Chapter III

Beware! The Ides of March Approach

Disturbing Faculty Meeting

Yesterday, the first part of our faculty meeting was devoted to pupil retention policies in the Santa Rosa County Schools. They are based on state statutes, and as is the case in so many places in the country, such statutes are often flawed. The goal of legislators is to guarantee that learning takes place and to reassure the public that no one passes from grade to grade unless he or she performs at "grade level." The concern for learning is, of course, commendable, but the grade level hang-up is a sugarcoated illusion. It may be good politics but it is terrible education.

Any heterogeneous group of children at any grade level will reflect a wide range of achievement levels regardless of what politicians or pundits say. But policy is policy and so we meet to decide how to legally "fail" students who we know are doing their very best. As elementary school principals are wont to say, "Regardless of policy, when our students start shaving, they're out-a-here!"

In addition to retention, we review testing and assessment of students' performance. You guessed it, by grade level. The national love affair with "standardized" tests is great for test manufacturers and politicians, but not necessarily for learners. Tests for diagnostic purposes can be very helpful if they are directly related to the curriculum—to what is being taught. But tests used primarily for purposes of comparison are questionable, in my judgment. And they invite all kinds of strategies to "beat the system." To falsify results or tamper with the actual tests is dangerous and, contrary to public perception, is probably rarely practiced. But there are more insidious practices that produce better results. One is the practice of "educational triage."

As in the medical application of triage, when resources are limited, those patients who have the best chance of responding get the most attention. That may be an oversimplification, but it is the general idea.

The child who is very low in performance and ability will be given "standard" instruction and perhaps a little extra. The teacher knows it is probably hopeless, unless there is a miracle, so invests his or her additional effort and time in the child who is in the mid-range of performance. This child can probably perform much better with additional intense assistance and produce a significantly higher score, thereby influencing the comparative scores of the total group. High performing students will gain from regular instruction but do not, surprisingly, justify additional assistance, as the real gain would not be that great. It is a trade-off. Help the ones where the help will probably produce the greatest gains in *scores*. That's the logic. Well, not at Munson!

But the Ides of March approach and the dreaded tests will soon be upon us. We had better be ready.

Tests, Tests, Tests

"Why do we have to go to this room?" is Tommy's gloomy lament. It is more than a question for he already knows the answer. It is a statement. Tommy and all of the fifth-grade pupils have to be assembled by grade level in preparation for the three-day barrage of standardized tests that is approaching all too quickly.

Our combination classes present a problem; it is necessary to administer the tests by individual grade level, rather than class. This requires separate space and additional test administrators.

Mrs. Janice Schultz, the school system's visiting speech pathologist for this area, graciously adjusted her schedule and will administer the tests to Mrs. Coogle's third-grade pupils. This will be very helpful. Ms. Cadenhead, our multi-talented P.E. teacher, will administer the tests to all fifth-grade students thus freeing Mr. Johnson to be with his fourth graders and Mrs. Rogaliner with her sixth graders. It is a makeshift arrangement caused by our small size and combination classes, but it will work.

Although test results are not driving our instructional program, we want to be certain the children are as comfortable and as knowledgeable as possible in the matter of test taking. No child at Munson, if we can help it, is going to be disadvantaged because he or she is "spooked by some old test." This means practice and more practice and building confidence and familiarity with testing procedures.

Tommy's fellow fifth graders, some from the fourth/fifth combination class and some from the fifth/sixth combination, are brought together in the multi-purpose room, the only room large enough to accommodate the group. It is a windowless barn of a room and not the best environment—but it is all we have. Furniture in traditional rows, a chalkboard and clock suggested it is serious business we are about. And it is.

Simulated test questions in every subject are part of the exercise. This is important; a child may know the material but not understand the manner in which the question is phrased. In a normal classroom, a pupil might ask for clarification. Not here. Also, the subject may be math, for example, but reading or vocabulary limitations can easily create problems that cause a child to become confused and miss the question. In theory, test makers take these matters into consideration. Children are not accustomed to such rigid test procedures. But this is the world of standardized tests—the tests we use to judge children, instruction, teachers, schools, systems and the state of education in the nation.

The children practice and practice. They are familiarized with rigid time constraints, fatigue, bathroom needs and on and on. When fatigue begins taking its toll, the teacher quietly walks by each desk and leaves an individually wrapped candy. And, of course, there is always the seventh-inning stretch or a "time out" jog around the room for everyone. Little strategies like these work and will help Tommy and the others when the real tests come and they rub their eyes and grip their pencils until their small hands are white with tension as they struggle desperately with question after question.

Some children complete the simulated exercises long before "time" would be called. This is always worrisome, for in most cases there are many unanswered questions—questions they may not have understood.

Statistics show that at this point, when they have already tried but to no avail, a guess, preferably an educated guess, pays dividends. So we encourage children to return to unanswered test questions and try again. It could only improve their scores because unanswered questions, by definition, are always marked incorrect. They have nothing to lose and much to gain. It is the general practice and we are going to avail ourselves of every legitimate strategy that will give our children a competitive edge.

Learning the test subjects is essential. But learning how to take tests gives the child an advantage in a very demanding, stressful and competitive exercise. At Munson, we do both. These children are not going to be shortchanged. Tommy is a good student, but his test scores the preceding year were dismal; this year will be different.

As confidence grows, a smile appears now and then and the agony of test taking becomes a little less painful. The actual tests begin soon. We are urging parents to be calm and to insist on plenty of rest for Tommy and all of his classmates. At school, Edith prepares some of the most delicious and nutritional menus of the year.

When testing days arrive, little did we know what an extra burden some of these little ones carried until sobs of frustration and tears of worry and fear told us. "Mommy said if we didn't do good on the tests they would take away our little school. Will they, Dr. D? Will they?"

And then I lie. For in truth, if test scores do not improve it is almost a certainty Munson Elementary will close. It will be an agonizing two months before we will know the verdict.

Thoughts That Wiggle in My Mind (What I Want for Children)

I gave a talk the other day to a civic club, and the members asked me about Munson and about America's schools and America's children. They know I am the dollar-a-year principal. No ax to grind. No agenda. No future, either. They just want to know what I think is important in education. What do I really want for our children? I thought, and I answered as best as I could.

I want children:

- to learn to read and enjoy reading.
- to learn to write and to express themselves well both in the written and spoken word.
- to know arithmetic, science and technology and be able to apply this knowledge easily in life.
- to know this planet, its people, its places, and its history.
- to appreciate music, art, nature and all beauty everywhere.

I want them to know about our flag, the stars, the colors— what they stand for and how important they are; to respect the flag; to meet and respect military men and women and the many others in our nation who place their lives on the line each day for us and for our freedom.

I want them:

- to learn that freedom and responsibility go hand in hand.
- to learn about volume control.
- to learn to eat with their mouths closed and with utensils, not only fingers.

- to say "please" and "thank you" and show respect for each other, for their parents and teachers, and for all people and property.

I want them to understand and respect courage, sacrifice, faith, hard work, honesty, commitment and kindness.

I want them:

- to respect the differences that exist among us.

- to give as well as to take.

- to laugh.

- to cry.

- to play.

- to dare, responsibly.

I want them to love and be loved. I want parents to listen and to hear and I want them to know the joy of their children's love, just as I want children to know the depth of their parent's love.

I want children to be the very best they have the capacity to be and schools and communities that will support this goal and will settle for nothing less.

These are some of the things I want for our children. Maybe I want too much. But that's what I would like for our children.

Mary's Diary

Last night I dreamt of little Mary. I found some pages from her diary. Although it was only a dream, I must ask, why are we so insensitive?

Dear Diary,

I have a wonderful new friend. Her name is Sarah. She has been in school for a while but I didn't really get to know her. Then they put her down in my grade. I don't know why. In a lot of ways she is real smart. Anyway, she sits close to me and now we're great friends. She doesn't smile very much and really doesn't seem too happy but I like her and I think she likes me. She doesn't have any brothers or sisters like I do. She's been in a lot of different schools.

I know I'm a lucky girl. We live in a nice house, have a lot of fun and go exciting places. Last summer we went to Alaska and I learned so much. I didn't know America was so big. The year before we went to the Grand Canyon. That was wonderful. I learned about Indians and all kinds of things. I never knew how a river could make such a big canyon but I know now.

My daddy is a whiz at numbers. He is always teaching us things about arithmetic. When we take a long drive, he gives us all kinds of interesting problems to solve. We have to do them in our heads. My brother usually gets the answer first. But not always. I'm pretty good.

Every night my mother reads fun stories to us and things like that. And then we have to read to her. There is hardly a night that we miss our "story time."

At first I wondered what Sarah did at home. She doesn't have a daddy any more and her mother seems to work all the time. She is alone a lot. One reason I think she is real smart is that she plays the violin. I can't play the violin. It's hard. She came to our house once and played for my family. It was so beautiful. My mother cried and hugged Sarah. She liked that. She doesn't get many hugs. I guess Sarah spends most of her time at home just studying and practicing. It seems so lonely.

Sarah is smart all right, but there are a lot of things she just doesn't know. The teacher tries real hard to help her catch up. Every lunch hour Mrs. Schultz gives her special help. After school too. They work very hard. I've seen Mrs. Schultz secretly turn away and cry a little in her hankie because Sarah is trying so hard but has so far to go. I bet she is learning three times as much as I am. Of course, I am learning new stuff too so she is still behind. Sometimes I think she will never catch up. She can't help it she is behind. She didn't have a daddy to help her learn arithmetic or a mommy to read to her. And she didn't have any brothers or sisters and never got to go on any trips. Never! Never even once.

We had the big awful tests last week. If only Sarah could take a test on the violin, she would be at the top of the class for sure. But I guess the violin isn't important. Poor Sarah. She had a terrible time with the tests. It was like she was being whipped. Every day she came back and was whipped again. They say the tests will tell us how good our school is and how good our teacher is. I don't know how they can. Sarah is behind but she is learning so much. It's not her fault she's behind. It's not Mrs. Schultz's fault either. Sarah shouldn't be whipped. Neither should Mrs. Schultz. It's not fair.

Please, God, please help my friend Sarah. And please help Mrs. Schultz too. Please. It's just not fair.

Mary

Chapter IV

Spring Fever

Fashion and Other Matters

Immediately following the marathon days of standardized tests the weather turns warm. Of course, this is no earth-shattering matter. The Panhandle of Florida has lovely seasons but when the warm weather approaches it comes on fast. However, the warm days present problems at school for which we seek all the help we can as reflected in the following letter to parents and guardians.

> *Dear Parents and Guardians:*
>
> *We are very proud of the boys and girls at Munson Elementary and the way they conducted themselves during the Comprehensive Test of Basic Skills (CTBS). It is*

an exhausting experience and they all worked very hard. They are great children.

There is one matter that comes up about this time every year on which we need your help. When warm weather arrives, shorts that are too short can be a problem at school. We do not want to embarrass your child so we would appreciate your support. Most children have grown since the last warm season—or the clothes may have shrunk as we adults say—and that needs to be taken into consideration.

Many schools have found the following specific information useful for parents:

Shorts should be <u>at least finger tip length</u> (whether worn with an oversized top or not).

Clothes that show undergarments or midriff or are low-cut or see-through may not be worn. (This includes tank tops, halter tops, etc.)

In the interest of safety, flip flops, wedges (or any backless shoe) or cleats are not approved.

Tops with inappropriate language or advertising, etc., need your control.

When students tell you "all the other kids wear them" it is probably not so. It's an argument we have all used with our own folks. Usually, it didn't work!

Most of this is covered in our Student/Parent Handbook but we thought the emphasis might be helpful as the warm weather approaches.

If you have any questions, please call. Teachers will be glad to help.

Sincerely yours,

John Dunworth, Principal

We are ready but so are the "schoolhouse lawyers" in the student body. The policy is first challenged by requesting a definition of "finger tip length." "Which finger? My little finger?" says Miss Innocence. That addressed ("Your longest finger"), the next ploy is to use elastic waistbands that place the shorts at the proper length when leaving home but may easily be rolled higher when at school. Clever!

Oversized long tops are the next technique to conceal the rolled up shorts. However, when bending over, the situation is far from concealing.

It takes about a week or so and constant vigilance, but the message finally gets through. In the process, no child is ever embarrassed and reminders by ladies on the staff are kind, private, and effective. The change is obvious when mothers drive over to school during the day and unobtrusively deliver a garment of appropriate length. The caper of short shorts is over.

Of course, there is still spring to deal with when girls pay particular attention to boys who pay particular attention to girls. And many do. Interest is high. Schools are places that teach more than the 3-Rs and where lessons can really be fun.

We take advantage of that interest to help the older girls with matters of appearance, skin care, and the judicious use of makeup. Purple nails only go so far!

Mrs. Marmount, our vivacious teacher assistant, had once served as a cosmetic expert. She was good. Her extra classes for the upper-grade girls are tremendously popular, and the results are clearly apparent. She provides a great service to these young ladies and a boon for the boys. We may be a little rural school but we're pretty "up town."

Speaking of fashions and spring brings to mind the story of the Ice Cream Tie.

Thanks to my very thoughtful wife, I have in my wardrobe a tie depicting a delicious ice cream cone with seventeen colorful scoops of ice cream and sherbet. It covers the entire tie and looks good enough to eat.

Well, I was not prepared for the reaction. The little children would swarm around that tie and poke their little fingers at their favorite flavor.

"Dr. D, Dr. D, I like that and that and that." And another adds, "And that. It's my favorite flavor."

All the children think it is wonderful every time I wear that tie. In the school cafeteria, ice cream sales soar. In the spirit of fun, I finally buy ice cream for every child in the school. No one is left out.

That tie cost a small fortune but it is worth every penny. I'm going to frame it. When I look back through misty eyes and clouded lens, it will say, "Remember the wonderful days of lime sherbet and little noses buried in the ice cream promise of spring?" And I will remember.

The Absent-Minded Principal

Mrs. D threatened to disown me if this little story were ever published. But she has threatened before...

It is a true story. It happened just the way that I recorded it in my notes.

Today I forgot my pants! Well, not exactly my pants—actually, my shorts. Well, not exactly my shorts either. For in place of shorts I was wearing the bottoms to my shorty PJ's. I didn't know it.

Now that didn't mean anything to anyone but me. Tonight, just before showering, I was looking all over the house for my pajamas—everywhere. Finally, I asked my wife, "Dear, have you seen my pajama bottoms?"

There was a pause, a sly grin, and then, "Why yes, dear. You're wearing them!"

There is no question I am frequently preoccupied with the cares of being a principal. Also, I confess to not being entirely awake at 4:50 a.m. when the alarm calls. Or perhaps it is incipient Alzheimer's. I hope not. Whatever, it wasn't as bad as the day I put my boxer shorts on backwards. Now that did present a problem.

Setback

We experienced our first major setback. It will not be possible to launch a Pre-K program this school year. We have tried everything. There are insufficient numbers of eligible children at this time whose families meet federal or state income guidelines.

We'll try again for the fall if there is a fall for the little school.

Preschool programs, as vitally important as they are, are not part of the regular school curriculum and are not funded by state formula, as are all other grades. Funding comes primarily from federal and state programs for the disadvantaged. If your income is low, your child may be able to participate. If your child has certain impairments, he or she may qualify. But if you hold a job, earn certain levels of income that exceed the guidelines and your child does not have special needs, you do not qualify and your child cannot participate. That is an over-simplification of a complex issue, but is generally the case.

The irony is that although we are a poor area and are classified as a high poverty school, our families generally work hard, exceed the income guidelines a little, and are then denied access to the program. A few qualify on the income issue but not in sufficient numbers to begin a class. Charging a monthly fee was considered as an alternative, but would be so costly for parents that it is not considered feasible. As I told my wife, "Can you imagine? Children and parents are ready, eager and willing to come to school, but our doors are closed to them."

We are not giving up! If there are fifteen children whose parents meet the income guidelines, we can start the program almost immediately. New families in the area might make the difference.

In the meantime we will think positively, move forward with the refurbishing of an old classroom that will make a fine facility, and continue to remind the public that it is still our intention to begin the Pre-K class as soon as there are sufficient numbers of eligible children.

Young children learn at a prodigious rate. They are ready and eager to learn. A stimulating environment that can help them with language, numerical development, reading readiness, conceptual development, and a host of other things will impact their entire lives. Parental education is a vital part of this program, too. If we want to have "smart kids" in America, and indeed "smart adults," we will need to review public policy in this area and make early education available for all children.

In Trust

Early in my career I served as an administrator in three different elementary schools. All included kindergarten through eighth grade. All were in California and all were large. One had an enrollment of 700 pupils, as I recall. Another, over 1,400 and the last, where I was the principal for three years, had an enrollment of approximately 1,200 pupils.

Two of the schools were on double session. That meant that one group of children arrived in the morning and a second group of equal size arrived in the afternoon. Teachers too. Children were in school for four hours per day, the minimum number of minutes required by law. Teachers were there much longer. The turn-around time was at a premium. Thirty minutes to clean, organize and air (no air conditioning in those days) every room in the school. Teachers had to be flexible and resourceful. Children and parents too. But this was Southern California during the days of unprecedented growth. The school system was attempting to build a new school every month. It wasn't an optimum situation, but remarkably, children learned.

In Munson, our concern is that there will not be enough students to justify the continued existence of this little school. Clearly, if a large group of students graduates in the spring, and a small group enters the next fall, we'll have a deficit. We can't count on a large new influx of families, as in California. The area will undoubtedly grow but slowly and orderly. Indeed, this is the very best way to experience growth.

Each spring, elementary schools conduct registration for the kindergarten children who will be entering school the next fall. It is essential for planning and equally helpful for parents. Birth certificates, immunization records and several other documents must be available. Hopefully, parents will have an opportunity to meet their son or daughter's first teacher. It is an exciting time for everyone and a critical time for schools, particularly this little school.

A year ago, only four students enrolled during kindergarten registration. A few more enrolled later, but that turnout sounded the death knell for Munson Elementary School. There were indications all along that parents had lost confidence in the school, that they wanted to be here but did not trust the place as a suitable learning environment for their children. The feedback had been informal, but in these parts, it is usually the most reliable kind. However, the registration of only four new pupils was a devastating and irrefutable sign. The school was doomed.

When you consider it thoughtfully, parents are making a tremendous leap of faith when they place their most precious "possession" in the hands of others to teach, guide and help that little child to maturity. We are very hopeful that the people and the program at Munson will be worthy of the parents' trust. We try to make it so.

Understand that there are no secrets here. Everything that happens in this place is discussed at home. Several of our staff live in the community or are related to local people. We hide nothing; so parents know. And they should, for we are asking them to say, "I trust you." Not in some abstract way, but with the very life and future of their sons and daughters. We take that trust very, very seriously. They know that too.

There is another key factor that will influence many parents this year, and that is the kindergarten teacher herself. Mrs. Sanders is phenomenal. She is knowledgeable, wise, warm, enthusiastic and absolutely dedicated to her children. She has high expectations and high standards. She loves every child in her care and every child loves her. She also has high expectations for parents. They will become partners and the results will be astounding.

Mrs. Sanders' reputation preceded her, for on kindergarten registration day this spring, we enroll 19 students, several more than will be graduating from the sixth grade. And more are to follow. The deficit in enrollment is over. Trust has been re-established. Munson is a good school and everyone knows it. Projections for the 1998–99 school year suggest a steady rise in enrollment. We have won on this front.

But still no word on test results.

Chapter V

The Final Bell

The Message

Kathy had left a note on my desk.

Mr. Russell just called. He'll call back as soon as possible, but he left a message. "Congratulations!"

I reread the note and almost hold my breath. If he was saying what I thought he might be saying…I considered…

For some time now, the superintendent had been making public statements that Munson is now one of the most cost-effective schools in Santa Rosa County and that the instructional program is one of the best anywhere. Children are clearly learning, progress is palpable and the taste of success permeates everything. Also, parents are enthusiastic and reflect a new confidence in the school, in the teachers, and in what we are all about. Still, we have no hard data, no standardized test scores, no so-called objective independent outside assessment to confirm or deny what we know but cannot prove. I am cautious.

We have all seen TV reports showing seriously malnourished children in Third World countries, literally starving. It is devastating. Even with help and proper nutrition, some will never make it. For others, the deprivation will have a lasting impact on their fragile lives and futures. Even with the strongest, few would be expected to become Olympic champs.

This is similar to what I call academic malnutrition. Some children will never really overcome the impact of such deprivation. Those who do have a hard struggle. Even with the best academic diet, they will have to play catch-up. However, while they are struggling to move forward as fast as possible, their academically healthy peers are also moving ahead, often leaving the others still behind. It is a terrible load for a child to carry.

In the face of this, considered opinion was that while Munson children would probably improve academically, as reflected on the CTBS standardized test scores, that gain should not be expected to exceed five to seven points. Even that might be optimistic. It would show progress, but would it be enough?

"Sir, Mr. Russell is on the line." I take a deep breath and lift the receiver gingerly.

"John," he says warmly, "I want to congratulate the children, the teachers and all of you at Munson. I have some preliminary test data you'll be interested in. As you may have heard (I had) we have a couple of computer glitches that will delay getting the data published and out to the media. However, I wanted each school to know. (That's just like Benny.) We'll send you a brief summary later in the day. The full report will be out next week. Anyway, here are the highlights.

"Munson had the greatest gain of any school in the entire system. Last year the composite score for Munson, as you know, was 44. This year it is 59. That is a 15-point, or 25 percent, gain over the preceding year and considerably higher than the national average. A tremendous accomplishment.

"Your upper grade students—remember the difficult class you frequently mentioned? They had a 20-point gain from 46 to 66. A wonderful achievement.

"It looks too as though the school will win the $2,200 computer and software award for the largest percentage increase on math scores for 1997–98. Great!

"John, I want you to particularly convey my congratulations and appreciation to Mrs. Sanders. Her first-grade children scored higher than any first grade in Santa Rosa County!

"I know you're well aware that every child did not achieve at these levels, but many did. We're proud of all of them. My special congratulations to the boys and girls, to their parents, and of course to the teachers. Must go. The summary report will be out later today."

I hardly had time to say, "Thanks, Benny. Thanks for everything." I am stunned. It is better than anything I could have imagined. In fact, it is overwhelming.

The message is disseminated to teachers, children, parents, staff, volunteers, the entire Munson family. Heidi Nieland (Hall), the quintessential journalist with the *Pensacola News Journal*, had already read the signs and wrote the first story even before the test data is officially available. Its headline read "Munson Makes the Grade," followed by "He's done it—turned Munson Elementary School from a faltering institution on the verge of closure into the little school that could."

I hadn't "done it." A lot of people had "done it." But it was nice to hear. *Pensacola News Journal* reporter Elizabeth Lee soon follows up with a front-page story with a headline that says "Students Catapult Munson Test Scores." The world knows. The message is out.

The Verdict

There are now only five days of school remaining. Only five days before summer vacation, with its lure of leisure and the stilling of clocks that have sliced the silence of the night and ripped open the curtains of sleep for so many for so long.

The days would be busy and today promises to be no exception. In fact, it seems particularly demanding. Staff, parents, even children and volunteers keep me very occupied and closeted in my tiny office. The break comes about 1 o'clock when one of our most delightful and responsible girls appears breathlessly at the office door.

"Dr. D, Dr. D, you're needed in the cafeteria right away!" she exclaims.

Her demeanor suggests a serious emergency. She is clearly disturbed and is urging haste. Has someone been hurt? Has there been an accident? Has Edith or one of the staff had a heart attack? I am out the door in a flash. She is ahead of me, her shirt billowing and her hair flying. She opens the door to the cafeteria and I dash in. Then I stop cold in my tracks. I freeze.

"Surprise. Surprise!" and then tremendous applause! All of the children, all of the staff as well as many parents, volunteers, the superintendent of schools, members of the board of education as well as top district personnel and key faculty from UWF are present. All are standing.

Enter Mrs. Dunworth. She also receives a rousing standing ovation. She has known all the time!

To this day I marvel at how they pulled it off. All my meetings and busy schedules must have been carefully choreographed well in advance. They were all in on it including the children. Still, I'm the principal and am supposed to know what is going on. Obviously, I don't. I bet even the cats knew! And the little actress who lured me to the cafeteria—what a masterful performance!

It is a beautiful occasion. Children have prepared thank you messages in pictures and words. Some read them aloud. They are so real, so very touching. The superintendent and several others express their heartfelt appreciation. Mr. Johnson's warm, humorous, and organized manner keeps things on track. He is very skillful.

Mrs. Coogle, on behalf of the school, presents a large beautifully framed portrait of "Dr. D" which is to hang in perpetuity in the halls of Munson Elementary. Her words are like jewels. "He believed in us," she says. "All of us. And therefore we believed in ourselves." A framed poem by one of Mrs. Coogle's third-grade pupils will hang alongside the portrait. It concludes, "Dr. D, you are a star to me. You are the light to me." It was signed Tori.

Recognizing that it will be very difficult for everyone to come to the school board meeting the next day in Milton, when formal action would be taken, the superintendent makes the announcement everyone has been waiting so long to hear. Munson Elementary School will remain open and, in effect, will be an important part of the Santa Rosa County School System as far into the future as anyone can see.

Board members smile enthusiastically and nod imperceptibly. Tomorrow, they will vote officially.

The verdict has been rendered. It is done.

I am speechless. It really is a very poignant moment in my life. I do not know if the right words are said; however, I do believe my appreciation, my admiration, and indeed my love for everyone in that room comes through, for it is there in abundance.

The next day at the meeting of the board of education, I am officially paid my famous $1. Appreciation is expressed by the board to the community, the children, the parents, grandparents and guardians, volunteers, staff and especially each teacher. The Dream Team has achieved the impossible.

Mr. Johnson is appointed principal. The school will have superb leadership in the form of this highly competent, dedicated and respected educator.

My work is almost done.

There would be ceremonies and celebrations, accolades and awards, graduation and the inevitable good-byes. There would be tears, joy and there would be thoughts—thoughts that would fill a page or two, and thoughts that would fill a lifetime.

Thoughts That Wiggle in My Mind (On Caring)

Caring starts with mothers.

Parents caring, helping their children grow to fullness, is love expressed in a thousand ways. The demands on parents are incessant and exhausting but caring comes before all. A little infant or child denied care will wither. With care, the child will blossom.

Children reflect the love of their parents in the mirror of their faces, the song of their voices, the joy in their steps, in their striving and work at school and at play and even in the mischief of their ways. Sometimes they say it in pictures and even in words.

All of this is cherished deeply by both children and parents, forever. It is expressed by two children from my mind who represent all children in "A Letter to Mommy."

Dear Mommy,

I guess I should have written to you earlier but like most little boys, I just forgot. Our teacher told us that isn't an excuse. So I thought and I thought and this is what Sis and I want to say.

Little Sis and I really love you Mommy—the way you look at us when we're good or when you think we're not looking. Also, the stories you read to us and the stories you help us read to you. Little Sis is reading real good. Your cookies are the best cookies in the whole world and our house is the best house with the biggest wheels. I watch you iron Sis's little dress when you are so tired and I know why they all say she's the prettiest girl in the first grade. Somehow you came from work to hear us sing and to see me in the play. Sis and I was real proud. I think you was proud too. You had that beautiful smile you save for special times.

I know we are bad sometimes but you don't never get mad. You help us learn right from wrong. You can say "no" real good and we know you mean it. But I can't think of one day that you don't give us a big hug. When daddy had to leave, it was awful. Sis and I cried and cried, but those hugs somehow made us brave and strong.

You teach us so much. To care, to be honest, to work hard, to be kind, to do our homework, to do what the teacher tells us and to say our prayers and be a good boy and a good girl. We really try, Mommy, we really do. Sis said, "Mommy is our light." I like that because I think so too. Somehow your light is always there. Always.

I really am sorry I didn't write to you before, Mommy, because now I don't know what to put on the envelope. They said that was alright. So little Sis and I held hands and went up together and put our letter gently by the yellow rose in your folded hands. In your beautiful new dress you will be the prettiest lady in heaven and you will always have our letter to read.

Oh, one other thing, Mommy. Don't worry about little Sis. I promise, I promise I will always take care of her. Always. You taught me that too.

We love you Mommy, forever and ever.

Your little boy and girl,

Timmy and Sis

The Final Bell

The story of Munson Elementary, of the little school that wouldn't die, is a story of teaching and learning, and of resourcefulness and determination. But more importantly, it is a story of faith and caring: every soul in that place caring for every other and for every child. Their faith glowed. Love and faith were rekindled and expressed in action—from the encouragement, expectations and invaluable help of individual parents and volunteers to the determination, persistence, patience and tremendous skill of teachers striving every minute of every hour to reach and help each and every child. All this is reflected in the lives of the children: in their caring, in their striving, and in their determination to do their very best. It was a driving force. We really should not be surprised at the results.

It is the afternoon of the last day of school. The final bell has rung and the halls are empty and silent.

Tearful farewells have been taken and the last school bus has left emblazoned with the words in large print, "THANKS DOC."

This gesture was courtesy of one of our most dedicated and dynamic parents and her pals. It is completely in character and a beautiful "thank you" I will never forget.

I return slowly to my office. It is over.

And then Gail steps in briefly to exclaim, "There is this huge 18-wheeler parked in the school's drive! It looks as though it has come a long way."

I can only think, "What now?" However, before I can move, a giant of a man comes directly into my office with a purposeful stride, stops in front of my desk and pauses. Lord, I thought, it really *is* over! But then he smiles, extends his large hand and says, "I just want to thank you personally for what you have done for our school and for my little girl. I'm away a lot. But I know." As we shake hands, he looks me squarely in the eye and adds, "God bless you and Mrs. D too." And then he is gone. A few moments later as I look for him, all I can see is the giant rig making a lumbering turn onto Munson Highway and a hand extended in a salute of farewell.

That Sunday afternoon, Lavona and I visit the school for the last time. We stand under the big oaks on the empty playground, join hands, and lower our heads in thanksgiving for what God had wrought in this place. At that moment I feel certain I hear the distant sounds of boys and girls at play and a strangely familiar voice quietly say, "And God bless these children and this little school, forever and ever. Amen."

Part II

The Principal

My Personal Road to Munson

Chapter VI

An Odyssey of Discovery

Okinawa—1964

It was last August during typhoon Flossie. The night was inky black and the landing strip approach lights formed a prophetic blurred cross through the driving rain and the 60–90 knot cross winds. Maj. Rex Floyd, the Air Force officer accompanying me, was calm and collected.

The pilot had made three passes over the runway in a vain attempt to land and we all had considerable time to meditate. I could only think that visiting schools in California had never been like this. It used to be so easy and yet as a Superintendent in California, how many times had I let administrivia stand in the way.

It's different now. On July 1, 1964, I became Superintendent of all Army, Navy, and Air Force Dependents schools (now referred to as Department of Defense Dependents Schools) in the Pacific and Far East. We have over fifty million square miles in our "district," probably the largest in the world, and many of our schools are as far away from the Area Superintendent's office as Los Angeles is from London! If we're lucky we can reach most of our schools in eight to ten hours by jet. If we're not so lucky it can take twenty to thirty hours.

On July 1, the Department of Defense reorganized the Overseas Dependents Schools and divided the world into three geographical areas: Pacific, Atlantic, and Europe. Each branch of the service acts for the DOD in administering the schools for a particular area. In Europe schools are the responsibility of the Army, in the Atlantic they are under Navy, and in the Pacific and Far East they are under the Air Force.

Our task is to provide quality education for children of military personnel stationed overseas. There are over 40,000 of these youngsters grades K-12 in the Pacific and by anyone's standards most of them are receiving an exceptionally fine education.

To get the job done we have sub districts for Japan and Korea, and for Okinawa, Taiwan, the Philippine Islands and Southeast Asia. The Area Superintendent's office and staff is in Honolulu (Hickam Air Force Base) with the Pacific Headquarters of the respective military departments. However, the District Superintendents and their staffs provide the on-the-spot guidance and leadership for the more than 1,500 teachers who staff classrooms.

Thanks to the support of the military, it is not unusual to find a fully equipped library and trained librarian in many of the schools in the system. Many large elementary schools will have a full-time trained counselor as part of the staff, in addition to a speech therapist, art teacher and special music teacher. Special education is provided in most cases, just as in California.

In many classrooms individualized instruction, and the new approaches in math, science, English, and other curricular areas are common. Excellent science laboratories, business departments, and language labs are not unusual in the large high schools and even in some of the smaller facilities.

Children attending our schools in Japan, for example, have the opportunity to study the culture first hand under trained Japanese cultural teachers. The sharing of experiences with Japanese boys and girls is an invaluable part of learning in the rich environment of a different culture. Field trips are daily occurrences and are excellent sources of inter-cultural exchange and a boon to our "People-to-People" program.

But like yours, not everything is perfect in our system. The cooperation of the military has been exemplary. School buildings are often the finest buildings on a base, in spite of a few glaring exceptions, and teachers usually live in the best quarters that are available. Sometimes these facilities are not like home but it is to be remembered that the primary use of our defense dollar must necessarily be for military deterrence and essential preparedness, not for comfort and classrooms.

Our teachers and administrators are some of the finest. The Government pays for the transportation of each teacher to his or her assignment. If single, she is usually provided bachelor quarters on base and if she lives off base the Government provides a housing allowance for both housing and utilities. If assigned to certain remote areas, a differential ranging from 10 to 25 percent is added to the salary. She has a rating equivalent to that of a commissioned officer. She is encouraged to undertake summer university work and if she desires will be flown home and back at Government expense every summer for this purpose. And there is the opportunity for travel and the adventure of an exciting experience abroad.

It is a challenging and exciting responsibility representing American Public Education on the frontiers of the free world. But be it in Manila, Tsoying, Yokohama, or Los Angeles, when the bell rings our job is the same and our effectiveness will be judged in the lives of the children and youth we serve. In the end, be it small, or the "largest" in the world, a school district can only be measured in terms of its impact on the life of each child.

And, by the way, we landed on one wheel on the fourth pass!

(California School Administrator Vol. XIX, No. 5 November, 1964 California Association of School Administrators, Inc., Burlingame, California)

My personal road to Munson was exciting, arduous and enlightening. The peaks, valleys, twists and turns of the road led me to some very important insights about education in general and teaching, learning, and leading in particular. To me they were eye-opening revelations and have since become an integral part of who I am and what I believe about education. I brought them with me to Munson and applied them daily. Some other particularly intense experiences taught me a lot about me. Let me share these with you first.

"Doc," shouted the seaman in his wet oilskins, obviously under stress. "We need you bad on the boat deck. Jake has crushed his hand in the chocks." Our two-ton lifeboats are secured to chocks. Anything caught between that metal hull and the block on which the boat rests is bad news. I went immediately, of course. I was the ship's "doctor."

Shortly before, I had been chosen to receive approximately 90 days of intensive medical training followed by a 30-day "internship" in a New York hospital. This was war and time was critical. My new responsibility, along with a long list of other functions, was to provide for the health of the ship's crew. On this voyage, it numbered 55 men including the Navy gun crew. We were in the middle of the Pacific Ocean, alone, rigidly observing complete radio silence. Our safety depended entirely on stealth. Once spotted we would have been doomed—a lumbering heavily laden vessel with limited armor and no speed. It would have been like shooting a duck in a pond—with sharks instead of gold fish.

We had morphine, sulfa, no penicillin yet and the usual supplies of a well stocked sick bay. We also carried ether for surgery but what little I recall of a hurried lecture on anesthesiology in a hospital hall suggested that would best be left to specialists. One sailor, with undoubtedly an inflamed appendix, begged me to operate and remove it. He had seen too many films. I told the Skipper I would kill the man if I attempted surgery. I told the sailor I would treat him conservatively and he would soon be well if he would follow my orders to the letter. He did, I prayed, and he recovered beautifully.

There are also other incidents during this period that are indelibly fixed in my memory—the autopsies we were required to attend every Saturday morning in the bowels of probably the oldest general hospital in Manhattan; the ER life and death experiences; the ambulance duty where the last admonition from the night nurses would be a hurried, "If necessary use your shoe laces." One experience took me into the moral realm as well as the medical...

"Stand aside for the doctor, please. Stand aside," said the heavily padded New York police officer at the site of the accident. It was 2:00 a.m., ice under foot with new snow forming a white wet blanket over the eerie scene. The flashing red lights of the police cars and the bright spotlight from the ambulance gave the intersection the appearance of a movie set. All that was needed was a director to shout "action."

The unspoken word came and I moved quickly with my faithful medical bag. I was it! Fortunately, the only injury appeared to be a lady with a possible fracture of her right leg. Ice had caused the accident. The lady was a passenger in the car.

Ever so cautiously and gently I moved her into a position where I could apply the prescribed splint and proceeded as I had been taught. I believe she was 40 years old. She wasn't hurting too badly but looked so helpless and so very, very sad. The gentleman driving the car did not appear to be her husband although her beautiful wedding ring suggested she was certainly married. And then softly and pleadingly she asked, "Does my name have to be mentioned when I go to the hospital?" Now it was clear. I continued methodically with my bandaging, said nothing and thought furiously. Of course, she would have to register—or would she? What could I do? What should I do? It is not my place to judge; I was taught that lesson as a boy with the biblical admonition, "Judge not..." Also, I was taught to be honest. And then I answered her question. "I am afraid you will, Mrs. Miklovitch, although if you are not up to it I am sure the office will take my word. They know me pretty well." For a fleeting moment her gaze was quizzical and then tears silently rolled down her cheeks accompanied by the most beautiful smile I had ever seen. You see, Miklovitch was just the name of a dry cleaning shop across the street.

To my knowledge it all worked like a charm. Her leg was not broken. The police officer got some names for his report, I received an "A" in First Aid and Mrs. Mary "Miklovitch" was released from the hospital and on her way home before breakfast. When a storm hits the city, it can mess up schedules something terrible! I prayed that God would forgive my transgression.

There are probably a vial or two of lessons in this unusual medical career which the reader, if interested, can easily ferret out. By the time the war was over, I learned that I liked to mend hearts but not necessarily other parts; medicine would not be for me. I also learned that there is no substitute for solid, rigorous education and training in every walk of life. It is a must.

The Odyssey Begins

The odyssey started at the University of California in Berkeley, California. Actually, it started long before that with my parents who came to America from England bringing with them experiences and values that shaped my life in profound ways. They also brought my sister, Margaret, who guided and befriended me as a child and enriches my life immeasurably as an adult. There were friends, family, teachers and colleagues who influenced my life in many ways. But this is not an autobiography. It is an odyssey in which certain experiences led to new insights related to schools and children, and these are the experiences we shall explore.

The University of California immediately following World War II was a bustling place. Most of the students had returned from war and were eager "to get on with their lives." I was one of those students. The pre-war perception of the university campus was gone. It was no longer a "community of scholars" where students and faculty members could be seen discussing the philosophical issues of the universe as they strolled leisurely through a cloistered cacophony of beautiful blossoms and manicured lawns. The lawns were there but that was all. For everyone, students and faculty alike, it was rush, rush, huge classes, long lines, and little opportunity for discussion except as related to "meeting requirements" for degrees and other program objectives. The "university" had become a vocational school. That was fine with me. Many vocational schools are excellent institutions. Research, especially at the University of California, considered to be one of the finest universities in the world, continued to flourish. But that activity primarily impacted Nobel Prize winners and would-be winners and their cadre of brilliant graduate assistants. Senior professors of great distinction in various disciplines would lecture occasionally, which added an aura of excellence. However, the bulk of the instruction was provided by underpaid, hard-working conscientious graduate students called Teaching Assistants. "TAs" are the unsung heroes of academia, especially on super-large university campuses.

There was serious debate (and some not so serious) at the University of California and it often took place at a campus location called Sather Gate—the major south entrance to the university. Here, the famous "free speech movement" flourished and no issue was sacred. Although controversial, it did lend an air of intellectual freedom and passionate integrity to the place, which was in sharp contrast to the orientation of many of the students. It became quite a spectator sport. However, you wouldn't find me at Sather Gate too often. I was one of the vocationally-oriented students who was "getting on with their lives."

It was during these years that things started to happen on the odyssey to insight. My own schooling had been in a typical college preparatory program followed by some higher education, the exigency of war, and the traditional academic demands of a distinguished university. By definition, such programs and such institutions have an elitist air about them. Some consciously encourage such a perception. For others it is simply a byproduct of the institution's record and tradition of excellence. "Berkeley," as this university often is referred to in California, is in this latter category. Some believe Stanford University is too, but that is sometimes debated, usually at rival football gatherings.

If you succeed in such universities, you receive the accolades and rewards of society. And over a lifetime they are many. If you fail . . . well, no one in the institution is too concerned. In fact, they may not be concerned at all. Large prestigious universities are often noted for the academic exclusivity of their student bodies achieved primarily through the combined efforts of their admissions offices and the "high standards" of their faculty. Compassion is not their strong suit. I began to realize the implications of this when I commenced serious study in preparation to serve all children and youth—rich and poor, capable and not so capable, motivated and those not motivated, of parents who valued learning and those who did not—in the bastion of all egalitarian institutions in our society, the American public school!

Courses in the School of Education were demanding but also enlightening. I was now in a world that said all human beings have value. That when a youngster "drops out" in the course of schooling, it is the school that in some measure has failed the student and not only the student who has failed. It said the potential in every human being is too precious to be squandered or discarded, that when children are "failing" we too are failing as educators and as a society. This was not only a profession I was entering, it was a "calling," or a way of life. It was consistent with my values. I believed it. I still believe it. I was ecstatic. There would be many twists and turns in the road before the significance of this would become an integral part of my being, but it was a wonderful beginning.

I eventually completed two degrees at the University of California and after several other twists in the road found myself in an eighth-grade classroom with 35 adolescents in a place called Torrance, California. In some ways, my education was just beginning.

Torrance, California

"Hi, Mr. Dunworth," said Sally, the ebullient 15-year-old eighth grader, as I was crossing the playground to the school office this beautiful Monday morning.

"Did you have a good weekend?" she continued.

"Sure did, Sally. How about you?" I answered.

"I had a swell time, Mr. Dunworth. I met these Marines and we went up to lighthouse point and ..."

Saved by the bell! "See you in class, Sally" was my parting comment.

The Torrance Unified School District was a very special place. Located in the South Bay region of the Los Angeles basin and close to the sea, it served affluent families and many of very modest means, as well. Our school served the latter. Sally was not typical. Indeed, I believe we felt there was only one Sally in this world. An outgoing child with a flair for color and design, Sally could barely read. She had been retained a grade along the way but that did not help. The best teachers as well as every specialist in the system worked with Sally but to no avail. No one ever gave up on Sally, but no one to my knowledge ever succeeded. I was no exception. We found the things at which she could excel and concentrated on those. Although she stood apart in some ways from the other children, she was well liked. She was just Sally. Every teacher learns, in time, that you don't "bat a thousand." It's a hard lesson.

In Torrance I learned in depth about self-contained classrooms. I became committed to this type of education. I still am. Upper-grade youngsters usually found themselves in junior high schools—large places where students moved from class to class on the assumption they were getting more academically oriented lessons and thus a better education. However, too often they were large impersonal places where too many students became merely numbers. A student could go day after day without his name being called once. These days, good middle schools address many of these issues with fine programs for older children. However, my eighth-grade class was self-contained. I was with the children every day, all day (except for shop and home economics that were offered by visiting teachers one afternoon a week). I was certified by the State of California to teach every subject in the curriculum from math to music and art to physical education. I did, but it was hard work.

Self-contained classrooms work when the classroom teacher has a strong support system: the help of teachers in a variety of specialized areas and an equally "full cupboard" of differentiated instructional materials. There are books, computers, TV and ideally whatever the teacher needs to get the job done. Anything less is short changing children and the teacher's ability to be successful with students.

Children feel secure in this home-away-from-home. Regardless of the size of the school, and these were very large schools, youngsters were part of a family. There is no question that the teacher became a surrogate parent as well as teacher, which in some cases was the only parent the child really knew. Standards were easy to establish and maintain, and children were proud of their accomplishments in all areas. They were also proud of the accomplishments of the group. School was a dependable place in their lives. School was even fun. School was where people cared and where you were loved.

Thirty-five youngsters is a large group, but that did not deter Torrance nor its teachers from striving for the very best education for every child. Expectations were very high. It was an inspiring place to work.

Torrance's vision saw learners as individuals: each different, each at a different place on the ladder of learning. Teachers were selected whose values, beliefs and skills were compatible with this view of learning. "Old timers" in the system came "on board" or left of their own accord. Teaching positions were readily available, for this was the period of the famous "baby boom" and increases in the school-age population were staggering. "Chalk and talk" teaching was out; engaging each student in learning was in.

Comparing children also was dropped. Report cards became "Progress Reports" of each child's individual progress related to his or her own ability and talents. This was communicated in frequent narrative reports and compulsory "parent conferences" with each family, often including the child.

Ideally all of this was good, but dropping familiar symbols was disconcerting to many parents and teachers alike; change was massive and fast. The amount of work was staggering and teachers started to buckle. Few could handle the pace with such large classes. Teachers who might complain for having "3 preparations" now, in reality, had 35 preparations. Carried to this extreme, it was clearly unrealistic.

In time, a middle ground emerged which combined the best of the past with the enlightened direction of the future. The wide range of differences in every classroom was recognized and addressed with differentiated instructional materials, flexible time allocations and differentiated homework and tests. Large classes eventually gave way to smaller classes and the ability to address the specific needs of each child was greatly enhanced.

I learned a lot in Torrance. Never again did I look at a classroom of children as a homogeneous group. Never again did I see learning as a process of pouring knowledge in but rather as a process of drawing knowledge out. With few exceptions, never again did I employ the "chalk and talk" method of teaching. And never again would I be so presumptuous as to believe the task of educating a child could effectively take place without full involvement, love and caring of the child's parent. Most importantly, I learned that unless the child is fully engaged in the process at the point where the child actually is, little happens that can be labeled "education."

I also learned some other things in Torrance. I soon learned that the eighth-grade teacher in the classroom adjacent to mine had been selected as the "Outstanding Teacher of the Year" for the entire system; that she would artfully wear beautiful high-heeled red shoes when we shared "playground duty"; that she was as sharp as a tack and cute as a button; and that we were madly in love. Our students never knew until the wedding!

Lavona went on in secondary education, continued with her graduate studies and in time became a wonderful university professor. I went up through the chairs in Torrance and neighboring systems serving as a vice principal, principal, assistant superintendent and, with my new doctorate from the University of Southern California, superintendent of schools—a normal professional progression for the times. But I will never forget Torrance. Without question, it is one of the outstanding school systems in the nation.

In each place I also learned something else—that one of the very best ways to strengthen the parent's role in the school-parent partnership is to be part of a strong PTA. The Parent-Teacher Association links your school to parents and teachers and many others in your region, your state and even nationally. The network is invaluable. Critical information is available, exchanged, and voices join others in helping to shape policies on behalf of children and families. Everyone is connected. "Going it alone" in today's complex world is difficult. I am an unabashedly strong advocate for the Parent-Teacher Association and for what it can do for schools. In school after school, I have seen the difference a PTA can make and the help it can provide in strengthening the all-important parent-teacher partnership. Invariably, children are the beneficiaries.

As I became a school district administrator, I also developed the highest regard for those citizens who stand for election and serve as members of a board of education. Well, most of them anyway. I once sent the following statement to the school board members where I served. I meant it then and I mean it now.

The School Board Member
By John Dunworth

Few people in public office have greater responsibility, contribute more, receive less, and are recipients of more abuse than school board members. You are remarkable people. You spend untold numbers of hours in interminable meetings. Your patience is inexhaustible.

You face the delicate problem of promoting the public good through education, which costs money, while defending the public purse through fiscal restraint. You are blamed if you do not do enough and you are condemned if you do too much. If you please one constituency you invariably alienate another. If you should, by chance, please everyone, your decision will undoubtedly be challenged in the courts. Your families are patient, too. But they do wonder about you. Are you really a saint or are you what the editor of your paper and the president of the teachers organization sometimes suggest. Indeed, when you win an election you are not sure whether to celebrate or to cry. You must often ask, is it worth it? Is it ever appreciated?

Well, let me just say, on behalf of the thousands of children and youth whose lives are in your trust, and on behalf of their families with all of their hopes and aspirations for those young people, and on behalf of a society which has literally placed its faith and its future in your hands, the toil, the time, and the tribulation are worth it. We honor you and we express our deepest appreciation for your service. In my judgment, there is no higher office in the land and no higher honor than to serve as a member of a Board of Education.

The Pacific

Although I didn't know it at the time, the sojourn in the Pacific was to be a period of transition from elementary and secondary education to higher education.

It started with a telephone call from Hawaii to our home in California. I knew I had been selected to head up the DoD Schools in the Pacific under the new structure established by the Department of Defense. Being new, everything was in a state of flux.

"Dr. Dunworth, this is Col. Patterson from PACAF—we met during your interview." I realized this would be a new culture and even a new language. I would have to learn quickly. After all, I am on the staff of each of the top commanders in the Pacific, CINCPACAF being my boss. "We need to know, Dr. John, where you want your office to be located—here at Hq. PACAF or in Japan?"

"When do you need a response, colonel?" I asked.

"Take your time, I'll hold on..." was his reply. Obviously, military types make big decisions quickly. Impressive. My mind raced. A rule of thumb I have always followed is that leadership and personal interaction are inextricably intertwined. To have an impact you need to be close—connected. If I were to be an effective advocate and leader, I had better know the key people, their values and the priorities that would drive their decisions. Perhaps I could change some of those priorities. And they had better know me and my vision for the education of the approximately 40,000 children of their "troops."

But there was another problem. The children, the teachers, the administrators, the parents and the schools were out there—all over the place. Where should I be to be most effective? Because of the vast distances, would I now only be able to exert leadership through others? It was a disquieting thought.

I shouted down the hall: "Lavona, where would you like to live—Tokyo or Honolulu?" She replied quickly. Fortunately, we were in full agreement.

"Hq. PACAF, Colonel, is where the DoDDS office should be located." Lavona and I were moving to "paradise."

It was a glamorous position and introduced us not only to Hawaii and Far East cultures, but the military community as well.

I developed a very high regard for people in uniform. They were professional, dedicated, refined and responsible. The security of our country couldn't have been in better hands. Lavona was on the faculty of the University of Hawaii and thoroughly enjoyed her work with prospective teachers. It was a pleasant life—at least for a while.

As I visited classrooms across the vast area, met teachers and administrators and discussed instructional strategies and educational philosophy, I was impressed. These were dedicated, competent people—some of the best. They were remarkable in their ability to adjust to almost any situation. They were creative. They cared for children.

Students in the DoDD Schools had another advantage. Parents were involved with their children's schooling, and in a majority of cases that would include fathers as well as mothers. Teachers and parents were a team. It made a big difference and strengthened my increasing awareness of the vital importance the home-school relationship plays in a child's success at school. I have never forgotten it.

There was no question that the DoDD Schools were "state of the art." *But that was the problem. Is "state of the art" good enough?* Can American education continue to move forward if we are too locked into the past? I found it in California and now here. I knew it could be better. The thoughts were both disturbing and at the same time exciting.

Long distance leadership was taking its toll. It was clear now that I would have to work almost entirely through others. However, I still had the need to be there to interact with "the troops," to listen, to learn, to reassure, to encourage, to praise and sometimes admonish, and most importantly: to guide. Although I was almost constantly in the air, it seemed the distances were impossible. If I were not visiting schools, I was at the Pentagon in Washington. Lavona and I were apart too much. Neither of us liked it. We enjoyed being together very much—that's why we married. However, things were going very well in all other respects. The transition was smooth. Children were learning and the system was firmly in place.

Running a "system in place" through directives and memorandums and an occasional ceremonial visit sounded perilously close to the duties of a bureaucrat. It is a very important role but I wanted more. With my new insight about the shortcomings of "state of the art" teaching, I wanted to be where I could challenge the status quo in education and where I might make the greatest difference in America's classrooms. It seemed to me that would be where teaching and learning is studied and where teachers and leaders in education are prepared.

When the opportunity presented itself, I made the move to higher education. "Paradise" had been fun for a while. The campus life would be even better.

Higher Education

All together, I spent 19 years in higher education. I learned much, fought battles, and in some measure influenced the way we prepare teachers, run schools, and teach children. This was accomplished partly through politics. But I am getting ahead of myself.

Generally, teaching in early days required no special training. It was felt desirable that the teacher know more than the students but that was about it. Pay was very low and the status of teachers was similar to that of farm laborers. Some feel things haven't changed that much! The growth of free publicly supported universal education, changes in the curriculum to meet the needs of the rapidly evolving society and new insights about teaching, learning, and child growth and development required a more professionally sophisticated, well-educated teacher. In addition, dramatic increases in the birth rate, more women in the work place, single parents, the acknowledgment and accommodation of diversity in the society, and the impact of television and other technologies—all influenced the kind of teacher America's schools would require.

The response was rapid. State teachers colleges emerged across the country. Many became state universities. Teacher preparation programs evolved. In time, most institutions of higher education would include a department, division or college of education offering programs to prepare elementary and secondary teachers, teachers of children with very special needs, school leaders, researchers and many others including those who would become the teachers of teachers.

An organization emerged representing colleges and universities that prepare teachers and other professionals in education. Appropriately, it was called the American Association of Colleges for Teacher Education. Most of the teachers in America are trained in member institutions, and most colleges and universities are active members of the association. I was invited to stand for election as national president of the organization and was chosen by my peers to lead this influential group. It was a unique honor.

Not only was I involved on the home front as president of George Peabody College for Teachers, a very distinguished institution, I now had the opportunity to utilize the bully pulpit of national office as well as personal interaction with leaders across the country to attempt to strengthen programs that served teachers.

I remember the critical need for the prospective teacher to become more deeply involved in the real world of children and teachers and communities and cultures. I was often on my "soap box" for change. "Why," I would ask, "cannot higher education go to the public schools, to the private sector and to the community at large and build a program that involves each agency as a meaningful contributor to the total process of teacher preparation? Public schools have developed many inspired teachers and educational leaders, yet too frequently they play only minor roles in the teacher education process." Now, of course, fine collaborative programs between schools, colleges of education and other agencies are the norm rather than the exception.

I remember, too, the concern that kindergarten be publicly funded in every state in the nation. Some states felt preschool activity was just "play" and did not deserve support from tax dollars. That was another "speech"!

In university "lecture halls" there was the concern that we model the instructional methodology we purported to teach. Too often that was not the case. If teachers tend to teach the way they have been taught, we could easily negate a good lesson with our own inadequate instructional strategies. The value system, indeed the reward and punishment system for professors, might be ranked in many institutions as 1) research, 2) publish (or perish), 3) teach. That is the reality in the world of academia—not in all institutions but in many. On the other hand, instructional quality has improved tremendously. Technology would bring about even greater change.

I became particularly interested in the concept of distance learning: taking education to the learner and, in some measure, redefining the "university" itself. I will admit that the "measure" was small but it was a start. Again, modern technology now facilitates departure from tradition without sacrificing quality and will continue to do so at an accelerated pace. It is an exciting area.

There were dozens of other important issues that needed attention, such as quality, accreditation, relevancy and diversity. One pervasive issue was the public's negative perception of teachers and schools. Scientific advances in the USSR and other nations suggested America was "behind" and that America's schools were at fault. We conveniently overlooked the fact that schools reflect the society of which they are a part: its values, priorities, its commitment to learning and to children as well as the changing lifestyles of all of us. Sometimes the concern was directed positively and produced federal funding for massive school reform and assistance. Sometimes schools and teachers were just the scapegoats for a concerned public. Other times the criticisms were valid and demanded action. In that regard, the criticism was helpful.

I was a reformer during many of these years and a strong advocate for the practitioner in education—particularly the classroom teacher. I remember writing a column on the subject which appeared in *Peabody Views* in 1977. I include it here because it earned the praise of my most insightful supporter and honest critic, Lavona. She does not know that I have cherished her informal note these many years. Although the article has appeared many places, it is as valid today as when it was written over a generation ago.

*a
Memo
to
John:*

*In my humble
opinion, this is
one of the best
articles you have
ever done. You really
say it like it is!
Cheers to our leader!*

*An ex-teacher &
loyal fan,
L.*

A MEMO TO PARENTS
By John Dunworth

*Contrary to the vociferous comments of critics, most
teachers really care about your children and work long
and hard on their behalf. It's a fact. If you don't believe
it, spend just one full day with your child's teachers. And
if you don't believe it is a demanding job, consider having some thirty youngsters delivered to your home*

tomorrow morning to spend all day with you. You're the teacher!

This is what could happen: in some instances the young people have been told you are incompetent and don't care. They may react accordingly. If you discipline them too harshly, you may find yourself in court or lose your job. If you don't, you may lose your job for being too lenient. Some of your "students" are eager to learn but many could not care less. Their parents tell you to teach them not only the basic skills required in a technological society, but honesty, integrity, morality, and thrift. They may forget to mention that the unit they bought last Christmas was to help spot "Smokey the Bear" so they could exceed the speed limit (without being caught). If you survive the day you'll be relieved.

We are all human—teachers included! If a community, and in particular individual parents, will support the efforts of their teachers, administrators, and school boards, they can have excellent schools. There will be disagreements, labor disputes, tensions, and honest differences of opinion, but these disputes are best arbitrated at the council table, not the dinner table. Undermine your child's confidence in his teacher and his school with criticism and disdain and you may do irreparable damage to your child and his or her ability to accept the guidance of any teacher in the complex process called education.

If you are concerned about your youngster's progress in school, make an appointment and visit his or her teacher. But don't expect more of the school than you are willing to expect of yourself. If you won't discipline your child, the school can't make up for that deficiency. If you won't help him in his efforts to learn, the school can't succeed alone. And if you don't love your child, and show it, the teacher can't possibly make up for that void.

For your child's sake, be a partner with your child's teacher. Start by sending a note of appreciation—today! Together you'll make an unbeatable team.

Higher education also provided some very unique opportunities and experiences. Under a project for AID (Agency for International Development), I spent several weeks—with Lavona accompanying me at our expense—trudging through much of Africa interviewing educational leaders for advanced training in America's colleges and universities. Trudging isn't really the correct word, for we were provided on-site logistical support by AID personnel which was invaluable. Yet, it was just the two of us who arrived at such places as Morocco, Senegal, Sierra Leone, Ivory Coast, Ghana, Kenya, Somalia and Ethiopia. We seemed very alone and very far away; we were!

South Africa was not on the itinerary. Apartheid was in full swing and to enter the country required certification of racial purity. It was offensive to say the least. Lavona, as a member of the Human Rights Commission in Indiana, used stronger words. Fortunately, our governments were not on the best of terms and South Africa was not part of the project.

It was a hard journey through Africa but it was worth it. Many of our "pleasing certainties," as Aldous Huxley would say, were gone. We had grown on the trip, for our perceptions about "we" and "they" were changed. In some ways the words became interchangeable, transposed. A wonderful lesson. Little did I know how important it would be.

Many events of significance occurred during these years. The magnificent response of institutions such as Ball State University in Indiana to accommodate America's ravenous need for teachers during the post war decades is service of the highest order. Some of the finest teachers and educational specialists in the country are prepared in this outstanding institution.

The dramatic story of the merger of prestigious George Peabody College for Teachers and the great Vanderbilt University, with the success that followed, is a book in itself. There is no question that the brilliant work of the Peabody faculty, both past and present, is the key factor in Peabody's position of eminence. It prepared exemplary teachers as well as teachers of teachers and produced scholars, researchers, leaders and a host of distinguished graduates. It earned national respect and the support of its patrons and friends. As a vital member of the Vanderbilt University family, it continues to do so with vigor and unqualified success. This heritage and continued commitment to the development of the potential in every human being coupled with its uncompromising expectation of excellence places Peabody today at the pinnacle of Colleges of Education and Human Development in the nation. Clearly its future is as brilliant as its past.

The evolution of a fledging program of education at the University of West Florida to full maturity as a College of Education of excellence and commitment is as inspiring as it is impressive. That most of the faculty at Munson Elementary School were prepared at UWF is high praise indeed and speaks volumes as to the rigor and quality of this young but very distinguished college.

I am proud to have been a part of each of these institutions of higher education. Each provided a profound contribution to my Odyssey of Discovery. Indeed, the years in academia were very special but time was becoming an issue. Could I apply my new knowledge and insights in the real world of schools, children, parents and politics? I would soon find out.

A Thousand Classrooms

I accepted the superintendency of the ninth largest school system in California located in a place called Santa Ana—not too far from Los Angeles. It would be my last position before formal retirement. I remember writing to a former colleague in higher education to share my reaction to the change. Superintendents reading this will probably chuckle; they know.

The issues in elementary and secondary education are well known, although experiencing them again first hand is fascinating academically and challenging professionally. I have referred to the superintendency as a high wire act without a safety net. In contrast to the role of dean, it does not provide the luxury of time—time to study, to consult, and to deliberate. Indeed, time seems compressed, for the complex problems are relentless in their demand for resolution. Schools are more politicized than in past years. It is fascinating to observe the political pressure and to experience the insistent and conflicting demands. The drain on energies, knowledge, skill and compassion, as well as the testing of values, is constant. As they say in California, it's "life in the fast lane." But I enjoy it!

For 50 school days, every morning, I visited classrooms in Santa Ana. One thousand classrooms. Actually, there were many more days and many more classrooms but 1,000 conveys the message: a visual image of a thousand teachers and thousands and thousands of children. What a magnificent panorama and what a tremendous responsibility.

I have always made it a practice to visit classrooms as often as possible. As an elementary school principal, I tried to be in every classroom almost every day. In some instances I was there as the authority figure—formally observing, evaluating, and assessing performance. Such visits were followed with formal conferences and were appropriately documented and reported.

And then there were the mini-visits. These were very important too, for I was present in a supportive, helping role. All school principals wear these two hats. Mini-visits lead to professional discussions about children and strategies, channels of communication open and trust is established. We are all colleagues working toward a common goal. Usually teachers are way ahead of the principal with wonderful ideas and creative approaches that produce great results. If the principal does the job right, teachers are "free to soar"—and most do.

Smart, secure teachers can have fun with mini-visits from the principal. On occasion, I would be greeted with great enthusiasm and everything would stop with the announcement, "Boys and girls, the principal promised he was going to visit us today and tell us a wonderful story about elephants!" Everyone gathered around with great enthusiasm while the teacher, with a big grin on her face, left for a quick cup of coffee and I proceeded to create out of thin air an exciting story about elephants! Well, at least the children thought it was exciting. It is that kind of rapport that makes a school hum. It is a precious thing for it frees everyone.

Mrs. Coogle used a similar ploy with "Dr. D and the Dinosaurs," but that's another story...

There was a very special challenge in Santa Ana. I quickly learned that many children who entered school did not speak English—nor did their mothers or fathers—and that some had never been in a school in their young lives. I pondered the educational implications of these realities and I would invite any educator to do likewise. For it will challenge your expertise, your values and your definition of democracy to the core. You're the principal. A beautiful child, perhaps 10 years old, with dark innocent eyes stands before you, head bowed as a sign of respect...no schooling, no ability to read, no common frame of reference and no common language. The child with her humble parents look pleadingly for help, for one precious chance to grasp the dream this magnificent country can offer. How do you respond?

At this point I urge the reader to lay aside this book and just think. It is a horrendous challenge.

As an educator, how do you respond?

As an American, how do you respond?

As a caring human being, how do you respond?

I found the answer begins with love—expressed in deeds. The law at this time did not demand that we inquire as to the legality of the family's status. We were not required to call authorities or forcefully return the little group to poverty, ignorance, fear and hopelessness. If it had been necessary, my mind flashed quickly to Mrs. "Miklovitch" in New York. Remember Mrs. "Miklovitch?" I smiled.

Our basic tenet that we "engage the child where he or she is" took over. We have programs for children with all kinds of special needs. We will make opportunities for these children. Of course, the school system was way ahead of me with many programs already in place. Beautiful programs. To exacerbate matters, more than 30 different languages were spoken in the system. The population density was so high that most of our 35,000 children walked to neighborhood schools. It was not unusual for several families to live in one house.

All needs were addressed. Learning English was the very highest priority. Instruction was constant and intense. But remember, at home and in the community children are surrounded by their primary language—even on radio, television, billboards and movies—everywhere. It is not an easy task for the child or the teacher. But every child learned English.

Reading skills were essential, too, and learning here began initially in the child's home language. The process is the same and the transfer to English occurred smoothly and as quickly as possible. An army of teacher assistants, all bilingual, were part of the team. Everyone was contributing 200%. Many teachers were studying hard and acquiring fluency in a second language. Community groups such as the Assistance League pitched in too with extensive dental hygiene programs—all provided by volunteers. Bowers Museum, a wonderful regional resource located in Santa Ana, was in classrooms constantly with superb programs—all on a volunteer basis. And there were many others.

The response was magnificent. Children were remarkable—their fluency in English, their proficiency in a new culture, their respect for authority (most of the time, anyway) and their love of America was a joy to see. They were learning and learning fast. We responded too. Respect for their heritage, traditions and culture was always in evidence. We all gained and were greatly enriched.

I am sometimes asked point blank if race impacts learning. Environment impacts learning. Poverty impacts learning. And culture impacts learning to name just a few factors. The priorities and values of a culture can make a tremendous difference. Although many factors impact learning, it is not the color of skin that is important, it is the "color" of values that makes the difference. In cultures and families that place a high value on education and learning and express that value through support, encouragement, high expectations, discipline and personal sacrifice—children learn and succeed even under the most appalling conditions. Lip service does not do it. Actions are what count.

In general, children from families who do not care about learning raise children who do not care about learning. When our children are not succeeding at school, we often fail to ask the question, "Why are those other children so very successful?"

They can't all be brilliant.

The teacher is the same.

The school is the same.

The materials are the same.

Something is making a big difference. In most cases we do not have to look far for the answer.

Santa Ana was a wonderful school system and it is today—with its 56,000 pupils—now the seventh largest school system in California. It is a school system that achieves remarkable results under difficult circumstances and deserves the highest praise and respect. It was a privilege to be a part of it.

As you can tell, I learned a bushel of things in Santa Ana. This was good, for the odyssey was coming to a close. Oh, there would be additional twists and turns in the road, but Florida, retirement, reflection and repose were calling. We were both tired. It had been a long journey.

Sometime later one lazy morning with the birds singing, the Florida sun filtering through the green canopy of summer leaves and the cats cozily at rest, Lavona said, "John, did you see the article in the paper today about the little school that may be closed?"

And so it was that my personal road led right over the rise to a place called Munson, Florida, and to the little school that could. It would be the greatest story of all! Of course, the Dream Team may see it differently. I wonder.

Part III

The Teachers
A Different Perspective

—Alisa A. Rogaliner, B.A.
5/6 Grade Teacher and Dream
Team Member,
Munson Elementary School,
Munson, Florida

Part III

The Teachers

A Dialogue Revisited

Chapter VII

In Their Words

The Scribe

To hear Dr. Dunworth, or Dr. D as we like to call him, tell the story of Munson Elementary is quite moving. What makes it even more so to us is that we were actually there. But it is still amazing. The story is sensitive and inspiring while sharing a wealth of information; yet, it stays faithful to what happened there. It has enabled you, the reader, to be part of a very special experience. At least it is very special to us; we are the five teachers who Dr. D refers to as "The Dream Team." We'd like to share some of the story with you as we experienced it.

In all candor, principals are important people but they really do not know everything! Every teacher knows that. For example, our Dr. D is the most articulate advocate we know for computers and technology in education but we're pretty sure he doesn't know the difference between a hard drive and the automatic transmission in his beloved Honda. We even witnessed him using the CD-ROM drive as a cup holder, but we won't tell him we saw that! He does, however, know an enormous amount about teaching, learning and running a great school. Perhaps most importantly, he knows about people – children, teachers, staff, parents, the VIPs in the district office and the fellow we often overlook who is digging the ditch on the outskirts of the school property along Munson Highway. Good principals are really "people persons."

Of course, principals have many other important attributes. They are the best "spin doctors" in the world. They can make the worst situation sound plausible, the most difficult child a joy, and a critical shortage of supplies and books a mere temporary inconvenience that can easily be overcome by "creative resourcefulness" (i.e. make your own!). Although we wouldn't want them to think these lines are really fooling us, they are pretty good. As for Dr. D, we do love him.

We have learned through our combined experiences that a good principal is an advocate, a friend, a helper—and a boss. A really good principal is consistent and has high expectations for all of us as well as himself. He or she also understands our shortcomings and sundry other things like "bad hair days" and Monday mornings. The principal is a change agent too, a catalyst for change. Change is what schools are about. Dr. Dunworth exemplifies this kind of administrator and we think he's a very good model.

As for our thoughts on the rest of the story, we've decided to compile our experiences and exploits in a somewhat chronological order. This will give you our perceptions of life in a little school that needs to turn a new leaf. Though our faculty is small, combining the cumulative thoughts and experiences of so diverse and versatile a team wouldn't be easy. So we set about to decide which one of us—with the input of Dr. D—would be the lucky person to be the scribe. At one of our famous "mini" faculty meetings I was honored with this task. I'm Mrs. Alisa "Lisa" Rogaliner, the fifth and sixth grade teacher. I hoped I was chosen as sort of a connoisseur of words and prose, but actually, no one else was available. I think they tell me that to keep me modest. No kudos here. Davina Sanders, like all kindergarten or K-1 teachers, tends to be monosyllabic, but with a slight warm Southern drawl. She would probably start with "See the book? Oh, oh, oh. Look, look, look!" That would never do. Mrs. Sanders is the member of the team who shamelessly captivated Dr. D with her gorgeous smile and sparkling personality. We think he hired her not only because she is a superb teacher but also because he knew that smile and personality would be a boon for the whole team as we faced the struggle ahead. And he was right.

Elisabeth Coogle (Beth, as she likes to be called) is a vivacious second/third grade teacher. She could easily complete such a task, but somehow keeps acquiring children. She now has five of her own! No time for serious writing in that household even if you did graduate at the top of your class. Cindy Cadenhead, P.E. teacher extraordinaire, could do it too. She is also a whiz on the computer but she does tend to punctuate everything with a whistle! Of course, David Johnson is making the transition to full-time administration and true-to-form would undoubtedly practice by delegating everything to us. So we would be back to square one. Well, so much for the shared decision-making philosophy! I win by default.

Most of our mini-faculty meetings like this are held outdoors right after the last school bus has departed. Seems reasonable, considering this is the single time during our schedules that we are all in the same place at the same time. We joke around and share stories to relieve the tension of the day; then we get serious. Though I am most likely chosen to run the school hospitality committee or organize a children's program, they were both serious and unanimous that I was the one who might possibly match Dr. D's propensity for big words. So I have been asked to tell the teachers' view of the Munson story – our thoughts and our hopes.

The Announcement

The news media is full of woe. Horror, mayhem and corruption are fed to us in daily doses. The day the local paper ran the story of a small school closing was no different; or was it? Would the little school soon be gone? Thoughts began to form, phones began to ring, and in a few short hours a new lease on life was being handed to the "little school in the big forest."

Each of us got the word in a different way, but nonetheless, a call came to a group of applicants who felt they could make a change. As each individual made his or her way to the School Board offices to drop off resumes, the familiar butterflies set in and last-minute preparations began to shape each of us into "the one who could help make a difference."

David would be the first. A small fishing boat is hardly the setting to be notified of an important promotion, but David is noted for being "laid back." His group, vaguely reminiscent of a scene from *Huckleberry Finn*, is relishing a warm Florida summer afternoon with the children. But something interrupts the languid laziness that surrounds the barefoot fishermen as they meander along the banks. Would you believe from among the stately oaks and moss-bearded cypress trees drooping lazily off the shore, a telephone would ring? Seems that one of them is more a '90s person than he is willing to admit. To David's disbelief, his wife Harriet, is on the other end of the line. David should come home quickly. The school superintendent would like to see him this afternoon! Well, with 20 years of perfect service to an outstanding county, what would you think? "I don't remember doing anything wrong! A principalship? My name came up on the list? Nah." David muses to himself. But after the closest scene to walking on water in this century, he will soon find out. He dashes home and in record time makes a more appropriately dressed entrance to the School Board office.

A promotion is offered for teacher / assistant principal with the possibility of becoming principal the following year—with all that entails. Mr. Russell, the superintendent, carefully lays out the goals for Munson. It is a Goliath task and a risky venture. David needs time to think. Certainly, that is fair and he takes 24 hours. After much consideration and prayer with his supportive wife, David makes the decision to accept. The look of relief is scarcely hidden from Mr. Russell's face as he hears what he has hoped for. Congratulations are made. A flurry of paperwork begins and Mr. Russell quietly turns and says, "David, on many of the mornings you drive up to Munson, you're going to ask yourself, 'Why am I doing this?'" Little did the superintendent know, he was a prophet for all of us. But for now, Munson has a fine fourth / fifth grade teacher and a new assistant principal. Let the learning begin!

The task of sorting through all the applications is not an easy one to say the least, but what of the applicants themselves? What would motivate a person to be willing to give so much of his or her time and self to save a small facility so far away from town?

For me, Lisa Rogaliner, there were myriad motivations. I truly love to teach and have had many successful years before I moved here. But recently having been on the receiving end of the famous "Don't call us, we'll call you" line, there was a sense of wonder and relief when I read the article in the local paper. I had no idea that the situation even existed; I found it remarkable—this Dr. Dunworth, a person who was not encumbered by a political agenda, would help this little place. It would be a breath of fresh air to work with such a person. I am always one to cheer for the underdog and at this point, Munson definitely was one. Then again, going the extra mile is never an effort if something good comes of it. "Seeing the joy in the eyes of a child..." Remember? As good fortune would have it, applications had not yet been closed and within moments of reading the article, with hopeful face, I was delivering the ever-expanding resume. It was one of many being submitted. Only God Himself knew if this was the right place for my future colleagues and me.

God was indeed all-knowing and close to Beth Coogle as she sat in church, slightly distracted by the news her family had just shared with her. Encouragement is an understatement with Beth's family, for you see she is married to a gentleman from the Munson area. As Beth found out soon after her wedding, she didn't marry just this fine, Southern man, she married his whole family. And in the South, that is how it should be. But we digress. Many a meal at the home of Granny and Papa Coogle has been spent reminiscing about "the good old days." One subject in particular always catches Beth's attention—Munson Elementary. After all, she is a teacher. When Granny had called, there was much excitement in her voice. "Sugar, have you seen the *Press Gazette*? You need to get over and apply. I put five children through that school, you know." Sure enough, Munson wasn't going to close after all! A Dr. Dunworth was working for Munson for $1! There would be four teaching positions. Beth felt she *had* to fill one of them. Highly educated with outstanding credentials, Beth has been choosing a different path. She cherishes every moment at home with her two little ones and would have made June Cleaver green with envy. Still, the "call" was there, the ever-present little voice that makes her question her own decisions. Should she apply? The worst that could happen is she would not get the position and would continue her pleasant life at home. It is worth the try. And try she does. Without a moment's hesitation, she set to work on her resume.

Resumes did indeed cross the School Board office desk in plenty, but among the most promising of them was one belonging to Davina Sanders. Knowing the area well, Davina had been made aware of the plight of Munson Elementary from inside sources. Davina was already a teacher in the school system at a lovely school. However, since enrollment was down and she was the last hired for kindergarten, she would be the first to be relocated. Pro-active person that she is, Davina asks her principal if there would be a problem looking for another position in case the enrollment did not rebound. She is told of an announcement received that very morning. Munson Elementary School is looking for new teachers. Would she be interested? Before Davina could fully digest the situation, her astute principal places a phone in front of her. Davina lives only about 25 minutes from Munson, a much easier commute than into Milton, itself. As fate would have it, the phone call is made, an interview scheduled and butterflies set in.

It had only been a year since Davina's initial interview in the county, yet it seemed like forever to her. She rushes home to share the news with her family. Her mother is more than excited. The whole story of Dr. Dunworth is a beautiful story and it has an especially poignant meaning. Saving Munson means saving part of her mother's contribution as a teacher in the county, for her mother had taught at the school that is now in peril. Her daughter, if hired, has an opportunity that few would ever be offered. Yet Davina was hesitant. Like Beth, she knew that one year might not be enough. If the school fails despite her best efforts, she would be without a position again next summer and would face the interview process for the third summer in a row. But something spurs her on beyond her own doubts.

Davina prepares for the interview and promptly at 9:30 a.m. walks into the intimidating hallway. After checking in with the secretary, she takes a seat and patiently waits. A tall woman, beautifully poised and beaming with a smile, exits and carries her briefcase down the hall. Every move she makes suggests she has the position. For a moment Davina recoils, but reaching for every ounce of pride at her disposal, she squares her shoulders and walks into the office with a smile that says, "Hire me, I'm worth it!" The panel of three interviewers rises to greet her and Dr. Dunworth acknowledges her efforts. "With a smile like that, we will have to hire you!" he says. Immediately, Davina is set at ease. The melancholy aura that tried to discourage her quickly evaporates with the congeniality of the panel. Her intensive 45-minute plus interview seems to pass in only 15. Just as with Lisa and Beth, something has clicked. The questions from Dr. Dunworth were concise and direct. Davina would know exactly where she stood with this man. She was impressed with his demeanor and his extensive command of pedagogy. She was amazed at his desire to have this little school succeed at every level. The little ones would be just as important as the older children who will be taking the tests that defined Munson's progress. Dr. Dunworth knew that the little ones would be the ones who keep Munson open in years to come. He is not just concerned with today; he wants a future for the little school.

Davina rushes home to call her mother. As she bubbles over with all that she has encountered that morning, she announces, "Mother, I have to have this job!"

"What brought about this change of heart?" her mother asks.

"John Dunworth," she replies. "He is the most intriguing person I have ever met. His enthusiasm and his mission are unreal and I want to be on his side. He is going to turn that school around." She and her mom reminisce about the days when Davina and her sister ran the hallways of Munson as little girls visiting their mom's class. Who would have guessed that the beautiful little raven-haired girl swinging on the swings or drawing on the chalkboard would one day herself stand in front of a class of smiling eyes, take them to that very playground and teach them in that very room. Daughter and mother share a precious moment, cry a little and smile.

The time passes quickly and who is on the other end of the telephone line only a day later, but Dr. D himself. "Mrs. Sanders, would you consider being our kindergarten/grade one teacher?"

Would she? Was there any other answer she could give? "Yes, of course I would."

The "Dream Team" was set and as Mr. Gill, Munson's custodian and resident philosopher, so wisely states, "We'll be just fine... with the help of the good Lord."

Preplanning: The Shock of It All

On Sunday afternoon following the School Board's appointment of Dr. D and David, they met at the school to get the lay of the land. It was shocking how dark and abandoned the little school felt. Scattered around empty rooms lay piles of bric-a-brac: a poster here, some pamplets there. The atmosphere was dulled by the insufficient lighting, as if the pair were entering into another time. Both could picture a day when the mess in front of them might have been usable but there was no rhyme or reason to the antiquated supplies. Yellowed and faded papers left in unmarked makeshift cartons gave little clue as to what was going on in the school. Certainly, the previous staff had ended its year under the impression its closing was the final one. Where should they begin? Several deficiencies stood out. With their usual insight, each set out an important goal: David's to end the confinement of four classes in closed spaces when adjacent rooms stood empty and Dr. D's to give them light. The District responded with a promptness that amazed all of us.

With only a few weeks left until school, things began to happen. Electricians appeared with miles of wiring and jingling belts ready to give us the energy we needed. Exterior doors were painted and new sinks were installed in the primary classrooms. Not just sections, but whole walls began to come down and things became much brighter for the school. Is this foreshadowing our future?

Soon, a gray Pontiac filled to the brim with boxes and charts and dreams and books and maps and a starry-eyed teacher pulls up in front of a neat set of buildings to join those who had already begun their pilgrimage to a new Munson. "This looks nice enough," I think to myself as I walk toward the entrance. A genuinely warm secretary, Judy, greets me for the first time and welcomes me to Munson. Aesthetically, it is a pleasing place to be except for the ancient orange carpet, immaculately clean, and screaming to be laid to rest from the years of dutiful service. "Hopefully, this will go soon," I silently pray.

I meet David for the first time as a tour guide at Munson. He is acting in Dr. D's stead since an important meeting away from the school required the principal's presence. Walking to the hallway, David shows me a collection of empty rooms, I mean seriously empty. Piles of scrap papers and boxes of old guidance office material lay scattered. One lonely table longs for companionship and Olympic-sized wooden wardrobe cases serve as the only storage available in the rooms. No windows. Moderate light. Tons of potential. There are only days until school starts! "Excuse me, Mr. Johnson, where are the textbooks?" He just smiles.

David continues the tour of the school, and he tells me about the vision they have. The excitement builds. Can we build Solomon's Gardens out of a deck of cards and cardboard boxes?

Surprise is an understatement for Davina as she enters the school filled with childhood memories. As she walks through the halls with Dr. D, it all looks so different, so much smaller than it did through the eyes of a five-year-old. Then, everything seemed so much larger. Davina remembers Munson as an open modular school. Classes had dividers but no doors; now there are walls separating the small classes. She had run hand in hand with her sister down this hallway. She pauses and smiles as Dr. D opens the door to her new classroom, the very one her mother taught in. A ghost of the past flashes quickly to linger in the back of her mind, while visions of the future rush in like a flood. Reality sets in quickly and she begins to plan for her place in the annals of Munson history. Knowing that she would need to add to her supplies, she makes some mental notes of the deficits she sees. Dr. D graciously excuses himself to let her begin her plans. Shortly after, she begins the first of many scavenger hunts for first-grade supplies. Having taught only kindergarten, she would need many more things. A local teacher is retiring and Davina becomes the benefactor of all her first-grade materials. Shortly, boxes begin to arrive at Munson in her green Explorer. Davina will indeed make a difference.

There is an old storage room with miscellaneous odds and ends, a virtual treasure trove of memorabilia from a time long ago. "I'll take this and this..." was met with "Mrs. Coogle already asked for it. Did you see this, though?" None of Munson's teachers ever have to want for much. It may have to be rebuilt and repainted but we find a way. We all begin to marvel at the unprecedented support from both David and Dr. D. If there is a need, they will find a way to take care of it. And you wouldn't believe the after-effect. The teacher response is amazing. Giving 200 percent becomes the norm because we know that it will be respected and supported. No one here leaves early. "Dawn to dusk" is not an unusual schedule for any of us.

A good example of this support is my primary concern logistically about student desks. I've taught sixth grade before. Students, who would come in short enough to be used for armrests at the bus stop, would soon tower over me with legs eight miles long. Nothing is quite as distracting as resting your desk on your legs because it is too short for you to sit under. "This will never do," I explain to Dr. D. Upon hearing my logic about the ancient fixed-chair desks (which was well versed, if I do say so myself), a phone call was made to the district office. I have a feeling it took a lot of calls but the problem was solved. And then I ask naively, "Now, where are my textbooks stored?" He smiles.

Meanwhile, a carnival-like atmosphere has transpired in the kindergarten class. How in the world a young teacher can have so much stuff is beyond all of us, but never accuse Davina of not being thrifty. Newly painted shelves stand covered with books and games and more books for little ones.

Primary colors adorn the walls in the form of posters and charts. And still there is more material being brought in. Davina wisely enlists the help of her mother, who is herself a first-grade teacher, and begins to sort through the endless parade of laminated alphabet animals that trail across the floor. Beth stopped by earlier to share some of our valuable thrift furniture and takes mental inventory of all the stacks on Davina's floor. Could she ever get through this by Open House? Not to be distracted from the task at hand, while the two share a lively conversation, Davina breaks into another stack of boxes.

Beth soon leaves to tackle her own Mount Vesuvius of packing material and sort through a never-ending menagerie of teaching aids here and there. The hours pass with little rest and much fatigue but Beth and all her energy has cleared quite a path across her room. She treats herself to a little break and wanders back toward Davina's class. "You're not done yet?!" Beth exclaims. Davina's bewilderment can hardly be mistaken. And though they had only just met, she thought Beth seemed like such a nice person. Laughter is truly the best medicine and we all soon find out that our petite little Elisabeth is also quite the firecracker. Only David can outdo her with a good prank.

"The chrome legs cost extra. But we're worth it," Dr. D exclaims as Larry proceeds to bring crate after crate of brand new student desks to my room. The logistics problem is solved, but with only one custodian for the moment who also serves as handy man, who would assemble the desks? "I'll get to them as soon as I can, Mrs. Rogaliner," Larry Gill replies as he sets the last of the crates in the room. Like Dr. D and David with the textbooks, I look at Larry and I smile.

For the next few hours my teenage daughter, Christa, and I assemble 30 shiny new adjustable desks and place the beautiful navy blue chairs underneath them. Life is good. Now, where are those textbooks?

"You've got to be kidding me" is the only response I can muster as I look at the piles of rustic, time worn texts that David has assembled in his room. Again, he smiles, but responds, "Apparently, Lisa, textbook forms had been filled out, but with the prospect of the school closing they were never ordered. We'll have to make do for now." A serene mood ensues as we leaf through the well-used pages of the antique math books some 15 years old. Still, math concepts rarely become outdated. Once a triangle, always a triangle.

First rule of teaching: be flexible. As we rifle through boxes and bags, we find several promising texts that can be used in addition to the class set. Slowly, the upper grades are taking shape.

The primary grades are facing the same challenges. "What must every new teacher do first?" Beth asked herself. "Go to the school and get your curriculum!" Wrong. Beth arrives at the school to see Dr. D trying to make sense out of complete organized chaos. He quickly leaves the office to give her the grand tour. During the interviews, Beth recalls, he had been meticulously dressed, and displayed a warm, highly professional side that no doubt he expected from those in his employ. She smiles with the thought that even now in shirt sleeves he shows a versatility that was equally friendly, making her feel at ease and completely comfortable in her new position.

Beth likes his sense of humor too. "You know why enrollment declined?" he asks. She looks around at the construction workers on ladders, lights littering the floor, concrete debris, books in piles. Where should she begin? "They've been losing the little ones down the toilets!" he says with a twinkle in his eye. The adult-sized fixtures did look massive in the small bathroom for first graders. He hadn't missed a thing!

By this time, the administration's goals for the building and grounds were being reached. She notices the openings in the walls that were created to make larger classrooms, lights that were brighter, paper towels that could be reached by students, and the list goes on. All these "little things" were to pay off big. They showed the students the school was for them. They weren't just temporary inhabitants of "our" school; we were here to meet *their* needs. Beth was amazed at Dr. D's insight into elementary education.

After the tour she also asks to see her curriculum, textbooks, and so forth. The answer would be the same: "This is it!" It would take literally weeks of digging, phone calls, and the patience of Job to finally sort through the piles. Beth, like Lisa, is appalled to find the latest math textbooks were dated 1970 something. These look like what she had used as a child. (Does that date our teacher as well?) Then she remembers that her husband's grandparents, who live only two miles from the school, got their first indoor bathroom the year that her "city" school got its first computers. These textbooks had been published the same year! The other subjects weren't much better. Beth understands she will have to develop her own materials if she will bring her students up to this decade! After all, the CTBS test they'll take in March was developed this decade.

By the end of many 10-hour days, classrooms begin to take shape. It will take more hours and the help of our children and friends, but by Open House we manage to pull it off. And by the way—never, ever open those Olympic-sized cabinets without a safety net!

Open House itself is a huge success. The faculty and staff meet with myriad applause after one of Dr. D's eloquent introductions. The official proclamation of Munson's "reopening" is read and again the crowd roars with applause. As Dr. D calls us to stand and introduce ourselves, Beth, like the rest of us, feels the awesome responsibility at hand. She looks into the eyes of the three other teachers, believing that we each have said a prayer that night. She is absolutely right.

Later, parents and students alike explore the freshly decorated corridors in awe of the physical transformation they see. Several recall youthful activities they themselves had within these halls. Beth finds she knows a lot of the faces from her Granny's kitchen and church. Davina also greets several family members and friends. Many of the faces are new and that is exciting. We are getting the families' attention. David is his usual warm and friendly self, making people feel at ease in their old but new surroundings. I join in the silent prayer vigil that is taking place that night, praying for guidance and wisdom to do the right thing for these families.

As Beth looks at the parents leading their children to the classrooms to meet their respective teachers, she is reminded of herself leading her own children to their pediatrician. "I know they're sick, but I'm not sure of much else. I need to call on the expert, our family doctor." These parents also feel that something has been wrong, not with health issues but with their child's education.

Because of her family association, she had heard them talk about their concerns at social gatherings, but they couldn't pinpoint the problem or offer a diagnosis. So they came to us. They were literally placing their children's lives in our hands. Could we really make the difference?

The First Week: Reality Check

If bureaucracy is the downfall of administrators, preconceived ideas will do the same to a classroom teacher. The cascading waterfalls of endless beautiful lesson plans and academic theory one brings to the classroom will soon give way to the monotony of "Johnny, please sit down." "Johnny, are you doing your own work?" "Johnny, we don't hit people in this school nor do we use words like that." And creative, positive classroom management becomes the topic for breakfast, lunch and dinner. This is reality. We dream grand dreams, but somehow, the students forget to read our script.

If you don't believe me, ask David Johnson. Walking by David's room was like walking by the soft side of an Army barracks. Everything was perfect. Everything has its place and every desk is in a neat row. (Desks in rows drive Beth and Lisa crazy.)

Textbooks are neatly organized and he even has all his board work up for the first day! He's done these beautifully coordinated lesson plan outlines for the whole year! Go figure? But we all admire David's skills. He is a master at working through difficult situations. So it was with the honesty of Abe after a week of school he said, "Hey guys, remember those great plans I made?"

"Don't remind me!" was the response.

"Well, I have to throw them all out! Yes, I looked at the cumulative folders and had everything prepared, but the student skill levels are in an entirely different range than I even imagined. We are going to have to give these children a lot of individual help."

Davina was extremely confident in the pages of lesson plans she had made. Hours of research into models of combined grades and first-grade skills were carefully outlined, categorized and expanded in her plan book. The children arrive and by the afternoon the plan book is in the wastebasket. She hadn't known the deficit of the children's knowledge. What a different world this is for her little ones. It is going to be quite a struggle, but with all her Southern confidence and charm (and a little elbow grease and lots of crayons) Davina will make the best of it. So she starts with each child and works her way from there.

These anecdotes emphasize the need for flexibility. Even the best laid plans can go to ruin if both sides of the educational coin are not made of the same material. Our children needed different approaches. We had to incorporate other teaching styles to reach out to the needs of particular kids. But boy, when we found that style, the sky was the limit. It was worth every page we threw away because we found a system that worked. It may have been altered 88 different times, but we tried until we found an answer. It was as though we were free. We supported each other in the process and we reached for the stars.

Another reality for us was that though they are polished and proofed a thousand times, many curriculum guides and standardized tests contain cultural biases. Beth had considerable insight regarding the needs of the primary children, having worked in the rural South previously, specifically in Edisto Island, South Carolina. She knew well the advantages and disadvantages our children possessed. Living among extended family members, farmland, and poverty teaches strong values. Children learn to look out for one another, to share, to respect experience, and they learn about God. On the other hand, she observed two major obstacles that must be tackled: grammar and background experiences.

Learning to read seems an arduous task for many youngsters, but when "book talk" doesn't sound like "real talk" the task is magnified. Our children's "real talk" is quite specialized compared to some of the more urban schools. For a child with a strong accent or dialect, learning to read is, in a way, learning a new language. The vocabulary changes. Word usage and sentence structure vary from what the children are accustomed to in their everyday conversations. Clues that the average reader relies upon are not so clearly evident here.

The lifestyle of this community also affects the way our children approach reading. We ourselves often check to see if our reading is on track by asking, "Does this information or word make sense?" For example, if children from the city read about a cow outside their bedroom window, it would seem out of place. Our students see this as quite normal. Compounding this problem, many students come from homes that have limited financial resources, therefore they are exposed to fewer opportunities to travel and amass material things. Beth observes that the children from Munson have to travel 30 minutes to a grocery store or a library and an hour to reach Pensacola, the nearest "big" city.

Needless to say, some of our students don't "get out" that often. The result is that our children often lack the background experiences necessary to make important connections. With this in mind, it is easier to see that a story about a pet store is hard for a child to understand who doesn't have the experience of visiting a pet store. Here, you just get a pet from your neighbor. A poem about sidewalks? What is a sidewalk anyway? What's a boulevard? Most farms don't have a sidewalk and we travel on roads and highways here.

Part of the teacher's job will be to give these students experiences to build their background knowledge. In Beth's words, "I will help till the soil so that the more seeds I plant, the more there are to actually take root." Will these plans work? Beth is able to test them after several weeks of cleaning, trips to the teacher stores, searching professional magazines, and dusting off textbooks.

Beth's classroom stood ready — ready for the little bodies that would come walking through her door that first day. She had watermelons everywhere. She knew Papa grew lots of watermelons in his garden, so she thought this would be a good theme for the Munson children to start with. If you don't know how to grow a watermelon, you may at least enjoy eating one. There was a snack center with watermelon Jell-O, a watermelon nametag for each person (even for Dr. D), a watermelon bulletin board, a collection of watermelon books. Well, you get the idea. Beth is a big advocate of teaching with themes. She'd begin "tilling the soil" to plant watermelon seeds! The children loved it and learning had truly begun.

Then There Were Five

Another gargantuan taskmaster that loomed over our little abode was the great grand monster of schedules: bus schedules, lunch schedules, library schedules, computer lab schedules, faculty meeting schedules, scheduled parent conferences, media blitz schedules, and on and on. But like the infomercial, "Wait, there's more!" The fiercest of all the schedule creatures was the dreaded P.E. schedule.

Although we all enjoy sports of some kind, just try playing kick ball in 90+ degree heat in a button-down shirt and tie or a dress, high heels and panty hose. We have images to uphold. But with all their wisdom, Dr. D and David are determined to offer the children an organized, structured physical education program. After all, a sound body breeds a sound mind! Out of our minds is more like it. The children can barely tell the difference. Beth and Davina can be seen on the playground during their P.E. times often playing "Duck, duck goose" or some similar game. David and I have the task of organizing the upper grades. David is much more astute at this than I am, so as an aspiring administrator, I practice delegation. I do make a mean third-base coach, though.

As good as we are, three or four weeks of this 30 minutes each day is as much as we can handle. Our guardian administration angels silently hover though and soon the call is out for a part-time P.E. teacher. We all wonder if the 40 applicants interviewed for our jobs were as colorful as the candidates we meet. Could God have possibly created a person who would mesh into our dream team with the same professional and personal fluidity that we found with each other? Then comes Cindy. Of course, academician that he is, Dr. D thoroughly scrutinizes her resume. "Top of her class, award, award, award…Let's go ahead and interview her." She instantly wins us over. She leaves the interview with a job offer practically in hand and a one-week notice to give her current employer.

Honestly, if you think classroom teachers are low on the career food chain, resource teachers are barely subsisting in the public eye. Yet, when dedicated to the children's needs as the focus of their job, their contributions rival any lesson created in the four walls of a classroom. Teamwork and sportsmanship cannot be learned from a book. They must be modeled. Cooperative learning that classroom teachers dare to use in limited amounts is the requisite learning style for physical education.

Our first-year teacher is incredible. "No" is not an option for her. With the same black hole of resources available to her that we had in the classroom, she somehow manages to make ends meet. A decrepit closet is miraculously transformed into an office. Faced with the challenge of storing her supplies (at this time, she has a few deflated basketballs, a busted hula-hoop or two, and a few things that seem to crawl on their own — oh, we won't count the dead rat found behind the shelves), she locates a space. With the same generous assistance from Dr. D, there will be a way to provide for the physical needs of these children. A day or two later she is called to the gymnasium to see some able-bodied Marines from VT-6 ready to take orders in her reconstruction project. Soon, her equipment storage area is immaculate and a few weeks later brimming with wonderful new supplies and equipment. Dr. D has done it again.

Munson Elementary has never had a P.E. department head before, so her work is cut out for her. The limited experiences that we had been providing were about as much structure as our dear children had received in the art of P.E. Then there were the attitude problems, but we will address that later in our saga. We are still in awe of the dedication and joy Cindy puts into her work. When she has a good day, and most are, we all benefit.

We classroom teachers will forever be beholden to our fair Cindy. She gave us children who could begin to think in terms of the group and work together better. She also rescued us from the P.E. schedule and gave us our much treasured, first official 20-minute planning time. Truthfully, P.E. is a 30-minute class but once a teacher gets the students there, waits for the change-over, goes in the office to check for mail and into the restroom, then returns for the students at the end of P.E. class, about 20 minutes are left. (If you have ever been in a job where you had to stay with your group from beginning to end and have to ask permission to leave your task and go to the restroom, you will appreciate this time.)

In all sincerity we do thank God and thank Cindy for the guidance she gives, the activities she provides for the children and also for that precious 20—uh, 30 (sorry Cindy)—minutes.

Classroom Management: Before and After

Sweet Pinocchio. Big beautiful smile. Sparkling eyes. Makes you want to do everything for him. Every class has one or two or seven. This is the precious child who never tells the same account twice, never has his homework (because he has the best-fed dog around), and never seems to see Mom or Dad to give them the behavior note sent home from school yesterday.

What do we do about little Pinocchio? The teachers at Munson all have different techniques (and those change hourly) to deal with these problems, but the most consistent factor is parent notification by telephone or certified mail. Parents must know both sides of the story. They must know school expectations and not just what Pinocchio tells them. For you see, we found Pinocchio always seems to leave something out. "I promise, Mom! I never said one bad word about him. I never called him one single name, and I didn't hit him first." What a master linguist at only 8 years old! However, he failed to say, "I said several bad words about him; I called him 20 bad names and I hit him as hard as I could after he bumped me first." Sound familiar?

Other good techniques we teachers use are: 1) Have Pinocchio call his parents from school and tell them directly about his infraction, with the teacher there to fill in the left-out information. 2) Have him present at the end of the parent-teacher conference to answer questions from both. We recall the time this worked particularly well for Davina, who sweetly asked, "Misty, would you like to tell Mommy what you did today?" Misty never repeated that particular offense again.

Sometimes classroom management can be made easier by listening to parents and not getting caught in another preconceived idea that often inhibits teaching: "I know better than they do because I am the educator." Teachers may be trained in a thousand different methods, but we don't live with the children. If you want to really find out what will motivate Johnny to learn these wonderful things we are teaching, include the parents and listen when they talk. Don't just wait your turn to tell them what to do. By respecting them and incorporating what they desire for their child, you can work through many difficult times and even make a friend for life.

Parents may tell you about troubles they have had in the past, then you take one look at their child and think, "What do they know? I can handle this little angel," only to be reminded that you should never judge a book by its cover. Not convinced? Ask Paul's parents. Paul was a special-needs child with a history of difficulty in school. He saw things differently and thought rules did not necessarily apply to him all the time. Trouble seemed to follow him, even when he tried his best to stay ahead of it. A pattern had been set. He'd been to several different schools and his past teachers tried diligently, but from all indications they used the traditional authoritative approach of "Me teacher—you student," which did not work in Paul's case. Munson would be different though. Munson still had a mission.

When I met with Paul's parents, they were tired of the run-around. They had tried to talk to the schools before, but no one would listen. However, I knew that Munson was not staffed to handle the emotional concerns I was seeing. We only had five teachers and were already stretched thinly enough to see through. Our 10-hour days were filled to the brim. This child needed special counseling time but counseling in the hallway leaves much to be desired. The parents, however, were adamant. They did not want their child in a different setting. They truly believed Munson was the best place for him.

Realizing that a power struggle would only make things bad for all of us, I tried a different approach. I invited Paul's parents to attend some special activities with the class. They were shocked. No one had ever asked them to be part of the solution during the school day. They accepted with enthusiasm and showed up promptly for the first activity. I was a bit nervous at how they would respond to my difficult group. With 25 different personalities all struggling to be in control of my class, there was a constant battle with classroom management. Paul's special needs along with the five other high-needs children only compounded the battle.

To say Paul's parents were amazed after their visit would be an understatement. For the first time, they were able to observe their child in a group setting with the high academic demands placed by state and local criteria. After the second visit, I seemed to win their trust. Requests and suggestions were taken warmly. "I don't know how you do it with this group," Paul's father admits. "With much love and a big bottle of aspirin at home," I say with a laugh. Soon, Mom and Dad see Paul in a different light and realize that he needs extra help, not because he is a *bad boy*, but because he learns differently and he needs help that his present classroom cannot afford him, just by the nature of classroom dynamics.

Paul writes me a note:

> *Dear Mrs. Rogaliner,*
> *I am having fun now. I like my new school. We do a*
> *lot of neat things here. Thank you Mrs. Rogaliner,*
> *Paul.*

Each of us has similar victories we could relate to this topic. Beth makes such a difference with her endless phone calls and personal visits to help out not just the children, but their families. For when we have Mom and Dad on our side, little Johnny is much easier to reach. Once reached, little Johnny also must be supervised, especially when he is only three feet tall and there are 24 of them.

Our little staff grows one more time. Davina is doing a masterful job in her class, but with the combination first-grade and kindergarten with many children who had never been in a school setting before, time was of the utmost importance. Davina's time becomes much too fragmented. A teacher assistant is needed. Divine Providence intervenes again in the person of Mrs. Debbie Marmont. Debbie had worked in professional office work and was used to dealing with a rather elite clientele. This mother of two young adults now desires to do something different with her time and energy. She is just what the doctor ordered and quickly wears many hats around the little school. She runs the office at Mrs. Baxley's side one moment then tutors sixth-grade English the next. Moments later we find her in a first-grade reading circle as little eyes glow with delight while she shares a favorite story. Davina notes about her class assistant, "Debbie's presence made the difference with our class. She was able to work with one group so that another group could receive the more individualized attention they needed. I think our test results show this."

Managing children has many different facets and controlling class size is paramount. With too many students in a class, regardless of age, opportunity for problems and discord increase exponentially with the addition of each new student.

Munson becomes successful for many reasons, but among one of the most prominent is attention to the needs of individual children. Because class sizes are monitored closely, children are not forced to be a student number in the central computer. They are not faceless entities that are counted to secure the school budget for the upcoming year. They are the school. They are the reason we come to work each day. They cannot have a price tag placed upon them. Although it is true that money cannot fix education, it is required to hire the excellent teachers, teacher assistants and administrators who can. It is required to hire enough of them so that students can be heard, taught and cared for. Thank goodness, Dr. D knows this too. (We are beginning to wonder what he doesn't know.)

First Contact: A New Journey for Cindy

We know that our first experiences with Munson were quite eye opening, but by this time we classroom teachers are becoming accustomed to the ways of life that our children are exposing us to daily. Cindy, however, missed the early shock we experienced and had to brave through strange new waters on her own, so to speak. She missed the "pre-planning" time that teachers have at the beginning of the year, but she was afforded three whole days to get her materials together and be ready to teach.

Cindy greets her classes with the same enthusiasm that we all have the first few days of school, only to meet a more hostile group of students later. At least in the classroom, teachers can immerse the children in academics and textbooks, and therefore keep them distracted from thoughts that lead to trouble. We teach children to work quietly and focus on one thing at a time. In physical education, however, students must perform through movement and noise. For the Munson children, it is not an outlet, it is a war.

Cindy recalls the first days. "My first contact with the children was scary. The children had been playing kickball for a long time and they must have been playing for blood. They were too competitive: in an unhealthy way. They did not enjoy the game for the sport of it; they must win. When the sixth-grade class arrived, I could almost see the chips on their shoulders as they seemingly dared me to knock them off. The looks on some of the girls' faces, especially Jackie's face, made me wonder what I was even doing here and if I really belonged. I could feel the tension, as though they had been dumped on many times before. Undoubtedly, I was not going to be given their respect. I would have to earn it."

Cindy knew that respect is central to a successful program for her P.E. classes. Her greatest challenge would be to create an environment where the children would feel safe and important. They need to be taught skills for games and sports; they need to learn about physical fitness, but more importantly they need to learn how to work together in a productive way. Teamwork would be stressed and competition would be set up on a personal level and not against other classmates.

Opportunities for success find their way into Cindy's plans, and the students begin to see that they have found someone who believes in them and someone they can believe in.

Struggles and Successes

It is often said that anticipation is greater than the event, but that did not hold true for us. Though the beginning of our year was stressful, it was also filled with multitudes of goodness and joy, of growth and beauty, of accolades and pats on the back for a job well begun. Appreciation and recognition are definitely fuels for success. The teachers and staff at Munson were "walking on sunshine," to borrow a song lyric. Students blossomed under the steady guidance of experience and foresight. The school building itself was transformed into a virtual museum and art gallery, with endless exhibits readily displayed. Teachers provided encouragement in student performance and self-esteem building.

But too much sunshine makes a desert. Rain is necessary to make the flowers grow. Unfortunately, many of us are not overly fond of rain or the mud we have to walk through on the way to the garden.

When the initial fanfare and hype were over and the dust settled from the workers, we began to settle into a routine. We all loved what we were doing but the challenges became more and more apparent. Days became longer and the harder we worked, the further behind it seemed we were in reaching our own goals for our students. Dr. D stays the ever-present silver lining to the clouds that threatened the blue skies above our academic abode.

It is fall now and though we have been together for what seems like a lifetime, we begin to notice we have differences in points of view even when we share so much in common. Each of us has a very different setting in which to work that special magic. To our credit, we handle these brief moments with respect. There is no time or place for backbiting or complaining in a successful school.

Then there are personality conflicts among children, even among families. Some of these children have been together a long time and are more like siblings than schoolmates. Finally, there is the personal evaluation every good teacher makes of herself or himself as the year progresses: "Am I doing a good job? Are the children in my class really learning? Do I need to do something different?" Still, our little group manages to forge ahead.

We get a few new textbooks and become the most cunning of scavengers by seeing potential in discarded materials from a variety of sources. But the outside accolades have largely dried up. No one is there for the bedraggled staff and faculty who are beginning to show the wear from endless hours of labor. Burnout was looming ahead but we hold on to our vision. Like battle-weary soldiers charging under the skillful eye of their tried and true General, we are determined to succeed. We will not buckle; we will find a way.

When you read *Cinderella*, the beauty and delight of the ending often clouds the heroine's path to reach the end of the rainbow. Remembering that path doesn't remove the glamour of success, it merely reminds us we are human and life is full of staunch realities that can impede our success if we choose to let them.

At this time in our school year, David gives a perspective that holds very true for all of us as teachers and as human beings; he describes the typical business part of a teacher's day. You see, by the end of the school day you are wasted: physically, but worse yet, mentally exhausted. Start with getting up around 5 o'clock in the morning. Quick shower, dress, gather your things from the night before, make sure you have any necessary items for today, prepare breakfast for your family and then head out the door by 6:15. Drive 30 to 45 minutes from your home through an eternally endless forest to arrive between 6:45 and 7:15. The children report to their rooms at 7:30, so there is only a short amount of time to make sure preparations for the new day are in order. Basically, Munson teachers are on task with children every day from 7:30 a. m. to 2 p.m. with no relief all day, except for the short break during P.E. class and a brief hiatus for a lunch, which is often eaten in the classroom.

"Most people have no idea what it is to be an elementary school teacher. If you are good at what you do, you are 'on' all day long," says David. "At the end of the day, after the children have left and you review the success of your seven or more lessons in different subject matters, you look to your desk to see stacks of papers that need to be graded or checked. You look into your plan book and realize the next week will be here in a few days. What will you cover then in reading, math, spelling, social studies, art, music, language arts, writing and science? How will you present these concepts in ways that 24 children at different levels will grasp each concept? What about the materials you need? What about that child who has been absent for three days? And, oh yes, we've got a faculty meeting this afternoon, your professional development paperwork is due and you still need to take one more class to recertify your teaching credentials. Oh, what's wrong with this computer? 'Yes, I am here. Mrs. Smith wants a phone conference now?' Most people could not be an elementary school teacher. They just couldn't."

If there was a knight in shining armor, we found it in Dr. D. He demonstrates the requisite skills of an adept administrator as he realizes what the insurmountable stress is doing to each of us. He begins to solicit help from countless sources. Slowly but surely, volunteers begin to emerge taking small groups for tutoring, giving make-up tests, working one on one with the child who needs not extra moments in his day, but extra hours. The silver in the lining of the cloud spreads as the warmth and concern of our principal helps renew the sunshine in our days. We have stresses still in just managing all the volunteers, but they are good stresses—the kind that challenge us and make us grow. And grow we do.

As a note, many factions often focus on making teachers more accountable. Yes, we should have special credentials and know our subject matter, but Dr. D realizes just how much more there is for which we have to account. We can make beautiful and exciting lessons, but we can't make kids learn. We can't open up their heads and pour it into them. That's not learning anyway. Yet if they choose not to do their parts, it reflects on us. We feel trapped between a rock and a hard place. What more does the public want a teacher to do? But all the while, a skillful hand keeps the rudder of our little ship on the straight and narrow—sometimes with a forceful command and other times with a gentle grasp but always with our best interest and the interest of the little children at heart. We would later learn that for every hour we spend wrestling the demons of apathy and disparagement, Dr. D spends three. Interestingly enough, he exhibits the quintessential core of the successful administrator: he never lets it show.

Throughout the fall, we traverse hills and valleys. We take three steps forward to one step back, but at the very least we were going ahead. A little boost in energy comes as parent volunteers organize a Fall Festival. Homemade games, food and prizes bring the whole community out for fun and fellowship. It proves to be a rousing success. Food and prizes dangle from chubby little hands, while Mom and Dad share a social time with friends and family. Fun is the theme of the event and all of us experience a little boost from the joy of the evening. Our vision for the school, the children, and ourselves is rejuvenated as we all realize that much like an automobile, a human being cannot run on an empty tank. He or she must be fueled with encouragement and the success of reaching goals, however small they may be.

Plans begin to form for the holidays ahead. With the success of the festival, we dare to venture into thoughts of more energetic activities. Thanksgiving indeed brings special thanks from our Munson family as we look at how far we have come. Children are enjoying school. Parents are happy with the progress they are seeing and teachers are watching with bated breath as little buds of knowledge begin to develop into leaves and flowers of thought in the minds of our students.

Our Thanksgiving celebration day dawns bright and sunny, yet with a slight chill in the air. The long hot Florida summer that lasts well into October is beginning to dissipate. Again we marvel as what seems to be a multitude of people illustrating a wide range of ages and faces arrives at school. Each Thanksgiving, the community is invited to join the students and staff of Munson for one of Mrs. Edith's famous holiday dinners. Family and friends from all over the forest gather to share in this special time. The school buzzes with the sights and smells of Thanksgiving.

The children are active participants in this presentation to the community. Glue, paint, construction paper and scissors cover desks in the classroom as students proudly show off the results of their artistic labors. Sixth graders are much too old to dress up for the pagentry of the day, so they elect to decorate the formidable cafeteria. Munson pine trees have some of the most beautiful pine cones; you would not believe what incredible replicas of turkeys can be created. My students gently carry in the centerpieces for the tables. After hours of patience and gentle guidance, Davina's little cherubs show up adorned with Pilgrim and Indian gear created from brown grocery bags. Beth's children have worked equally hard and join their fellow sojourners with appropriate headgear and smiles that would win any pageant. The fourth and fifth grade students from David's room also have grown beyond the dress-up stage and instead create an Indian village for families to admire as they visit the school.

Parents, grandparents and neighbors seem impressed by the opportunities we are providing for their children. We indeed are happy with their response to the day. Who wouldn't be? Yet all the while we fight the nagging question, "Just what was life like in Munson before Dr. D?"

We quickly dismiss such thoughts and look again to the smiling faces of the day. A little fuel has been added to our academic automobile and we all smile at another success, small as it may seem. We have made another step forward. Isn't there an adage that reads, "A journey of a thousand miles begins with a single step"?

Half Way Home

After Thanksgiving, we all begin to notice the calendar. Christmas vacation is only three weeks away and we are half way home. But, with all our exuberance over the days that begin to come more and more swiftly, we can't neglect Christmas. At a scheduled faculty meeting, we discuss the safety of appropriate lighting for Christmas trees in our rooms, parties, gifts, and adjusted schedules for Christmas dinner.

Beth and Lisa have a brainstorm! Wouldn't it be fun to have a school-wide theme? So with input from Beth and Davina, I put together a proposal. I guess it is a little too formal, because the next morning Beth heads into my room and says, "Lisa, you might want to pull that memo from the teachers' boxes. Seems like we should have taken a different route to bring this up for discussion. " Apparently, in my verbose written articulation, my suggestion came across as a direct order. The first thing that crosses my mind, besides "Uh oh!" is a line from the *I Love Lucy Show*, "Lucy, you got some 'splainin' to do!" And explain I do. I go straight to Dr. D who with his usual spry humor teases me about taking over his job like the "Munson Mafia." He is such a good sport. Then I talk to David, reiterating that my note was merely a suggestion and not an edict. He also understands and we have a good laugh about my pro-active initiative.

After this we all decide it is best to pursue the Christmas theme in our own ways. David has a terrific Christmas party planned for his crew. All kinds of goodies and treats are brought in from the students and parents alike. Beth, Davina and I have a little different idea. Although a party is still part of the plan, music plays a larger part.

Each of us puts together a medley of Christmas music for our children to learn. The students have a ball. Laughter is heard down the corridors, and Dr. D is delighted to hear something he hasn't heard from these children for some time — music! It is lovely. I guess of all the teachers, I am the most surprised. I put together a rather complex set of songs from different lands. Learning words in other languages presents a difficult task and several of my students rebel at the thought of singing in front of their peers.

After what seems like unending practice, the day finally arrives. Everyone, including myself, is amazed. The children are perfect! Primary children wear costumes to represent the traditional Christmas songs they chose to perform. The older children in "Christmas uniforms" of white, green or red shirts with dark pants look equally impressive. Just wonderful! Not a missed note. No one is punched or tickled on stage. The props are in order and even though we had not had a chance to practice with the other classes, it appears to be choreographed to the letter.

After the 45-minute pageant, parents hug their children with pride. Teachers beam. Dr. D smiles in recognition of the major accomplishment of his little ones, and we all sit back in wonder as our children seem to grow before our eyes. What a great way to end this half of our year. We all leave for Christmas vacation more optimistic about the spring.

Testing

As the year progresses, we begin to focus on the bane of our existence: standardized tests. We have worked hard to this point, remediating, playing catch-up, and moving forward with our students as quickly as they can go. Music is not as readily heard as is the recitation of math facts and voices in reading groups. Students continue to respond in each classroom as the teachers narrow their focus. The knowledge seems to be there, but we still don't have the level of performance on paper that we would like. We incorporate an additional skill as we begin to help these students learn "how" to take a test. As we meet at the bus ramp, we compare notes about our children's test-taking abilities. Across the board the skills are quite low. Content is certainly important, but if a student doesn't understand the question, it doesn't really matter what the student knows.

Dr. D and David have the foresight to see that extra materials are needed and within days we are looking at boxes of practice material for our grade levels. These resources are a tremendous help to each of us as we incorporate test-taking skills into our daily lessons. Dr. D also enlists the help of Dr. Rex Schmid of the University of West Florida, who provides invaluable service. Days tick away like a metronome on the grand piano of time. We guard every second jealously and make the most of every teachable moment. Still, we remain mindful of the mental fatigue that can take its toll under such a demanding load and we intersperse our lessons with fun activities and outdoor lessons as the weather permits. The testing schedule looms until weeks become days, and days turn into hours. Arrangements have been made to assist us with the combined grade levels. Even the County Office has been enlisted to assist. We are armed, and prepared. We will prove our worth.

We've gleaned every possible strategy we can. Like the Olympian on the day of the big race, teachers and students alike enter the school with exuberance and fear. The time is here to assess the fruits of our labors as "Testing Week" begins. We look at each other nervously; can our students do it? We put our faith in them, just as Dr. D has done with us. There are procedures to follow. Books are checked out each morning, tallied after testing and returned as gingerly as top-secret, classified material from the CIA. We can only hope now. We have done all we know how. With smiles of encouragement on each of our faces and a "can do" attitude, each group settles into the three days of testing. A sigh—more like a gasp—of relief hovers over the school as the last of the tests are sorted, labeled and packed. Under the watchful eyes of Dr. D and David, our precious cargo heads south to be scored and recorded into the annals of time. Testing is over and so we focus on the remainder of the year. We can breath a little bit better now. Win or lose, we gave it our best. Only time will tell.

Classroom dynamics change after testing. Each teacher begins to teach in more creative ways, releasing more and more of our unique talents and skill. Beth goes full force into her thematic teaching. Her Trojan horse will long be remembered by all. She raises baby chicks and puts on a Greek feast complete with food that some of us had never seen before, but her good cooking skills convinced us to try it.

Davina sets about the business of spring. Paper flowers and fuzzy cotton chicks dot her room. Her famous lap sits begin, and Mrs. Dunworth becomes quite the celebrity in her room. Evidence of new reading skills and language development is everywhere.

David proceeds with cooperative learning and group centers. His students move through their activities like a well-oiled machine. Can it be possible that these are the same children who began the year?

My sixth grade ventures into "the land down under." With the help of my student teacher, Lisa Murphy, our classroom becomes a true mastery, whole-learning classroom. Children move from center to center with passports in hand, visiting over 30 different activities. Anticipating behavior problems is really wasted worry. Again, I marvel at the maturity that seems to be filtering into my class of 25. Students work in groups without criticizing or quarreling. They support each other and they begin to function as a team. I look toward graduation for this class with both excitement and remorse. They are part of my life and I will miss them all very much.

As our summer countdown approaches, Cindy plans our first annual Field Day. No teacher in the history of P.E. has ever had the vision or drive of this young woman. She single-handedly heads this fun-packed competition. She is also quite adept in delegation of tasks—a talent learned by observing Dr. D, no doubt.

With a legion of volunteers in tow, Cindy begins Munson's Field Day Olympics. The whole student body is divided up into four groups, with a teacher as leader of each team. Each team has a color (T-shirts are ordered to match) and a flag. In the morning students go from station to station completing individual activities for ribbons and stickers. Lunch is shared in color groups, then teams assemble for water sports in the afternoon. As much as we dearly love Cindy, we still owe her for the "squeals of delight" she allows our students to have at our expense. Cold wet jeans don't make the most comfortable attire, but it is for a good cause. Plus we get to toss water balloons with the kids. Talk about therapy!

The Countdown

Learning takes place through a variety of measures. Some things cannot be internalized deeply unless you experience a moment so true that it penetrates the very core of your being. Such is the case with what we experience this day. The spring morning dawns warm and clear. The dogwood in the courtyard presents a pristine white canopy for the ceremony about to take place

The student council has worked for days on landscaping the entrance to the school and everything is in full bloom. Only moments now before the dignitaries will arrive. Men and women in crisp white uniforms appear. The Congressional aide is arriving on behalf of the Congressman. The Commandant of Whiting Field appears, escorted by his entourage of service men and women.

Dr. D calls the event to order as the whole school is seated around the courtyard. Patriotism has a very special place for Dr. D and among the inheritance he wishes to leave these children is a spirit of pride in community and country. The assembly today celebrates those ideals. We honor our country with a very special flag and we honor a local citizen who has meant a great deal to the school and the community.

God surely smiles on us as the day is a handcrafted masterpiece. My sixth graders have been training in our flag corps. Four students in crisp white shirts and black trousers stand at attention. A hush falls over the audience. The four young people advance to raise the American flag. This one has special meaning. It was previously flown over the Capitol. The team moves with precision; every step is in place and the flag is raised swiftly. The team returns to stand at attention as a quartet of heavenly voices give an a cappella rendition of the National Anthem. The voices from the Navy choir that harmonize as we look upon the symbol of our freedom will forever be etched in our minds. Stirring words issue forth from our esteemed speakers about the importance of the American flag and all that it stands for.

As those remarks draw to a close, another special presentation begins. Our superintendent, Mr. Russell, presents our former school secretary with a commemorative plaque from the school and accolades from the county for a job well done. A dry eye cannot be found. Even the smallest of the children is caught by the awe of the morning's events. Dr. D has indeed left an indelible mark upon our hearts and spirits. "Let freedom ring."

Much laughter can be heard in the hallways and classrooms as the days roll by and summer looms ever closer. Regardless of what our scores might be, we can see a difference. Children who were not especially interested in school, or any learning for that matter, are now eager to get to the library for a new book. They run (walk quickly—we don't run in the halls at Munson) to the office to share a good grade or a positive weekly report with Dr. D. Every teacher gets a hug from the little ones and we know each and every child by name. I remember one afternoon on the way to the buses feeling particularly proud of the school and yet a little sad when one of the second graders said, "Mrs. Rogaliner, all the flowers are so pretty. We never had real flowers here before."

"I'm so glad you like them. We put them here for you!" was all I could muster. I knew then that we had succeeded. The children do notice the little things their teachers do. They feel loved and safe and all the things that Beth had known they needed. They are proud of all they had done and we are proud of them. But the best is yet to come.

The Results

There is really no way to describe the scene before me as I enter the little work room that we used for assorted and sundry work throughout the year. There is a buzz of excitement in the air and I enter the room to see all the teachers huddled around a scattered set of papers, passing them around, comparing notes and then studying them over again. The test results were in.

David hands me a set labeled sixth grade. Dr. D would join us shortly—more administrative matters to attend to—but we are to peruse the information and he would walk us through it upon his arrival. Dr. D's job this time is really quite simple. He comes in with a sheepish little grin and calmly states that he's sorry he's a little late but he's been on the phone with the school superintendent. Seems that we have a little bit to be proud of. I am just in shock at seeing the numbers. Dr. D reminds us of Dr. Schmid's words, that a gain of five to seven points would be "substantial." Well, we are better than substantial. Davina has the highest scores in the whole county for first grade! All classes have shown dramatic improvement, with one group going up 20 points overall! What can we say? One would think we would be bouncing off the walls with excitement, but a calm is over this little group; or maybe it is shock.

Here we are all together in the little room that had been transformed into our work room, complete with giant paper cutter, and a transparency maker. Ambulance stretchers should be made available to help us out. Really, it is remarkable, wonderful, but mostly tremendously unbelievable.

As a scripture from the King James Bible states, "Little is much when God is in it." We know beyond a shadow of a doubt that

God himself must have sent John Dunworth and given him the insight to hire each of us. We all felt we are good teachers, but this is beyond our wildest dreams. And Dr. D is just a little proud. We make the papers and the local TV newscasts again so all is back as it was in the beginning. We have come full circle.

A special School Board meeting is held to present Dr. D with his official $1.00 check. There is not enough we can say to show our pride in him and the honor it was to work for him. Memories flood our minds. Problems that seemed to take weeks to overcome are now only fleeting glimpses of a struggle that was overcome. Pumpkins and Pilgrims, Christmas trees and flowers, flags and farewells seem only seconds in a day that went by too quickly. Then one by one, we are each called to join Dr. D on the stage and receive certificates of appreciation for our supporting roles in the Munson story. David is named the new principal with Dr. D's full blessings. We are happy.

Songs and Sunshine

In the summer of 1997, four very different adults made plans for their summers. Families decided vacation routes and children reveled in thoughts of swimming in the lake. In the summer of 1997, other families worried about their children's educational futures and children worried about the possibility of long bus rides before dawn. A superintendent and School Board spent sleepless nights in worry and wonder. In the summer of 1997, one single, kind-hearted man affected the lives of hundreds of people. He changed the attitudes and views of many. He reached out beyond the "what is" and grasped the "what could be." He changed worry and fear into songs and sunshine. In the summer of 1997, Dr. John Dunworth wrote a positive chapter in history.

Later, as we sit in David's room mulling over the textbook budget for the up-coming year, a mystical shadow quietly wisps across the room. Large manila envelopes are placed in front of each of us and the shadow disappears. Inside each envelope is a picture of us, "the Dream Team," with a personal message on each photo. David quickly glances up and instinctively reaches for the tissue box for his staff. "He is so special," Beth remarks quietly. "He walked out of our lives as quickly as he walked in."

Martin Luther King, Jr. once made the point that if anyone were to be asked to do a task, any task, be it a menial job such as sweeping streets or a great artistic endeavor, he should undertake that task and do it so well that all the world would stop and proclaim his greatness. Dr. D wore many hats and we wouldn't be surprised if he raised his sleeves and even swept a few places along the way. But regardless of his position, we all know that here is a great man of whom heaven and earth can both be proud.

Dr. D continues to share in our lives. He offers support and guidance for our school and lots of laughter and smiles for the faculty and staff. To quote Davina, "Dr. D is a special type of person. They are few and far between. I thank him and I hope he feels our love." We all love and thank you, Dr. D. You are part of our lives and part of our family. Thank you for your example. Thank you for sharing you.

Part IV

The Tests
Assessment and High Stakes Testing

—Rex E. Schmid, Ed.D.
*Associate Professor, Division of
Teacher Education,
University of West Florida,
Pensacola, Florida*

Chapter VIII

The Rationale and the Reality

Darlene's Intuition

Santa Rosa School District educators and guests gather in March of each year for their Teacher-of-the-Year Banquet. Individual schools in the district select their teacher of the year in February from which one is announced at the banquet as the school system's teacher of the year. People dress up. Women wear new gowns and their men are dressed in tuxedos or dark business suits. The food is good and the tables have centerpieces and starched white cloth napkins. It is an evening for celebrating classroom successes and recognizing peers who, for this year, exemplified the best in every teacher. In 1998, I sat at one of the good tables up front with an elementary school's teachers and their teacher of the year.

The emcee was a personality from the local television station, and the guest speaker was a prominent political figure. Things started well. The introduction of the speaker was humorous but respectful. He set a complimentary course in his opening tale of a personal school experience with a talented teacher. Then, abruptly, he turned to his participation in the Washington education reform effort. He expressed concern about the failure of American schools to produce literate graduates, the need for stronger testing and accountability programs, and finding ways to fund parents who wanted to move children to schools of their choice. We politely applauded when he finished. In thanking the speaker for his remarks, the emcee couldn't resist adding his opinion that deleting education as a Cabinet Department should be a national priority.

The teachers, at least at my table, were furious. The only comment, however, was Melinda's, "Not too cool." Her look and tone, however, would have sent her kindergarten class scurrying for cover. As the program continued, anger ebbed and pride returned as stories of personal success and educational accomplishment were presented.

Dr. Dunworth has things that wiggle in his mind. They wriggle in mine. The first wriggle that evening was, "How did we develop such an incessant, pervasive compulsion for education reform?" Conventional wisdom is that social reform runs in cycles. It seems to me this current cycle began with four of President Reagan's education policies: (a) to concentrate the nation's attention on education reform; (b) to use federal government influence to stimulate reform initiatives in the states and local school districts; (c) to encourage specific reforms such as implementing "basic" academic curriculums and school choice; and (d) to reduce federal funding of education. Terrell Bell was appointed Secretary of Education in 1981 to implement the Reagan administration policies and succeeded by appointing the National Commission on Excellence in Education which, in 1983, issued its report, *A Nation at Risk: The Imperative for Educational Reform*. In melodramatic language, the authors of *A Nation at Risk* warned:

> *Our Nation is at risk. Our once unchallenged preeminence in commerce, industry, science, and technological innovation is being overtaken by competitors*

throughout the world. This report is concerned with only one of the many causes and dimension of the problem, but it is one that undergirds American prosperity, security and civility. We report to the American people that while we can take justifiable pride in what our schools and colleges have historically accomplished and contributed to the United States and the well-being of its people, the educational foundations of our society are presently being eroded by a rising tide of mediocrity that threatens our very future as a Nation and a people.

If an unfriendly foreign power had attempted to impose on America the mediocre educational performance that exists today, we might well have viewed it as an act of war. As it stands, we have allowed this to happen to ourselves. We have even squandered the gains in student achievement made in the wake of the Sputnik challenge. Moreover, we have dismantled essential support systems which helped make those gains possible. We have, in effect, been committing an act of unthinking, unilateral educational disarmament.

Our society and its educational institutions seem to have lost sight of the basic purposes of schooling, and the high expectations and disciplined efforts needed to attain them. (pp. 5–6)

The authors alleged the decline of academic standards and achievement in public education was, at the least, partly responsible for America's declining productivity and failure to successfully compete in global markets. *A Nation at Risk* received extensive media coverage and stimulated a subsequent series of similar reports by private foundations. As intended, the report spurred a torrent of education reforms over the next decade.

By the beginning of the 1990s, a majority of the states had passed legislation to increase the academic requirements for high school graduation, test children's skill proficiency at specific grade levels, and install competency tests as a condition for teacher certification. The education profession, reluctant and defensive, responded with an "effective school" movement in which: (a) the principal was to be a strong academic leader; (b) the teachers worked as a cooperative body to efficiently provide instruction; (c) the school clearly announced goals and expectations for students; and (d) the school assessed student progress toward the goals and expectations.

By the late 1990s, some form of education standard and/or curriculum framework and student-testing program had been established in nearly every state. A few, like Florida, had begun publishing annual "report cards" for individual schools which listed information about the school faculty, student body, improvement goals, and student performance on a variety of tests and assessments. Further, schools in which students were not performing at an acceptable level as measured by the state's tests and assessment programs would invoke state sanctions. Despite these and other significant improvements, continuous criticism since *A Nation at Risk* and three presidents who campaigned on the promise to "fix education" have produced a public perception that the nation's schools are failures and must be radically reformed.

As the evening's formal program drew to a close, table talk picked up with two and three simultaneous conversations. Darlene, a first-year teacher, turned to me and said, "Is it just me or do politicians and news people make everything sound like it's the end of the world? I mean, everything is gigantic or the ultimate disaster. All the stuff about education being so bad. If it's that bad, how come the economy is so strong? I think we are doing pretty good as a country." Before I could reply she was drawn into another conversation, so I just smiled and nodded. Another mind-wriggle began.

Maybe Darlene's intuition was on the mark. It does seem the hyperbole from politicians, policy makers, and media people is becoming more strident and extreme. Is it possible that Americans have become desensitized to anything but the most sensational revelations? You don't have to search for examples. Casual reading or watching TV provides ample exposure. A national columnist noted recently that the nation has expended billions of additional dollars on education over the past few decades yet schools continue to drop in quality. Most of those billions were for new buildings, teachers, and supplies to meet the requirements of ballooning school enrollments. As for dropping in quality, there are individuals such as Gerald Bracey (1997) whose analysis of test results firmly refute this perception of pervasive ignorance. With each interest group forced to one-up the competition for attention has our ability to discriminate wants, needs, and requirements disappeared? There may be a lesson in Darlene's common sense appraisal of forecasts for ruin and America's steady increase in standard of living and world influence since *A Nation at Risk*.

Flashback

It is one of those early fall days that occur only in Northwest Florida. Clear, clean air with the thermometer balanced precisely between cool and warm. On days like this it's evident why military personnel refer to Pensacola as Pensaparadise. Dr. Bill Evans, chairman of my division at the University of West Florida, knocks at my open office door. "How ya doing, ol' buddy ol' pal?"

He wants something! "Ol' buddy, ol' pal" is his cue that he has an opportunity to share and I'm correct. He wants me to volunteer some time with Munson Elementary School. "Just go out and talk with them and see if there is anything you can do to help with testing and assessment," he says. I call, talk with Dr. Dunworth and arrange a day to drive out and meet with his teachers to answer questions about tests and testing. Dr. Evans forgot to mention that it is a 45-minute drive from the campus to Munson Elementary School.

I arrive a little before the end of the school day so I putter around the school grounds and buildings until Dr. Dunworth is available. He provides an official tour, introductions to the non-teaching staff, and we talk. He has a vision for this little school and is determined to make it reality. After the children have left for the day we meet the faculty, all four of them, in the library. It is clear in the introductions and small talk that Dunworth's vision is infectious. He seems to have contaminated everyone with it. They also share a good deal of apprehension about the task of raising the school's test scores. After the ice breaking, Dr. Dunworth invites the faculty to ask questions. I don't remember if the first question was asked by the elfin Mrs. Coogle or the thoughtful Mrs. Rogaliner, but I do remember the exact question. "What is the difference between the unit tests I give in math and reading and the test the kids will take in March?" I had a feeling they already knew the answer but were really "testing" me, the so-called expert.

I start, "First, the tests you give as a teacher and the test the kids will take in March are totally different species. They differ in purpose, what is measured, how it is measured, and how the score is reported. Let's start with what you are most familiar with, classroom assessments."

Testing by teachers, in their classrooms, has two purposes. One purpose is more important than the other and should drive every assessment a teacher conducts. That purpose is to provide information necessary to make effective instructional decisions about individual students and about groups of students. At Munson, for example, Mr. Johnson must make decisions about when to move his class on to a new math concept, which children to put into groups for drill and practice, which individual students will need additional tutoring and practice, and what kind of homework is most likely to strengthen student skills and be completed. When to move to a new concept or instructional unit is a "clinical judgement." It occurs when a teacher is confident that a student or a group of students in the class have demonstrated they know the material and are ready to progress. If Mr. Johnson wants to form groups to practice three-column addition with regrouping, he has some choices. He can form groups in which all the members are on the same skill level or he can form mixed skill-level groups. To form the groups, however, he must know the skill level of every student in his class and this knowledge comes from his assessment activities. All instructional decisions like these should be based on assessment results.

Now, classroom assessment has many forms and goes by a number of names. Some of those names are curriculum-based assessment, objective-based assessment, direct assessment, and formative evaluation. The textbooks on tests and measurement describe each term as having a specific meaning, but for classroom teachers they all have one thing in common. Each is a measure of a student's mastery level of specific curriculum information and skill. Teachers evaluate students every day. Mrs. Sanders, for example, may read a story like *Put Me in the Zoo* to her kindergarten children at the beginning of the year, stopping after each page to ask specific children questions related to something they heard her read or something they can see in the story's pictures. She may ask Seth to show her something red, Dawn to point to something round in the picture, and Matthew to tell her what the word "spot" means. Kindergartners are expected to know colors, shapes, and infer word meanings. This is as much an assessment as the school district's readiness skill checklist completed for every child at the start of school. Mrs. Rogaliner does similar things every day with her fifth and sixth graders to check their mastery of the skills and knowledge she is teaching. Another assessment all of you do each day is check the seat work of students to see who is "getting it" and who is not. In second and third grade, Mrs. Coogle probably tests her class on spelling and vocabulary words every week. The point is, every teacher conducts classroom assessment activity on a continuous basis in order to make instructional decisions. Basically, you use a lot of questions and probes to check your students' knowledge and skill proficiency for a small segment of curriculum.

Mr. Johnson interjected the second question, "You used the words assessment and tests. Are they the same thing?" Ha, I'm being tested again! David's question was astute. I paused to think.

The terms are often used as synonyms, but they are not the same. Tests and testing are part of a larger process of collecting evaluation information about a student or group of students. The larger process is called assessment and the information collected is used for making educational decisions. That's why I used "assessment" to refer to the variety of ways a classroom teacher collects information and "test" in reference to spelling and vocabulary. Some textbook publishers provide unit and section mastery tests that can be used with students to measure their acquisition of the knowledge and skills described in the scope and sequence charts for their curriculum. These are usually paper-and-pencil exercises most associated with the word "test." In contrast, the Direct Instruction method of the SRA reading curriculum integrates continuous skill performance evaluation into the daily instruction activities.

Dr. Dunworth had been quiet and thoughtful during the questions and discussion. "You said earlier that there were two purposes of classroom assessment. You never got around to the second..." and he paused waiting for a response.

The second purpose is to provide a rationale for a grade given on a report card. For too many teachers this is the important purpose—especially at middle and secondary schools. I understand and accept that teachers have to give grades. That is part of the American school culture and not likely to change soon. Grades, however, should be the by-product of classroom assessment, not the primary purpose for evaluation. I insist that classroom assessment activity ultimately be for the purpose of gaining information to make good curriculum decisions and guide daily teaching activities.

"Rex," said Dr. Dunworth, "you know that the survival of this little school depends upon the success of our pupils—on whether or not we have this kind of educational program where children are clearly moving forward academically and in every other way. However, much to their credit, never once has the Superintendent or anyone in the system ever suggested that a score on a standardized test be the arbiter of the decision. What we have to deliver is a sound instructional program for every child. Test scores will take care of themselves," and then he paused.

"But I wonder. After all, one of the reasons this school was declared to be in trouble was that it posted the 'lowest test scores in Santa Rosa County.' Clearly, in the public's perception, scores have to improve. Right or wrong, such perceptions can even 'out vote' elected officials. What is your 'reading' on all of this?"

You could hear the capital letters in the words "test scores" and see the tension increase in each teacher.

Dr. D's assessment is absolutely "right on." It is called "high-stakes testing." In Munson's case the stakes are absolute: improve or die. The tension continued to increase exponentially.

There are claims that public schools in the United States administer more than 250 million standardized examinations a year, including achievement, IQ, readiness, and screening tests (Salvia & Ysseldyke, 1998). The scores Munson students have to raise are on the standardized achievement test given each spring to students in the Santa Rosa School District as part of the state and school district yearly assessment program. Each school's scores for selected grade levels are forwarded to the state while the scores for all the schools are reported in the local media. From this and other data, the state prepares and publishes an annual "report card" for every public school in Florida. Schools not meeting state guidelines for minimum student performance face State Department of Education sanctions. Two schools in an adjacent school system have been notified that they were on the state's list of schools at-risk for sanctions. Local school districts, too, invoke consequences for their schools not performing adequately. In Munson's case, the stakes could not be higher, the consequences more severe.

Standardized Terror

Standardized, norm-referenced, group achievement tests are developed and marketed for the purpose of comparing the score of one individual student with the test performance of a large group of his or her peers. If Jim, a Munson fifth grader, scored at the 65th percentile on the Santa Rosa achievement test, it would mean that he performed better than 65% of his peers with whom he was compared. This is similar to the comparison method used for visual acuity. If one has 20/20 vision it means that he or she sees the same things at 20 feet that people with normal vision see at 20 feet. A student with 20/60 vision, however, sees things at 20 feet that people with normal vision see at 60 feet. However, it is somewhat easier to measure vision than it is to measure knowledge. Thus, an achievement test score can be quite useful as one part of a screening procedure. Identifying children who may be eligible to participate in an enrichment program for talented and gifted, for example, might require teacher recommendations, examples of creative and/or advanced academic work, an individual IQ test score of 130 or better, and achievement test scores above the 91st percentile.

Given the immense revenue from the sale and servicing of achievement tests, test publishers are extremely careful to create valid, reliable, and technically correct tests. Great care is taken to ensure the domains included in an achievement test are aligned with the scope and sequence of the nation's school curriculums. The Metropolitan Achievement Tests, 7th Edition (Balow, Farr, & Hogan, 1992), for example, are standardized group achievement tests designed to measure student achievement in reading, language, mathematics, science, and social studies. Test specifications were created from an extensive analysis of curriculum guidelines, course syllabi, and textbooks used in America's schools. Of course, if the textbooks your children are using are 20 to 30 years old, it could impact the results. The test has 14 levels from kindergarten through twelfth grade. This broad scope is also a weakness because fewer test items per skill must be used to keep the test a manageable size. The Metropolitan Achievement Tests-7 have only 72 test items to sample all the mathematics concepts, procedures, and problem solving skills at the fifth and sixth grade levels. Tests like these do not have enough items to pinpoint specific academic strengths and weaknesses, but are useful for estimating a student's current general performance level and the extent to which an individual has acquired the skills and concepts that his or her peers have acquired.

To further facilitate precise comparisons, test authors and publishers are also careful to standardize the procedures for test administration and scoring. The intent is for every individual to take the test in as exact a manner and under the same conditions as possible. Scoring too must also be the same in every case. For example, in March each of you will read the directions for the test without deviation and the time permitted for completion of each portion of the test will be specified by the test publisher.

In a norm-referenced test, Jim is compared with a group of his or her peers previously tested by the test author. This peer group is referred to as the norm or standardization sample. The size of the norm sample is usually large for group achievement tests. The California Achievement Test-5 (CTB/Macmillan/McGraw-Hill, 1993) included 115,888 students in the spring norm sample and 109,825 students in the fall norm sample. About 250,000 students comprise the norm sample for the ninth edition of the Stanford Achievement Test Series (Harcourt Brace Educational Measurement, 1996). These norm groups must have the same characteristics as the population to be tested. Characteristics relevant for most tests include: student's age, school grade, gender, geographic residence, racial and cultural background, and general intellectual functioning, as well as the acculturation of the student's parents. However, it is not enough simply to have the right kinds of students in the norm group. The relevant characteristics must be represented in proportions that correspond to the population to be tested. In evaluating a test's norms, not only whether the norms are generally representative should be considered, but also the age of the norms, the relevance of the norms, and the appropriate use of the norms.

"I wonder how many children in the norm group live in the middle of a forest?" Dr. Dunworth mumbles. Good question.

All four teachers were squirming. Mrs. Sanders got it out first, "But the test in March is used to judge how well we are doing as a school!" The others all agreed that the March test scores were not being used to screen or help place children in beneficial programs.

"Yes and that's the rub," was my answer. Growing in strength over the past two decades has been an extensive perception that public schools fail to adequately educate children. Local school districts are held accountable for the academic performance of their pupils because citizens want to know the extent to which students are profiting from their school experience. So standardized, norm-referenced group achievement tests are being used to document achievement of a student population that grows more diverse each year. Some states like Kentucky have proposed including test scores among the determinants of teacher pay increases. The 1994 Educate America Act contains specific provisions for states to develop high education standards and to use tests to measure how well students are meeting them. The Improving America's Schools Act of 1996 mandates schools to assess and report the progress of all students. The Individuals with Disabilities Education Act signed in 1997 requires schools and states to report the performance and progress of all students with disabilities. President Clinton included in his 1997 State of the Union Address a call for voluntary testing of all fourth-graders in reading and all eighth-graders in math.

Our state has invested millions of dollars in the development and administration of a standardized, norm-referenced achievement test, the Florida Comprehensive Achievement Test (FCAT), specifically for use with Florida's public school children. The scoring procedure for the FCAT and other achievement tests produces a simple, straightforward numerical index that permits schools to be ranked from lowest to highest. Bottom line: these tests provide a relatively inexpensive and efficient method of producing the school performance data mandated by all levels of government. Like it or hate it, public school children's academic progress is going to be annually measured with achievement tests and the results of that testing will be used to evaluate the performance of individual schools.

The discussion among the six of us began to shift toward how best to focus classroom instruction and remediation to meet the needs of individual students and increase the academic performance level of the school. Evidently their vision and determination was contagious. I agreed to arrange for students in my tests and measurement class at the University of West Florida to perform diagnostic testing on every child at Munson.

During the drive back to the campus, my mind was full of wriggles and a few of Dr. Dunworth's wiggles. Could they make their vision reality? Geez, they had a lot of negatives. The momentum for mediocrity among the students and community after years of neglect was going to be difficult just to slow, never mind reverse. The pressure for satisfying all three conditions to keep the school open—academic, financial and demographic—could grow into a crushing weight squashing their enthusiasm and will to succeed. Dr. Dunworth had not been given a specific level to which he must raise test scores, and this unknown could add to the stress. I guessed that an acceptable level would be the 50th percentile if the other two conditions could be met. Still, that was a six or seven point gain, which would not be easy.

On the positive, they had some luxuries most failing schools do not have. They had a clear vision to which each adult, including non-instructional staff, was committed. All four (soon to be five) teachers were new to the school, so academic experiments and risk-taking would not be hampered by past experiences and failures. There was an expectation that teachers would teach and children would learn. They had access to a large pool of help. The University of West Florida and military personnel were providing almost too many volunteers for tutoring individual kids and working with small groups. Linking the pool of volunteers with results from diagnostic evaluations to focus on specific weak areas and missing academic skills should increase the rate of learning. The community had a direct stake in the outcome, so children went home to families concerned about their academic progress. All-in-all, I gave the venture a 50-50 probability of succeeding.

The winter months of January and February in Northwest Florida are not warm and balmy. They are sufficiently cool enough to wear wool and gloves and, unlike south Florida, provide a mild change of seasons. This particular afternoon was windy, overcast and cold as I drove north toward the Alabama border and Munson Elementary School. After my earlier visit we completed a diagnostic assessment of every pupil enrolled and plotted strategies and tactics for the most effective use of resources to get maximum learning from each class. The faculty was creative and motivated, but mostly they were persistent. Don't be misled by tales of daily high adventure in the classroom. The daily routine is often long stretches of dull repetition between moments of learning when a child suddenly "gets it." It was several months since my first visit, and every teacher was still committed to the vision and wasted little opportunity to improve the skills of their children.

The March Tests were approaching and anxiety was starting to grow. It was growing in the community, too. I'd stopped by the country store just before the Christmas holiday and talk was about the school and "what are the chances of them getting their scores?" This visit was to brainstorm ideas and develop a plan for the final effort of preparing for March.

We were barely settled around a table in the media center when the first question popped out, "Are we teaching to the test?" There was real concern in the question that an ethical misstep had been taken.

"Teaching to the test." Four words so often misunderstood. You want to teach to the test under most classroom circumstances, in fact you've an obligation to do so. In the context of classroom instruction, teachers select from the curriculum specific knowledge and skills they are going to teach in a specific time period, inform the children what they are going to learn, and then set out to do it. In preparing his math lesson plans, Mr. Johnson sees the next unit to be taught is simple fractions. On the Monday after the unit test on long division has been reviewed he announces to the class or to a specific group, "For the next two weeks, we are going to be studying fractions. When we are finished you'll know how to..." and proceeds to begin instructional activities. Is he teaching to the unit test on simple fractions? You can bet he is. The unit test should indicate whether he can move on to the next math concepts or if he needs to continue with fractions. This is curriculum-based assessment and we most definitely teach to the test in this case. It would be unethical and educational malpractice not to teach to the test.

The question, though, was really asking if we were teaching to the March achievement test. I don't believe a teacher can "teach to" a good quality standardized norm-referenced achievement test in the same sense we do for curriculum-based assessment. Remember the Metropolitan Achievement Tests-7 with 72 test items to sample all the fifth- and sixth-grade math skills? We would have to present the entire curriculum in order to prepare for the 72 test items. There is a short cut, unethical and unconscionable, in which we "teach the test items." Sometimes teaching to the test is used when teaching test items is what is meant. Don't misuse the two and don't engage in teaching the test items, because it's illegal in Florida and most other states.

Preparing

"So what do you suggest we can do to prepare...legally?" Mr. Johnson wanted to get on with preparing for March.

"You are already doing the best thing: effective daily instruction. You've selected children for tutoring and extra help based on the diagnostics and your classroom assessment." I suggested, "Experiment with 10-minute reviews of knowledge and skills you've previously taught. Add them to your daily routine. Maybe two or three times a day do a time-out and have the kids work for 10 minutes on something you taught two or three units back. After the class or group gets used to doing 10-minute drills, put a stopwatch on them so they can get used to having time limits like the March test will have."

Here's a half-dozen other ideas I provided that have some promise. First, work into language arts instruction some daily work on reading and following directions. Integrate words from test directions into weekly vocabulary lists. Write directions on the students' seat work and drill exercises like the directions on achievement tests. One of the most common reasons for error on tests is not reading and not following directions, so give as much practice as possible. It will be especially effective if it is imbedded into classroom instruction and teaching materials for the whole year.

Second, experiment with making instructional quizzes and unit tests that have formats similar to achievement tests. If the achievement test requires bubble answers, have students bubble answer exams. If separate bubble sheets are used for the achievement test, then teachers should sometimes use bubble sheets for classroom tests. Computers and printers can make bubble sheets that look like standard commercial bubble sheets. Practice will eliminate some errors due to getting an answer bubbled in the wrong line. Practice erasing answers from bubble sheets, too.

Next, I suggest something not usual to prepare students for test taking. During the test the students will be expected to work silently, independently, and with attention focused on one task for 20 or 30 minutes. The fourth, fifth, and sixth graders may be expected to go 45 or 50 minutes on one task. In our daily classroom instruction we rarely ask every child to sit in one place and focus on one task for a half hour. We may do eight or nine minutes of instruction, 20 minutes of independent seat work and small group instruction, followed by some whole-group discussion. Two or three times a week, do a task in which the whole class is expected to work independently on one task and build up to 25 or 30 minutes. Put a stopwatch on the class, too. The students have to get used to working under time limits and that takes practice.

Fourth, provide activities that can be done if a child finishes a task early. When the actual test is being administered the last thing desired is a child who finishes ahead of the others and then becomes a distraction. Some children will finish early and a few of them may become a nuisance to the children still working. Get the whole group in the habit of engaging in appropriate activity if they finish early and you solve most of this problem.

Fifth, consider where you test. If you are going to test in individual classrooms, which is the most common and best arrangement, consider how the room furniture and materials can be arranged to provide the least distraction and the greatest efficiency for the testing process.

Lastly, get volunteers to help. I will guarantee that at least one or two children will get sick and one may leave lunch on the test booklet. There will be errands to run and glitches you didn't anticipate. You have one class that should have two adults in the room during the test and probably one or two special groups. If nothing else, teachers may need a bathroom break during the test sessions.

Oh, we talked and talked that day. The teachers and Dr. Dunworth had all sorts of ideas once they got started. We talked of cues and prompts to teach kids so a testing session didn't have to be interrupted to manage behavior. We talked of rewards and consequences. Mostly, we talked of good teaching techniques and proactive planning to avoid difficulties. We spent a good deal of time talking about the pressure and stress of getting ready for the test and just a teeny mention of "if the scores don't go up."

The mind wriggles were intense on the drive home. What if the scores didn't go up? Dang Dunworth! Now, I had a personal stake in the kids' performance and no control over the outcome. I remembered a comment by a high school assistant principal in one of my graduate classes, "Everybody is accountable for test scores except the kids making them." It does seem odd that poor test performance has no direct consequence for the students.

The Goal: Fair Testing Programs

I have strong reservations about the distress of teachers, children, and parents produced by high-stakes testing programs. Judicious levels of anxiety enhance human performance. Levels too high and too long lead to irrational behavior. The staff at Munson all mentioned some sleepless nights, worry, and irritability in relation to the March tests. The learning climate of a school has to degrade under these circumstances with the largest penalty paid by the youngest—and the most vulnerable. In addition, accusations of outright "cheating" are reported by the media with disappointing regularity. Texas, for example, is reported to be investigating Houston and Austin School District 1998 incidents in which test answer sheets were allegedly altered to produce higher scores. The unrelenting criticism and assertions of teacher incompetence and school failure by "talking heads" and columnists (experts in nothing with opinions on everything) take a toll on enthusiasm and job satisfaction. If states operating lottery enterprises fund programs for compulsive gamblers, then perhaps states operating high-stakes school assessments should provide programs for the negative side-effects of testing. At the least, we ought to determine if the benefits of high-stakes testing justify the human consequences and financial allocation.

The perception that accountability testing programs are coercive perplexes me. Classroom teachers continuously assess the performance and progress of their children in order to make instructional decisions. The accountability testing mandated in many states has little use for making these decisions and teachers resent the theft of instructional time and scarce financial resources diverted from their classrooms. They also detect a trace of retribution ingrained in this kind of testing. In describing their proposed *A+ Plan for Education*, Florida Gov. Bush and Lt. Gov. Brogan (1999) write:

> *The private sector has long used incentives to improve performance. It works! The public sector however sometimes confuses uniformity with fairness. The true measure of fairness is when compensation matches the quality of work. Beginning next year, schools that receive an A and those that improve at least one grade...will be rewarded with up to $100 per student...The highest performing and improving school will also be deregulated and given the freedom to manage their own budgets and use innovative strategies to produce even more dramatic improvement.*

Schools with added challenges need our help and attention. They need our best teachers, our strongest partnerships, and our most determined parents. Schools performing at a failing level will be given two years to improve during which they will receive assistance from the school district and the Department of Education. If the school fails to improve beyond an F in the second year, it will be subject to State Board of Education sanctions currently provided in law. The Bush/Brogan plan proposes that parents will be offered an opportunity to send their children to a higher performing public school or private school of their choice. (p. 5)

Despite the wording, educators in Florida and other states with similar proposals sense a "get even" mean-spiritedness in these programs. A fifth-grade teacher told me most reform proposals reminded her of her childhood. When she had an accident or made a mistake, her stepfather would tell her, "This is for your own good so you won't be so stupid next time," and then thumped her. She doubted then and she doubts now that thumpings were "good" for her or for her brothers and sisters. At best, her stepfather could only punish the children into surface compliance. Current reformers using accountability testing as a measuring gauge may or may not intend retribution for the schools they identify; nonetheless, "retaliation" is the perception of their potential targets. Humans at any age despise coercion and retribution whether real or perceived and resist. Acceptance and genuine support for accountability testing programs will not occur in the nation's classrooms until perceived as compassionate and beneficial for children and their teachers.

The last wriggle of the day was a consideration of what classroom teachers learn early in their career: equal is not fair. Children come to our classroom in all shapes, sizes, and backgrounds with vast discrepancies in readiness to learn. BobbiSue's daddy disappeared before she was born, her mother works nights for minimum wage, and breakfast and lunch at school are her only two guaranteed meals. Katlin, on the other hand, is privileged, traveled, and entered school having already mastered the first years' skills. To treat BobbiSue and Katlin equally is neither fair nor moral. Most classroom teachers view accountability testing in the same manner. At BobbiSue Elementary School, 93 percent of the children qualify for the breakfast program and free lunch. There are no books, newspapers, or magazines in their homes and conversation with adults consists of orders and admonitions. Six of every ten children who enroll in the fall will be in another school by spring and may have attended as many as four different schools in between. Conditions in many of the nation's school districts have not changed since Jonathan Kozol documented BobbiSue and BobbiSue Elementary School in *Savage Inequalities*. For many of America's schools, accountability test results indicating under-performance may be accurate. But these results do not report the extent of progress in reaching that level nor the extraordinary effort of many teachers to get there. BobbiSue enters school with negligible readiness skills and little motivation. Katlin enters school intensely motivated and a grade level advanced. The annual district test results indicate BobbiSue has mastered only three-quarters of the skills for the year while Katlin is a half-grade level above her placement. Who is the success story?

Fact is, teachers in schools identified by accountability tests as low-performing may be responsible for more skill improvement in their pupils than that accomplished in over-performing schools. Fact is, working classroom teachers just want fair, not equal, in reformers' testing programs.

By the time I reached home, I'd had about all the wriggling I wanted for one day. I wasn't sure what would happen with Munson Elementary School or if they would satisfy the three conditions set for the little school to remain open. After watching Dr. Dunworth and his team pursue their vision since my first visit, I'd revised my estimate of chances for success to seven of ten. Not good enough to bet the bread and milk money, but good enough to wager the clothing budget.

Can the Kids Do It Again?

David Johnson became principal of Munson Elementary School after Dr. Dunworth was paid his dollar for the year. He and the teachers have continued working to make their vision for the little school a reality. They continue the intensive classroom instruction and to hold high expectations for each child. Now that the school board has agreed to keep the school open, the community has relaxed a little. However, March Testing this year created as much anxiety as the year to "improve or die." This year they had to prove last year's test score gains were the result of good teaching and hard work—not luck or some other phenomenon. The question down at the Country Store was, "Can the kids do it again?" Well, the preliminary results have been reported and it appears the Munson School test scores will improve at least another four or five percentile points. I'm willing to bet the bread and milk money now.

Bibliography

Balow, I. H., Farr, R. C., and Hogan, T. P. (1992). Metropolitan Achievement Test-7. San Antonio, TX: Psychological Corporation.

Bracey, G. W. (1997). "What happened to America's public schools?" *American Heritage*, November, pp. 39–52.

CTB/Macmillian/McGraw-Hill (1993). California Achievement Test-5. Monterey, CA: Author.

Governor's Office (1999). The Bush/Brogan A+ Plan for Education. Tallahassee, FL: Florida Governor's Office.

Harcourt Brace Educational Measurement (1996). Stanford Achievement Test (9th edition). San Antonio, TX: Psychological Corporation.

Kozol, J. (1991). *Savage Inequalities: Children in America's Schools.* New York: Crown.

Lopshire, R. (1988). *Put Me in the Zoo.* New York: Random House.

The National Commission on Excellence in Education (1985). *A Nation at Risk: The Imperative for Educational Reform.* Washington, D. C.: Superintendent of Documents, U.S. Government Printing Office.

Salvia, J., and Ysseldyke, J. E. (1998). *Assessment* (7th edition). Boston: Houghton Mifflin.

The Dollar-A-Year Principal's Principles

Good schools have a set of principles or guidelines that define what they are about. They describe, set conditions and establish the mind set that can make the difference in achieving success. It is best if they are stated in words that everyone understand—words that feel comfortable.

In a good school everyone respects everyone else. Everyone. This is basic. Also, a good school is a safe school. This is basic too.

In a good school greater emphasis is placed on individual objectives than on grade-level objectives. A good school has high expectations for everyone. However, how quickly you learn is not as important as how thoroughly you learn. Comparing children is negative and counter-productive. Recognizing children for reaching objectives is positive and very productive. Reflect this in the practices and policies of your system or school (grades, report cards, tests, etc.). Think of it as an attitude. Don't sweat the labels.

Schools should be judged on whether children are improving, are learning. There will be ups and downs and plateaus but the bottom line is, are they moving ahead on their individual learning tracks? Are they excited about learning? If children, teachers and parents are excited about progress, you don't have to worry. When the progress of learning is stalled, worry.

It would be trite to say that good schools have good teachers— or good students or good parents or good anyone else. Good schools see the potential in everyone and work to develop that potential. That's the key. Teachers are human beings, with all that implies. All are different. Good schools make good teachers just as they make good students.

Elementary school teaching is a unique profession. It is completely demanding and completely consuming. It takes study and preparation and, most of all, it takes commitment. You can't be a half-hearted teacher or a halfway teacher. It is a contradiction in terms. It is all or nothing. A few people try to be half-hearted teachers. They don't belong in a good school. Indeed, they don't belong in any school. There are proper ways to deal with this. Use them. A good school creates an environment that releases the potential in almost everyone it touches, including teachers. If it doesn't, it is not a good school.

Technology and good schools are close friends. Teachers need all the assistance they can obtain if they are to help each child reach his or her next step on the ladder of learning. That's a lot of ladders and a lot of steps. Computers, the internet, instructional television and related technologies can help. They are the bright screens on the horizon of learning and are bringing, and will continue to bring massive changes in the way we teach and learn. A good school will reflect and facilitate these developments.

To be a good school, you must believe you can be a good school. Everyone must believe, including the "front office." That means tangible support, encouragement, flexibility, faith. That is *absolutely* essential. Systems and communities that do not provide *all* of these ingredients, that do not support their schools, are not serious about having good schools. Criticism is not support. Rolling up your sleeves and helping is support. The public needs to be reminded of this.

In a good school parents and teachers are a team. Each respects the other's role. Parents can do much to reinforce what happens in the classroom. Indeed, they must if it is going to be a good school. For example, parents must teach respect and responsibility at home; teachers, at school. If necessary, bring in experts. Have parent workshops. But work on this and all aspects of parenting.

Parents must listen to their children. Also, little things like having your children read to you every day, just for a few minutes, can make a huge difference. You read to them too. If these things aren't important to you, they won't be important to your child. It's that simple. And that important. In choosing between the demands of living and the demands of loving, choose wisely.

One absolutely essential characteristic of a good school is good leadership. The research is unequivocal on this point. All of the things that make a good school happen only if there is a dedicated, skillful and insightful principal working around the clock to make them happen. Without exception, leaders of good schools represent the most insightful leadership in the world of education. Seek their input and listen. Also, nurture and cherish them. They are invaluable. Being astute people, they will agree.

Legislatures and State Boards of Education want good schools. Hopefully they will encourage, support and reward but not dictate. "All fourth graders must..." is nonsense. Fancy guides and rigid standards are usually not too helpful. Objectives are important. Direction is important. And funds are very important to reach those objectives. Schools and school systems and local school boards have the difficult responsibility of making it all happen. Give them the resources and the latitude to do the job and hold them accountable. But reduce the horrendous amount of reporting and administrivia. Not one child learned one thing from the dollars invested in these "'round and 'round" nose-to-tail exercises.

School systems in turmoil do not foster good schools. Continuing labor problems, school board conflicts, funding disputes or any system-wide turmoil seriously detracts from the business of teaching and learning and impinges on the quality of all schools. In the interest of children, resolve these disputes quickly.

A really good school will provide support, instruction and programs for the youngest children in the community, and of course, their parents. That means early childhood education must be available to everyone. States that do not fund such programs are shortchanging their citizens. Just because people know how to make children does not mean they know how to raise children. They need assistance and information and support.

The early years are the most important years in a child's life. Helping children and families during this period is the best investment a society can make. So if your state does not provide for such programs, fight for them. And fight hard. Good schools are advocates for children and the things they need.

If too many children in a school can not read adequately or spell or write, communicate or compute or behave responsibly, it clearly shouts "problem." But do not jump to conclusions. Children will be at different places on their individual learning tracks but most should be making progress, good progress, demonstrable progress. In judging "where they are" you must also consider "where they started." The operative word is "progress." If teachers or administrators aren't doing their parts, fix that. If the support system is inadequate, address that. And if the home environment for students is negative, hit hard on this. In the case of external factors such as bad legislation, questionable court decisions and the like, seek public support for change. In the mean time, ignore as many of these factors as prudently and legally possible. But use care. "Dead" leaders don't make good schools.

Tests are part of schooling. Unfortunately, standardized tests are used primarily to compare. Many feel they are excessively demanding and time consuming and should be challenged. They are expensive too. Teacher-designed tests, based on your own school's curriculum, can tell much about your children, their specific needs and their specific accomplishments. Encourage the use of this type of test.

Good schools have small classes. But small classes alone will not make a good school. The other ingredients are necessary too. It is not enough to reduce class size but it is a good beginning - a very good beginning.

Big schools can be good schools. It may be more difficult, but that's all. Little schools have the advantage because people know each other and reinforce each other. That's family. But a large school can also be family, a wonderful family. Big schools have the advantage that they have more resources. Both can be excellent schools. Size is not the determining factor.

A structured, pat formula to make a good school misses the mark. Each situation is different. Anything can happen. Someone may come along and offer to work for a dollar a year. You never know. A good school seeks good help where it can. Invest your faith and support in teachers, parents, children, friends and the principal and _you_ can have a wonderful school. Remember, leadership is important.

Who is _you_? All of us. Because schools belong to all of us and should be treasured by all of us. It is a thought that bears repeating.

The principal, the teachers, the children, the community and especially parents will know when a school is a good school. They will also know when it isn't a good school. Ask them...all of them...and if most of the informed people say "yes," you are there. All you have to do now is keep up the good work. You can, if you believe you can.

Part V

Messages and Lessons

—Daniel A. Talany, Ed.D.
*Principal, Village Elementary
School, Hilton, New York*

*Adjunct Professor, State
University of New York,
College at Brockport,
Brockport, New York*

Introduction to Part V

Aside from being a great story and an inspirational experience, *The Dollar-A-Year Principal* gives us much more. Imbedded in its fabric are a number of very important and meaningful messages and lessons. The ones I found particularly profound were those that spoke about leadership.

Before I begin, however, I want to explain briefly about two characteristics of the "Messages and Lessons" section. First among these is that I believe it is easier to understand things, especially concepts and making connections, if there are examples or metaphors for the reader to consider. I, for one, tend to think in metaphors. So, as I attempt to share what I see are the messages and lessons of the story, I will from time to time inject an example or a metaphor that hopefully will help you better understand what I am saying.

The second point is that I see recurring messages and lessons in the story. Furthermore, I believe that there are subtleties within each of the messages and lessons that are equally significant. Therefore, I will return to common themes throughout the section so as to underscore the important and essential nature of the message and lesson. You will find this particularly evident as I continuously refer the reader to the *goal*. I make it emphatically clear what I believe was the *goal* of John Dunworth's experience. And, without apology, I focus on the importance and critical nature of that goal in my comments. To me, the relationship between the *goal* and what happened at Munson is where it begins, is how it is guided, and explains in large measure its successful outcome.

Daniel A. Talany

Chapter IX

The Inside Dimension

Knowing Ourselves

I believe that all significant human endeavor begins with strong personal commitment. Moreover, if people are to be successful in that endeavor, they must have an equally strong sense of themselves, and the will to act upon their commitment. In essence, it begins with what is *inside* us and is judged by how we take it *out*. The story of the saving of Munson Elementary School begins with who we are on the *inside*. It is all about beliefs and how people act upon those beliefs. I have always believed that one pillar that supports success in schools is that a committed effort can only be achieved if words are matched by actions. I suggest that what you have just read about the saving of Munson Elementary School is just that.

The philosopher Decartes is claimed to have coined the phrase, "I think, therefore, I am." That statement may be adequate to describe humanity if you wish to merely show evidence of the fact that we simply exist. However, I wonder how Decartes would respond to this story. I wonder if he might consider expanding on his famous statement with proclamations such as,"I believe, therefore, I have a vision," and "I see, therefore, I act." Existence without purpose is meaningless. Purpose without action is missed opportunity.

The foundation of the miracle of this story is a message about the fact that we must know ourselves and use that knowledge to make a difference. The substance of who the author is, and his beliefs and purposes, are laid out in "The Dollar-A-Year Principal's Principles" and in his "Odyssey of Discovery." Having beliefs about who we are and what we expect of ourselves is important. However, relatively speaking, I think this is the easy part, although it is where it all must begin. Doing something with those beliefs takes us to a level of courage of which we all hope we are worthy and capable. This is the first *message* the story of Munson Elementary School provides. The implication for us is that our success in meeting our responsibilities will likely depend on how well we know ourselves; what we believe and what actions we are willing to take to implement those beliefs.

In this story, we see that the principal understood that if he were to be successful in this endeavor he needed to begin with himself. It is as if he knew instinctively that he needed to take stock of what he believed, not only to make sure he could clearly articulate it, but also, as I suggest, to reaffirm in his own mind that he was armed with the spirit to see this challenge through successfully. The review of his personal resources appears to me to have been an assessment of his most cherished beliefs. In doing this task, we can review "The Dollar-A-Year Principal's Principles" section of this book as well as the "Odyssey of Discovery" and consider a number of important lessons about *leadership* in school reform.

It may be so obvious as not to actually require a statement, but the first *lesson* of leadership we can garner from the action to review personal principles is as follows: Effective leaders accepting responsibility for affecting the lives of others do not take that responsibility lightly. We saw in this story that leadership meant engaging in a substantial amount of soul-searching. It suggested that reflection and self-analysis were not only initial steps in the process, but also an integral part of the experience. The *lesson* is that self-analysis and reflection is necessary to maintain the balance between where we are and where we want to be.

Acting on Our Beliefs

More than a reminder for educators, there is a *message* to a broader constituency. The story and its *lessons* poignantly remind us of the importance of having principles by which to live. As Stephen Covey would point out, success comes as a result of knowing and living your own "principles of personal vision." (Covey: p. 66) Effective leadership has a vision. Effective leaders have a clear vision which they are able to articulate clearly to those around them. This story suggests that this is exactly what happened. More importantly, the story of Munson Elementary School shows us that vision can be turned into actions and decisions. The actions and decisions made by Dr. Dunworth in leading the school and the community toward the goal was grounded in his vision of what Munson Elementary could become and the ultimate impact on each child.

To me, having principles, knowing them, and living your life according to them should not be options, but requirements. This goes beyond education. It's about life!

Another *lesson* from the *inside* is that effective leaders consistently re-educate themselves by doing exactly what we see happened in this story. It is in that constant review and reflection that we refine our beliefs and appraise our actions against them. Reflection is more than an occasional mental and/or spiritual exercise to be conducted whenever discretionary time allows. Rather, reflection must be a constant in one's life. It allows us to make sure we are who we want to be, and not who we are at that moment. In a sense, reflection provides the opportunity for a kind of re-teaching. In his best-selling book, *On Becoming a Leader*, Warren Bennis calls this "You are your own best teacher." Like a good teacher, you first begin with the students, what the students know and bring to the situation. Reflection means that we are our own students and therefore we begin with ourselves. During the story, we see that the vision is revisited constantly by everyone and the principal saw to it that referring to the vision was integrated into the routine of the effort. We can learn from this story that when we review our beliefs and study our vision, it not only rejuvenates us, but also reaffirms the challenge we have set for ourselves. In other words, effective leaders say to themselves on a regular basis, "If I am to be an educational leader, I need to know what I am about and what I am willing to do to achieve my goal."

There is a subtle, if not implied *lesson*, that comes out of "The Principles." Although not stated explicitly, the suggestion is that we must first be prepared to change our own attitudes, as well as our actions and decisions, before we can expect the same in others. This speaks to the leader's responsibility to model the process. We frequently hear the mantra, "Walking the Talk." When a leader "walks the talk," as happened in this story, we see how powerful the model can be. Suggesting that a leader conform in some ways may contrast with other statements regarding successful people knowing what they believe. Some may argue that if you know yourself, then you need not change. I would offer the opposite conclusion; it is my contention that consistent review and reflection upon one's beliefs imports an understanding and a capacity to change. Effective leaders are like well-navigated sailing ships. The heading is true, but the winds may force us to maneuver about, tacking side to side, but always on course. It is almost as if the more we stay the same in our minds and hearts, the more we are easily and likely to change. Change is a reality and an on-going process. It happens to us whether we want it or not. Successful leaders know change happens and accept it. They use the reality of inevitable change in the world and in themselves rather than have it use them. They establish a practice of personal review and self-reflection. Successful leaders recognize that this process is simply a natural process that successful people use to manage change. They empower themselves to control how the change will impact them, and do not allow themselves to be victims of it. I believe this is yet another *lesson* we can learn from this story.

Effective leaders use their understanding of change to plan and act. They have the capacity to influence change to sustain their effort toward a desired end. Effective leaders know that although they may have been effective in their own personal review and self-reflection, if they are to be successful, as in the saving of Munson Elementary School, those associated with its salvation would need to share the same experiences. Therefore, we see in the story that the initial actions and decisions about what to do and how to do it began with having the stakeholders participate at various levels with discourse about beliefs, visions, and goals. Effective leaders recognize the power inherent in this process; without this focus the desired transformation will not materialize.

The literature of self-improvement, self-assessment, and self-direction are so pervasive today that it could be very easy to over-look it and take it for granted. The Munson Elementary story is compelling evidence that focus on the inside is real, important and critical. Knowing who you are and what you believe is not just an exercise at a seminar or during those rare moments when we allow ourselves the opportunity to reflect. The final lesson of this message shows us that we must act on these beliefs in ways that make a difference. Actions must be consistent, thoughtful, and purposeful. Each day as we address our tasks, constant reflection on beliefs and the congruency of our actions in relation to those beliefs is one way to separate effective leaders from those who aspire to be effective leaders. It is also a means for us to gauge our progress. The rebirth of hope in the community around Munson Elementary School is a living testament to the fact that it must begin inside in all of us. It is also evidence that acting on those beliefs is what makes them real. The implications for leadership and responsibility in all of us are immeasurable.

Warren Bennis (*On Becoming a Leader*, 1997) also wrote about two dimensions of the *inside*. Bennis described this in terms of *knowing yourself* and *knowing the world*. Bennis states that effective leaders engage in a lifelong continuous process of self-appraisal. *On Becoming a Leader* suggests that effective leaders immediately resort to the process of self-appraisal first when faced with deci-sions and especially with regard to critical situations. Effective leaders gauge all decisions and plans against the *inside*. This is not an uncommon theme in the lexicon of leadership research.

You may be thinking that this *message* and these *lessons* are not for you. You hear yourself saying "I am not a leader" or "I do not have the responsibility to use what is *inside* me to advance a cause." If these are your thoughts, then let me suggest that you may underestimate yourself and are missing a very important personal message this story has sent you. We are all leaders in education. Our leadership responsibility is predicated on the fact that we are members of a society. Our membership in this group requires us to play an integrated role. Every action we take impacts others.

Education is too much a part of our society and our lives for us to be passive and unconcerned. It is a responsibility we cannot escape. Some may choose to ignore it, others distort it, but the responsibility does not go away. Every child's face is a reminder of our responsibility to the future. It is our legacy, our connection to immortality. Munson Elementary School showed potential leaders that sharing what we are *inside* allowed others to rediscover what is *inside* them. When that combination of beliefs and concerted effort toward a common goal is blended and finally unleashed, great things can be accomplished. In this story, we see how effective leadership combined the energy of everyone in and around the school. As a result, Munson Elementary School was saved. Once the energy was harnessed and focused, what happened afterward was a matter of will, persistence, and patience.

Context and Potential

Effective leaders recognize that knowing yourself alone is not sufficient to sustain making the entire difference. Having knowledge of the world around is also critical. In this story, knowing the Munson community, its history and traditions, was important. Effective leaders know that they work in a context, and knowing that context is a primary responsibility. Failing to know the context, failing to know the "world," will invite disaster. Disaster was averted at Munson Elementary School because attention was paid to the "world" of the school.

Knowledge of the surrounding world, however, does not simply mean recognizing history and traditions. It also does not end with simply understanding that there are hurdles and limitations to address and overcome. Rather, an effective leader understands that it is necessary to approach the "world" in which one will work with a comprehensive, if not global perspective. There are relationships among the things in the world, and effective leaders realize this. An effective leader studies the situation and becomes cognizant of the many "stories," and "baggage," as well as "history." All of these are wrapped in emotion and viewed differently by every person involved. For this reason, effective leaders listen, look and consider "potential." The circumstances give effective leaders clues about the "potential" of the situation in which they find themselves. "Potential," thereby, can be equated to an opportunity to apply the vision and to assert the goal. Effective leaders see an opportunity in every challenge, while less effective leaders see a challenge in every opportunity. One important *lesson* in the Munson Elementary School story is that the leadership approached circumstances by thinking about their potential, about the opportunities to move toward the goal and to live the vision.

If we appreciate the importance and value of potential and the opportunity it imports, we imply learning. Effective leaders are learners. It is what they do, model for others, and empower others to do. The Munson Elementary story clearly describes the journey one man took to learn about being successful. Learning about how to achieve your goal and live your vision makes sense. It is the recipe for success. Having the capacity to learn is effective when the learning enhances the vision and promotes the goal. As Bennis stated, "The capacity to learn is always present." (Bennis, p. 88) The Munson Elementary School story illustrates how actions and decisions that recognize the potential in the circumstances is an opportunity presented. The story of the "little school that could" shows us that when we allow our capacity for learning to move in harmony with our vision and goal, success is a likely outcome.

Chapter X

Clear Goals and Committed People

The Goal, The Goal, The Goal

Every school is different and yet every school is the same. There are different kinds of people from many different backgrounds and experiences, but they are still teachers, parents, students, and staff. There are wide differences in material and spiritual resources in every community, but it is more a matter of quality than it is quantity. Furthermore, sheer numbers of people do not equate to greater success. Instead, we must keep in mind that it is the depth of conviction and the persistence of effort that are the determining factors. Some schools are like rivers that are a mile wide but only a few feet deep. Others are like rivers that are a few feet wide but a mile deep. Somewhere in between is the place we want to be. *The Dollar-A-Year Principal* tells us an important *message* about purpose. It clearly underscores the principle that it is the *goal* that counts. Without a doubt, the means to achieve that *goal* are important, but without the clearly articulated *goal*, understood by all, the means can be distorted and inefficiently applied. The *message* given us by those who lived the rebirth of Munson Elementary School is that we must make sure that everyone knows what that *goal* actually is. As simple and obvious as it may seem, failure to make the changes needed to accomplish school reform begins with not knowing what the *goal* is.

So, what was the goal? The answer is likely to be described and articulated in many ways by those who read the story. Teachers, parents, policy makers, and principals will read this story and conclude what the goal was. I have read and re-read this story and admittedly have had opportunities to talk with John Dunworth. I believe that I can offer an interesting perspective about what I feel was his goal. I am not apologizing for my advantage in having first-hand knowledge. On the contrary, I offer the following as another piece of the puzzle that I hope will fit into the picture.

I suggest there was one primary goal. I also offer a position that what many readers would see as the goals were actually the objectives Dr. Dunworth anticipated and planned for. Furthermore, the many tasks and activities that paint the canvas of the story were not really goals. They were but stepping stones the Munson Elementary community used as it marched to its goal.

If we peel away the layers of perspective and motivation, the goal is that kernel just below the surface and somewhat beyond the first view. If we peer carefully and listen to the story as it unfolds, the goal becomes most clear. The goal, and only goal that makes real sense, is found in the fundamental principle that every child must learn. The goal was about learning for every child. The goal was about learning in its broadest sense. It was about learning of the heart and soul, as much as is was about learning of the mind. The goal was certainly not merely to raise some obscure test scores. Although improved test scores could provide some evidence of learning, it certainly was not comprehensive or conclusive, and it would not accurately predict future success. For sure the public audience, especially the policy makers and district level administrators had to have their needs addressed. But I am talking about "learning" that transcends test scores. I am talking about learners who know they are learners, are proud they are learners, and who believe in themselves as learners. No test can give a child that. The "learning" by which the Munson community would judge its school was not numbers from a standardized test, but intuitively what they recognized in the hearts of their children. It is called hope and faith. These, too, are elements of education. The story of Munson Elementary School, if nothing more, is the rebirth of hope and faith in the goal that every child can and will learn.

One test or even a battery of tests cannot measure the sum total of a child's learning. Logically, the goal must be larger than passing a test or even what one test can measure. Therefore, test scores could not be the goal in and of themselves. Raising test scores alone could not be the means to judge the success of the goal for this school. The relationship between test scores and learning is indirect at best. We all know how it feels when we know we understand much about a subject and then receive a poor score on a test. Test scores do not tell the full story of what we know and have learned.

And the goal was not merely to save the school from closing or to give back to the Munson community its sense of accomplishment, pride, and identity. There is no doubt that a school is often the centerpiece of pride in a community. Make no mistake about it, the feelings of achievement of banding together, laboring as a community, and rallying around a common belief is something of which we may be proud. Overcoming great odds and significant challenges swells the hearts of those involved to be sure. I would argue that there is a deeper appreciation and depth of pride that comes from knowing that above and beyond the improving of test scores and the maintaining of "our" school's survival, the parents, teachers, and community had recognized that quality learning had occurred in their children. The quality was understood to be more than improving the minds of the children. If there were successful learners in this story, their numbers include both parents and the community at large. There were *lessons* learned by everyone about their hearts and souls, as well as their minds.

I believe I have made a strong argument that the goal was learning. Make no mistake about it. If you read the story carefully and think deeply into John Dunworth's words, the story makes that emphatically clear. The actions and decisions around saving Munson Elementary School were not focused on the test, nor on just keeping the school doors open, nor was it a means to build community pride. Effective leaders know they must address test scores, cultivate community pride, and improve their schools. However, effective leaders look beyond these "incidentals," the trappings of school success, and focus on the goal. Reading the story, the reader realizes that what was being looked for, sought, and worked for, was student learning.

To accomplish this, the story celebrates the establishment of a child-centered school where all children, regardless of who they were or where they came from, regardless of their experiences, good or bad, were expected to "learn" and that each of them mattered. Effective leaders begin with themselves and what is *inside*, but they go beyond themselves and help everyone reinvent their dreams.

People Power

The goal was manifested in the singular vision attained by the staff of Munson Elementary School. As in the story, effective leaders instill in their school staff the goal of teaching every child so every child learns; teaching all children so they learn more than they thought they could at levels of achievement higher than others thought they would. This sense of empowerment and responsibility for self-improvement may have begun with the five teachers and the cadre of dedicated staff, but it soon spread. We see in the story how this spirit was inculcated in both parents and the community. There was a wellspring of expectation that every child would learn, and that each child could be empowered to make the differences in their own lives and not to depend on outside factors. The story describes the actions that were designed to make everyone personally responsible for learning through self-improvement and to look beyond the horizon to a point that was important. That point was learning.

The message here is that successful endeavors begin and end with a commitment and focus on a goal. It is equally important to know what the goal is and to ensure that everyone knows and believes in it. It means not losing sight of the goal and allowing ourselves to be distracted by related, but not essential things. There are lessons in history outside the schools that can show what happens when the goal is not clear. The phenomenon of not knowing what the goal is does not apply exclusively to a school organization. For example, at the turn of the century the railroad industry believed their goal revolved around trains and tracks. The railroad industry was the dominant form of transportation for people and commodities in the country at that time. The leadership of the railroad industry, their decisions and actions, were predicated on the belief that they were in the train and track business. Within the first few decades of the twentieth century, however, the automobile industry with its trucks, and eventually the airline industry showed them how incorrect their perspectives and assumptions were. The railroad industry was in the *transportation* business and not the train and track business. When they finally realized this, it was too late, and the rest is history.

When we look at the great works of literature, there are examples of how tragedy was perpetrated on the main characters because they failed to properly identify the goal. We can think of the tragic figures of many a familiar classic tale. These tragic figures made assumptions about people and things that were incorrect. Their decisions and actions were ill fated because their goals were not aligned with reality and their vision was not grounded in reality. Such stories are ostensibly reflections of life, and as in the classic tragedies, are played out in real life as well.

There is a powerful *lesson* to be learned from the story of Munson Elementary School about *knowing the goal*. There are many people that are very happy that the goal was clear.

Armed with their goal, the people of Munson Elementary School were ready to act. Effective leadership cannot be satisfied that the goal is known. What is equally important to know is "what you are up against." In this case, there were some significant parameters and limitations to the situation. Effective leaders appraise the extent of the resources, both human and material. We see that John Dunworth assessed his resources and made conclusions about what could and could not be done. This is important to appreciate, because to be effective means that you often need to be creative and flexible. Often some resources are not available. More important is that effective leaders do not "throw in the towel" when what they at first believe is needed is not available. One characteristic of an effective leader is resourcefulness, which implies that the leader finds ways to meet needs in different ways. The story underscores this leadership characteristic. Moreover, it not only was attributable to the principal; it also became a trait of others around the principal. Resourcefulness is an attitude, a manifestation of beliefs that is contagious.

Resourcefulness does not solve every problem, and no one believes there are not limitations. There are always limitations. Even though the Munson community worked diligently to acquire the material resources for the school and muster powerful human resources, there were roadblocks. There are many episodes in the story when the exertion of great amounts of energy and time acquiring and managing material resources could not overcome the appetite of needs. Effective leaders consistently re-evaluate their situation and regroup from time to time, as was the case in this story. At the same time, effective leaders keep one eye looking beyond the horizon just in case something comes along that may help them. This is what happened in this story.

There is no way we can ignore the support Munson Elementary School received from the community at large, the local universities, the military establishments in the area, and local businesses in addition to the Santa Rosa County Schools. However, it is still the leadership that brings attention to the goal and the needs that enable us to reach the goal. Effective leaders emphasize the mobilization of the hearts and minds of the people so they can "see" new opportunities and solutions. This is a significant *lesson* in the story. When engaged in a difficult challenge, and after being met with hurdles and barriers, it is easy to give up. Keeping the spirit of hope alive allows for the chance that new opportunities will arise. As you read the story, you see how this very thing happened over and over again with all kinds of people associated with saving Munson Elementary School. People you have around you are your greatest asset. In solving problems, the most effective way to begin the process for change or improvement is to begin with the people who are impacted by the situation. The story shows us most vividly and in a uniquely personal way that when you mobilize people around a belief system toward a clearly understood goal, you then find many different ways to reach the goal.

Depending on who you are and where you are sitting when you read this story, you can come to a conclusion about whether or not the Munson community had sufficient material resources. What we can conclude, however, from this story is that every community has assets and liabilities. There are abundances and limitations. I would suggest that the Munson community may not have been as blessed with material resources as others, although in some areas they had more than enough. This discussion is irrelevant because it was not the material resources that mattered most here. What we can learn about effective leadership with regard to resources is that as critical and essential as they are, no material resources could be utilized effectively without faith in the human resources. Munson may have been a small community, but that makes little difference. The sheer numbers of people affiliated with a school does not in and of itself ensure an adequate human resource pool. What does count, and what counted here was the quality of the commitment. In this story, we see how mobilizing that human resource around a common goal maximized the skills, abilities, and most importantly the will of a community. In many ways, I would argue that this is actually more important than numbers of people. Schools with far greater assets and a capacity to acquire assets have failed to achieve what the Munson community achieved, as Dr. Dunworth might say, "in spades." It demonstrates what committed people can do when they act together. It also demonstrates why good leadership is absolutely essential.

Chapter XI

Change

Change and Transition

It is hard to ignore the obvious connections between the Munson Elementary School story and the literature on change. *The Dollar-A-Year Principal* is certainly a story about change. As with the previous message about beginning with people, effective leaders recognize that what is needed to be done means change for every person. Effective leaders also realize that change means that everyone will be experiencing transitions. These transitions will be disconcerting to some, exhilarating to others, and passively received by still others. Effective leaders know that transitions will be required of everyone, regardless of perspective, if the goal is to be reached.

In his book *Managing Transitions*, William Bridges describes the process of change as a series of interrelated transitions by people who are impacted by a change. In the story of Munson

Elementary School, we see how the principal realized that the changes he envisioned in order to make Munson Elementary viable as an educational institution depended largely on ensuring that every person realized he or she was a vital part of the endeavor. Effective leaders understand that they are dealing with a psychological process as well as a physical one. "...You simply cannot get the results you need without getting into *that personal stuff.*" (Bridges: p. x) Understanding that the responsibility included making sure that every person had a personal stake in the rebirth of Munson Elementary School was essential for success. The meetings, constant conversations with parents, local and state school officials, and community members all demonstrated the scope of this understanding and the skill these actions reflect.

Think for a minute about all the innovative organizations and structures that emerged from the collaborative discourse surrounding the blending of the goal with the resources at hand. We see that Munson Elementary School structured student learning around multi-level classrooms, and depended on the multi-tasking capabilities of the staff. For most of us, these are not visions that come to mind when we think of our own school experiences. For educators, who have spent their lives in a rigid grade level school organization and have had their professional lives organized around fixed sets of regulations, policy, and contract language, these changes are not only substantial, they are mind boggling. Multi-level classrooms and multi-tasking staff responsibilities were not foisted upon Munson Elementary School by outside experts and consultants. Rather, they grew naturally from the dialogue of good people making tough decisions about their school. That made the decisions much easier to live with because they all shared the same goal. You will also recall that Dr. Dunworth never used labels. Rather, "Think of it as an 'attitude,'" he would say. The focus was on each child and that child's progress. That was the goal. Accepting change requires transitioning and effective leadership understands the dynamics of change. Effective leadership recognizes the need to help people move to new structures and practices. Effective leadership in this story, however, had a powerful asset. Everyone knew the goal. Effective leaders know that if the goal is clear and the plan reflects a clear alignment of actions with that goal, then the actions leading toward the goal will make the transitions possible for everyone involved. This may be the most important triumph in this story.

Change and Commitment

The message is clear, and undeniably essential. For change to happen, the leader must make a personal commitment to see that everyone who has a stake in the outcome becomes personally committed to the goal. If the majority of those involved believe, then they will make the transition, and provide support for each other as well. The support among the stakeholders will also have the effect of speeding up the process of change. The increased rate of change phenomenon comes as the result of growth caused by the intense and rich impact of human interaction focused on a goal.

The story of saving Munson Elementary School began with changing attitudes and commitment. Early in the story, we learned that there was some doubt in the community, and clearly at the district level, that saving Munson Elementary School would be possible. There were even sentiments of hopelessness. Changing that belief and doubt in the people who mattered most is an effective leader's first task. In this case, effective leadership was eventually successful because the goal was clear and the directives and ideas were succinctly and purposely framed. Because the goal was clear, decisions and actions were congruent with responsibilities. Admittedly, effective leaders acknowledge self-doubts and accept responsibility for mistakes along the way. However, with each bump in the road, effective leaders return to the goal to re-nourish their battered souls. Once they do, the beliefs are rekindled and that is what sustains them.

We saw from the concerted effort described in the story that the goal to improve learning for every child was a constant focus. First and foremost an effective leader must address beliefs of the various people involved. An effective leader realizes that the range in interest will be great. Some people will be highly invested, and others will not. With the range comes the challenge of managing interest. In the story, there was the challenge of changing attitudes and beliefs regarding how well students could learn, about how much every person could impact that goal, and what we could expect of ourselves. This was true of everyone. Effective leadership appraises the interest, assesses what will need to be done to fortify the vision, and then determines the actions necessary. The Munson Elementary School experience is like a roadmap that detailed in a wonderful story how effective leadership can accomplish this.

The children of the Munson community were typical of the region. Their needs, abilities, dreams and experiences were not particularly unique. All children want to belong, feel loved, and be successful. If you look at their faces you will see the same enthusiasm and light of excitement sparkling in their eyes that you see in the children in your school. Their history of success as learners, as measured by standardized tests, however, has not been evident. Leadership needed to address this, and it began with changing the attitudes of many people about how well the children could learn.

Let us look at the realities of the situation. As with most communities, the parents and citizens of Munson had years of experiences with schooling. They had acquired a history and lore about what schools were about and what their roles were. The world around them changed, but their memories and ideas about schooling were still in their own experiences. When they realized the circumstances and specter of what was going to happen to their school, they were understandably confused. For many the idea of losing their school was impossible to comprehend. The community of Munson woke up one day to find that the dynamic world they had heard about in the news was suddenly impacting how they saw things. Like most of us, the world had changed more dramatically in a single lifetime than the combined experiences of past generations. Like so many other school communities, they could not reconcile their experiences and beliefs about schooling with the changes in the world around them. Like many parents and teachers, they longed for a past that was good at the expense of what was reality. Effective leadership recognizes that when faced with inevitable change, and change they may not understand, it is natural for people to look to the past for answers. The past can provide information about the purpose and the goals, but the practices are context and time bound. In the story of Munson Elementary School the natural reaction to look to past practices surely was strong. We know that such a reaction may be initially popular and attractive, but it may be the wrong response. Think of the situation in Munson in these terms. The principal was the driver of a bus heading down a road with many passengers. The passengers are offering suggestions about where to go while looking into the rear-view mirrors. There are many stories of failed reform attempts, and well-intentioned efforts being lost because the urgency leads to quick and easy responses. Effective leaders know that the best decisions, those that sustain the change and achieve the goal, are the result of hard work and attention to the vision and beliefs. Effective leaders know that making these kinds of fundamental transitions is essential. Once it happens, everyone is empowered to make the changes necessary to achieve goals.

School reform encompasses improved learning and changes in organization and practices for the benefit of *all* children. The transition is the journey, the process, and the personal experience all rolled up into one. The change is your destination. In this story, the people of Munson traveled on a difficult journey. They endured and were successful. Their transition of beliefs was carefully facilitated and led by a dynamic leader. As William Bridges, author of *Managing Transition*, would say, "Change is what happens at the end, while the journey is about people making transitions."

The story of Munson Elementary School is about change. Specifically, it is about giving people a vision and a goal that they can readily understand and comprehend. If they understand and comprehend it, then they recognize the transitions that need to be made. They abandon ideas that are no longer relevant. They prepare themselves for transition. The story begins with episodes where these transitions took place. The lesson so colorfully portrayed in this story is that transitions happen to people, and therefore, if change is to be successful, it must be done at a personal level.

The lesson of transitioning for change permeates the story. Effective leaders know that success in facilitating the transitions for change begins with interactions with every stakeholder. This interaction includes meaningful dialogue about the vision and the realities with parents, teachers and just as important, Edith in the cafeteria, and everyone involved. The story is rich with examples that show us that effective leaders value everyone's input and feelings. Effective leaders recognize that transitions and changes in attitudes and beliefs are for everyone, and not just a few. The Munson Elementary School story is a model experience of how a leader helps everyone to accept and support a goal. One outcome of the transitioning effort is that it creates in everyone a sense of uniform purpose. We have all had the experience of being a member of a group, a team, or an organization that has a common purpose. It is a good feeling, and it gives a sense of empowerment and confidence that comes only as a result of recognizing that associates are thinking and feeling the same as you. It is apparent that this was happening at Munson, and it felt great.

Chapter XII

To Will, To Do, and To Dare

Real Needs

Having the will to accomplish your goals is another powerful lesson that the story taught us. We saw that effective leadership assessed the situation in relation to principles and articulated a goal. There is ample evidence to suggest that there was extensive planning and actions taken. In the story, we recognized how the leader "sized" up the level and potential for administrative support, found out what the constituents expected and believed, and went about the job of forming a coalition around those beliefs.

I teach a graduate course on "Educational Leadership" and the tale of John Dunworth's actions regarding assessing his resources and appraising the available attributes is an authentic example of how it can be done. His experiences with using what he had available to him, and helping those around him to consider more than what they believed they had, is a classic example of synergy at work. The lesson appeared to be right there, *"Spend less time on what I don't have and more time on what I do have."* Furthermore, the story showed me that "what you don't have, you can get" even though what you think you want may not be in the form you thought it would be. Please let me explain, as that may sound confusing. Often the critical step with regard to resources is a matter of knowing what you *really* need. Sometimes we think we know what we need, but if we had really thought about it in a different way, the need might actually be different. For instance, every day we face situations where we have decided that we need a particular item or believe that something must be done in a certain way. We have concluded that the only way to meet our need is to have that specific item in order to proceed.

Leaders must focus first on identifying *"real"* needs. The *"real"* need is often hidden in the answer to the question, "Why do we need, want, or do this?" If we keep our vision in mind and focus on every possibility, the result can often lead us to answers we never considered and options we never realized were there.

Will Power

What we also see in this story is will power. Persistence and dogged attention to the vision and beliefs can be attained only through sheer will. Effective leaders must be prepared to face the reality that their will is a powerful force in compelling transitions toward change. In this story, the principal "willed" things to happen by his insistence, his uncompromising focus on the goal, the intensity of his energy, and his unflagging commitment to empowering others. The resourcefulness and flexibility of his actions speak loudly about his pragmatism, but not at the expense of his vision or his goal.

There is a lesson for those who have been entrusted with leadership responsibilities. The story of persistence and will showcases how the effectiveness of a leader is not measured in how he/she acts alone. Rather, it is the consistency that the leader sustains in attending to critical and essential aspects of the goal. Furthermore, the impact of "will" often shows itself in how well the leader empowers those around him/her to become leaders themselves. The story is replete with examples where leadership was encouraged, fostered, and cultivated, leadership among the people who worked to save Munson Elementary School. Effective leaders point good people in the right direction and hang on. We saw in this story how effective leadership turned a small staff and cadre of support personnel into leaders.

The Capacity to Influence

There are lessons here for many people. First among these is the lesson for the people who are entrusted with the task or challenge. These are the people in the "trenches." In the case of Munson Elementary School it starts with the five teachers and the handful of staff. The lesson is that we all have the capacity to influence others and ourselves as well. In *Becoming a Person of Influence* (Maxwell & Dornan, 1997) influence is seen as something everyone has and can be nurtured and grown. An individual's own ability to influence can be developed. Effective leaders assess the capacity of the people to influence themselves and others. Developing influence in yourself and in others happens simultaneously. Maxwell and Dornan advance the idea that influence occurs through an interrelated process in four dimensions: *Modeling, Motivating, Mentoring, and Multiplying.* Within each of these dimensions are indicators and characteristics that not only describe the actions of a leader, but also prescribe a course of action.

Modeling as expressed by integrity has already been described in previous messages and lessons. *Motivation* is demonstrated by nurturing others, having faith in them, listening to their ideas, and understanding their needs and wants. It is evident in the principal's decisions and actions at Munson Elementary School. Moreover, it is equally evident in the actions of those who worked with the principal. *Mentoring,* as implied by the outcomes of this story, expanded the spheres of influence of everyone involved in the rebirth of Munson Elementary School. *Mentoring* was evidenced by how well John Dunworth helped people navigate the rapids and undercurrents that threatened the success of the effort. *Mentoring* continued to be the function of connecting with people and empowering them to take responsibility. Finally, as a result of the creation of and exertion of influence among all the people, influence *multiplied*, it reproduced itself in others outside the Munson community. The latter is clearly evident by the incredible interest across the nation in what happened at Munson Elementary School. The influence of the people went far beyond the boundaries of this school community. This story is testament to that.

Risk Taking

The other lesson I want to note is that with the capacity to influence is the responsibility to use that capacity appropriately and wisely. In addition, it is the strength of character to use this influence even when difficult. Effective leaders make a significant personal and professional commitment to a goal. There are rarely overt rewards, as in the case of John Dunworth, whose salary was a single dollar. Even for those of us who are compensated much more than one dollar, there is an understanding that doing the right thing has a reward far greater than can be reflected in a paycheck. Effective leaders do not expect public acclaim for their work. The Munson Elementary School community could have never imagined the national acclaim their effort brought them. The fact that it happened should be cherished, but for most leaders of tomorrow, it is usually "not in the cards."

It is easier to be the captain of a ship when the sea is calm and the weather fair. Effective leaders take risks. They do so when what is most important and critical to them as a human being and as an educator is at stake. Effective leaders place their beliefs and integrity on the line. The sea they sail can be uncharted and full of ill winds. However, as in this story, effective leaders who have a strong belief system and know their goal are armed with a true compass and a well-designed sextant.

Influencing people to accomplish great things requires a high level of commitment. There is considerable personal risk to the leader as well. Had John Dunworth failed at Munson Elementary School, there would have been no national news reports, no talk show invitations, no requests for speeches but probably considerable derision. Effective leaders know and accept the fact that taking risks, even for the most worthwhile purposes, has a downside. Failure is difficult to accept, regardless of how well you believe you tried. Effective leaders have the capacity to bounce back from such experiences and learn from them. It is an inspiration for all of us when someone has been successful and the world knows about it.

The *lesson* about taking a significant risk is important, as is the ability to influence others upon whom you depend for success. These two concepts are inseparable. Leaders should take stock in the lesson that "you cannot do it alone." Influencing others makes taking risks possible. Knowing the destination, the direction, and the course is what success is all about.

Chapter XIII

Reality, Response, and Reform

A Political Animal

Effective leaders are political animals. We may not like it or believe it but being politically astute is not only a desirable characteristic, it is a must. We know that decisions and actions are not done in a political and social vacuum. There is a message in the story about confronting people and ideas that deter you from achieving your goal. What we saw was an example of how a leader can be tactfully astute when and how he confronts "obstructions" to attaining the goal. Sometimes the "obstruction" can appear in the form of a regulation or mandate. In other instances, it comes in terms of an attitude or a personality. Most importantly, effective leaders know when to make a stand and when to retreat.

There were times when John Dunworth simply recognized the futility of "beating his head against a brick wall." He turned around and found another way to achieve the same objectives. Often leaders must come up with completely different ways of addressing needs. This happened frequently in the story. I hope the reader appreciates the genuine modesty exhibited by the principal regarding his contributions to the success of this effort. It should be noted that recognizing and mobilizing the resources of the local university and the nearby military base were impressive. The circumstances surrounding Munson Elementary School's situation should be understood. One might be inclined to think that when the new principal walked into the office on that first day, everyone was beating on his office door with offers of assistance and support. Although that did happen, much of what presented itself was the result of effort, nurturing, and a keen eye. Effective leaders know that opportunities do not always just present themselves. They have a keen eye, and the story tells us that one must always be watching for an opportunity. Much of what effective leaders attain in the way of support comes from being aware of the possibilities and giving others the power to think of ways to contribute. An effective leader sets the stage and watches for those who come up to play a part. We must appreciate that in this case, the principal recognized resources in places others may have overlooked. This is a gift.

Strong but Diplomatic

The problems and difficulties encountered at Munson Elementary School required strong responses and deliberate actions. Some involved working under conditions dictated by the school district and the state. Effective leaders know that although they swing a wide swath in terms of things they can do, they still live within the boundaries of the system. Effective leaders understand this. However, at times they are compelled by principle to confront bureaucracy and the expectations that are not congruent with their purposes. Effective leaders argue their positions, but do so civilly. They use their goal and supporting vision and beliefs to mount a principled offensive against whatever they feel interferes with the attainment of that goal. In the story of Munson Elementary School, the leadership engaged in this type of dialogue. The discourse of differing opinions and perspectives involved people from every constituency. This included other educators, administrators, and community members from all walks of life. Experienced leaders know what this is all about; there are those whose solution to a problem is to acquire more staff, funding, and resources. Others never reach a solution and seem happy talking about a topic forever. There are people who always seem to have a different opinion and have a difficult time joining in a consensus. The variety is endless. This is "process paralysis." The effective leader does not get upset at the diversity, but rather relishes the possibilities. We can imply from the story that the diversity of ideas was as great in Munson as in most school communities. All the more reason to appreciate the achievement.

Effective leaders understand that people impacted by change sometimes see the problem as "out there." It is difficult for people to look at the goal and begin to honestly question their own thinking and practices. In the story of Munson Elementary School, there were differences of opinion from the school district's central office staff. There were differences among the team. The strategy so well utilized in the Munson situation was to always return to the goal. What followed was a review of their own approaches and practices. They looked inward first to find solutions. There were times when the decision was the leader's alone. Effective leaders understand that there are times when even the most supportive people would rather have leaders make the decision. This often occurs when others recognize that the choices are not attractive. As in the story, effective leaders accept people for who they are and what they can do to support the goal. The lesson is thereby spelled out for us. Everyone must be considered an asset, and at Munson the sum total of the human assets turned out to be the difference.

In all fairness, Munson Elementary School circumstances were somewhat unique. The pending closure of a small rural school is not a common experience. Furthermore, having a highly publicized hiring of a former superintendent and college president to be the principal at an annual salary of one dollar is not something that many of us regularly see. One can conjecture on the thinking that took place at the school district offices about handling the new principal and the circumstances of his employment. The school district leadership had little to lose in granting John

Dunworth the opportunity to perform a small miracle. Yet, they too had lessons that are not overlooked in this story.

The Munson Elementary School plight may not be so unusual in a very important sense. It was a school that was failing to meet the needs of the community it served. As the story suggests, many, even in the larger community had resigned themselves to the fact that this little school could not be "fixed." Faith had disappeared under what appeared to be the insurmountable weight of apathy, inconsistency and "devastating reality."

Forget about the size of the enrollment. Numbers don't mean a thing here. The Munson community had lost faith in the system to save their school, and worse, until new leadership appeared, they had no hope. All district and state level educators could be asked, "Aren't there schools in your area, your county, or your state, where that same statement could be said?" So what can a school system learn from the Munson Elementary School experience?

Look for a moment at the circumstances of the Munson Elementary School situation. There may be a clue here. From what is read in the story, it appeared that in some respects Munson Elementary School was "left alone" by the district office. Not that it was isolated from the district or the central office expectations, but the circumstances that created the unique Munson Elementary School situation left the district office in a position to think about the small rural school and its community in a different way. That, in and of itself, is significant. In such an atmosphere, the district leadership was willing to consider new ideas and alternatives. The support provided by the district to Munson Elementary School was more than just tacit. No success story can occur in isolation. The strategy of providing more leeway, more options, and having more ability to make decisions at the local level was a very important aspect of the success of this story. The district gave Munson Elementary School a wide swath in which to roam, and that approach was not merely an instrument of circumstance and good fortune. Rather, the lesson is that districts may do well to look at their own practices with regard to governance.

Of course there were expectations for improved tests scores, fiscal responsibility, effective instructional strategies and practices, community support and efficacy, effective supervision of staff, and efficient allocation of resources. No one can run from these basic responsibilities. However, a considerable amount of flexibility can help people find different and hopefully better solutions. This is what happened in the story and led to the revitalization of Munson Elementary School. Examples of this were evident with the flexibility in scheduling instructional time, the process for the hiring of staff, and the careful assignment of responsibilities among the staff. In some instances the decisions that resulted from the flexible thinking might be considered controversial. There is compelling evidence in the story around multi-tasking of responsibilities. In some circumstances, multi-tasking job responsibilities are in conflict with school policy and union contract positions. Circumstance played an important role in this story with regard to this. On the other hand, the message about providing school building personnel a wide range of options is clear. We see in the story that the decisions about things like multi-tasking were not dictated by the principal, but rather were arrived at by a consensus of the people who were invested in the effort. Although not specifically stated, but surely implied, it can be assumed that there were some tasks and activities that were "abandoned" by the staff. Like the other decisions, the people of Munson Elementary School recognized that some things could not continue if they wanted to succeed. Thomas Sobel, former Commissioner of Education in New York, once said that "If we are to reform education…, then we must learn to do less better." His comments went on to include the notion that the term "less" also referred to the constraints on local school officials to make critical decisions around important issues and objectives. This implication can be extended to state education departments and school boards. The flexibility and authority to lead is an important message this story underscores.

The story highlighted the fact that teachers were making critical decisions about important issues. Empowerment was working at Munson. Self-assessment of instructional practices was conducted in open forums among professionals without the fear of retribution. We saw a climate where failure was accepted as a part of the process of learning, and reflection about one's own practices and actions was seen as a strength and not as a weakness. We saw that understanding the goal freed everyone to improve, to make the transitions of spirit and will that lead to positive change.

The lesson here is that school systems, regardless of how large or small they are, need to look at their own organizational and procedural practices and ask if these practices and parameters support or hinder learning. If learning for all is addressed, then improvement takes care of itself. Too much effort and talk about test scores is wasted when discourse about improving learning should be paramount. Assessment is a part of the improvement process, and continuous review of what has been learned, by whom, and how well must be made. However, as this story showed, real assessment is more than a test score. It should be enough to note that the assessment approach suggested in the story was likely more extensive and more authentic in its variety and validity than the results from a standardized test battery.

Those whose lives are not directly involved with the teaching and learning act may have an obscured view as to what are the best teaching practices. Experiences with schooling and concepts generated about schooling are often formed by tradition, personal experience, and romanticized reflections of a past that did not exist. Unfortunately, tradition, experiences, and romantic reflections lead to a mythological perspective about schooling, and how "good" our schools were in the past as compared to today's school.

There are some interesting myths about the "good old days" that are totally unfounded. One of these is the popular issue regarding high school dropouts. The percentage of dropouts is often quoted in the newspapers and other media, as well as suggested by many pundits who look at education, as an indicator of the failure of public schools. However, focusing on the dropout rate issue in the way it is portrayed in the media is wrongheaded. It would be false to state that there is no dropout problem in our country; the problem is not so much about the rate of dropouts, but more about the implications of dropouts. These implications have changed over time, and the implications of dropouts in our world today are the significant piece of information that is missing from the discourse.

People should be reminded how the dropout rate is computed, and more importantly, how things have changed with regard to the history of dropouts. Generally speaking, the dropout rate for most high schools is computed by comparing the enrollment of students when they are in tenth grade with the enrollment of those same students when they are scheduled to finish high school. What must be remembered is that this standard means computing of the dropout rate is relatively new. For much of this century, a large percentage of children left school before completing the eighth grade, and statistics about high school enrollments and the dropout rate in particular would naturally be skewed and misleading. Today, much of the common discourse about the dropout rate puts the average percentage of tenth grade students who do not complete the twelfth grade three years later somewhere between fifteen and twenty percent. Whatever the percentage, it is unacceptable to most educators, parents and policy makers alike. In truth, the school systems of thirty, forty and fifty years ago actually had very high dropout rates.

An essential understanding in this discussion is the fact that the economic world has changed. In the first half of this century a majority of children did not get a high school diploma. When our great grandparents and grandparents dropped out of school, they were able to move directly and easily into the economic world. Whatever schooling they received had prepared them well enough for the kind of work the economic system required. Our forefathers were hard-working and loyal. As a result of their efforts, they could earn enough to sustain a quality of life that allowed them to get married, raise children, and become upstanding members of their communities. Because of the economic realities of that time, a large percentage of our citizenry could drop out of school. Our economic system absorbed them and the social system did not penalize them.

The world has changed; no longer will a strong back and willing attitude enable people to enter the economic system smoothly or guarantee social equity with their peers. No matter how hard a person were to work today, without a quality education, it will be extremely difficult to be as successful in entering the economic system as it would had the person acquired a quality education. Moreover, the quality of education the present-day economic system demands of its citizens translates into requiring almost everyone to have the kind of education that once was reserved for the privileged few in past generations. As Samuel Betances, a professor and well-known public speaker once said, "In the future, everything from the neck down is minimum wage."

The Capacity to Reform

There are many other examples of preconditions and notions about the past that get in the way of change, progress and improvement. Effective leaders know this and address it. The leadership in the story understood and was prepared to deal with the myths of the past. Having an understanding of everything that can impact the success of an effort, and having the skill to respond is the mark of an effective leader. The concept of being able to assess, learn, adjust, gain insight and move forward toward a goal is what is referred to in the literature about school reform as *capacity*.

Phillip Schlechty, author of *Inventing Better Schools*, clarifies and defines the concept of *capacity*. He asserts that school systems, in order to sustain reform (e.g., change and improvement), must establish, nurture, and promote the system's capacity to sustain change. *Capacity* refers to the policies, procedures, practices, beliefs and goals of a system. It also encompasses the mechanisms within the system that promote and encourage the kind of work, effort, and outcomes that will support the reform. Schlechty underscores the reality that real change and improvement in the name of instructional reform takes time. The literature around the process and effects of change is clear about the relationship between significant and substantial improvement in student learning and time.

Appreciating that a successful school system must possess the capacity to reform or change is important. It was potentially problematic for Munson Elementary School. Without a systemic approach to sustained reform, success stories like this may be isolated examples of what can happen but may not happen unless the system is committed to change. School leaders at the district and state levels would do well to recognize that whether deliberately done, or the result of a series of unique circumstances, Munson Elementary School is a microcosm of how a school and a school system can change.

The empowerment of the Munson Elementary School community is a legacy of vision, tenacity, commitment and skill. The beneficiaries are the children and the heroes are all of the people who worked so hard to make the vision a reality. Or, as Dr. Dunworth succinctly says, "I just did my 'principal thing,' people got excited about the possibilities, everyone contributed 200% and presto, we were there! Well, something like that anyway..."

Bibliography

Bennis, Warren. (1989). *On Becoming a Leader.* Reading, MA: Perseus Press.

Betances, Samuel. (1992, July 13). Professor of Sociology, Northeastern Illinois University, Chicago, IL. Institute for Development of Educational Activities 25th Fellow Program Presentation. Decatur, GA: Agnes Scott College.

Blasé, Joseph and Kirby, Peggy C. (1992). *Bringing Out the Best In Teachers: What Effective Principals Do.* Newbury Park, CA: Corwin Press, Inc.

Block, Peter. (1988). *The Empowered Manager: Positive Political Skills at Work.* San Francisco, CA: Jossey-Bass Publishers.

Bridges, William. (1991). *Managing Transitions: Making the Most of Change.* Reading, MA: Perseus Press.

Coontz, Stephanie. (1992). *The Way We Never Were: American Families and the Nostalgia Trap.* New York: Basic Books, Division of Harper-Collins Publishers.

Covey, Stephen R. (1990). *The Seven Habits of Highly Effective People: Powerful Lesson on Personal Change.* New York: Fireside Books, Simon and Schuster Publishers.

James, Jennifer. (1996). *Thinking in the Future Tense: Leadership Skills for a New Age.* New York: Simon and Schuster Publishers.

McIntire, Ronald G. and Fessenden, John T. (1994). *The Self-Directed School: Empowering the Stakeholders.* New York: Scholastic, Inc.

Maxwell, John C., and Dornan, James. (1997). *Becoming a Person of Influence: How to Positively Impact the Lives of Others.* Nashville, TN: Thomas Nelson Publishers.

Patterson, Jerry L. (1993). *Leadership for Tomorrow's Schools.* Alexandria, VA.: Association for Supervision and Curriculum Development.

Schlechty, Phillip C. (1997). *Inventing Better Schools.* San Francisco, CA: Jossey-Bass Publishers.

Schlechty, Phillip C. (1990). *Schools for the Twenty-First Century: Leadership Imperatives for Educational Reform.* San Francisco, CA: Jossey-Bass Publishers.

From the File

United States Department of Education

The Secretary

September 19, 1997

Dr. John Dunworth
Principal
Munson Elementary School
11550 Munson Highway
Milton, Florida 32570

Dear Dr. Dunworth,

A Lakelander, Mrs. Gwendolyn Gallaher, sent me a clipping from *The Ledger* reporting on your new job and I just want to thank you from the bottom of my heart for your selfless devotion to the education of children.

President Clinton and I say often that it will take the involvement of all of us—parents, teachers, governments, businesses and other citizens—to achieve the educational excellence that each and every one of our nation's students deserves. Your coming forward as you have to take on the principalship of Munson Elementary (at that exorbitant salary!) to keep it from closing sends a potent message to the entire community there. They now know that the education of their children is your top priority. That is quite an inspiration, Dr. Dunworth, and I'm sure you'll find that many others will follow your lead.

Thank you again and best wishes for every success in your new undertaking.

Yours sincerely,

Richard W. Riley

Munson Elementary School
11550 Munson Hwy
Milton, Florida 32570

March 12, 1998

Memorandum to Factulty and Staff

From: Dr. D

Re: Monday Morning March 16th

UWF will be taking some video shots of Munson Elementary (classrooms, etc.) as part of a story they are developing for use on local TV. Thought I would let you know in case you want to wear your shoes, send someone to the office, put your animals out to pasture or paint your classroom pink (don't take me seriously, Mrs. Coogle).

It is "no big deal" but I wanted you to know what is going on.

MUNSON ELEMENTARY SCHOOL
11550 Munson Hwy.
Milton, Florida, 32570

June 2, 1998

Department of the Navy
Commanding Officer, VT-6
7700 USS Enterprise St., Ste. 102
Milton, Florida 32570-6153

Dear Lt. Colonel Mills:

I would be remiss if I failed to express the appreciation of all of us at Munson Elementary School as well as this community for your invaluable assistance in saving this little school. The men and women of VT-6 volunteered hundreds of hours to work with children and teachers in making this year a resounding success. They tutored individual children in math and reading and a host of subjects. They taught the meaning of patriotism, the responsibilities of freedom, the greatness of America. They exemplify the best in our country. They assisted in physical education and school events and were even involved in construction and painting and all kinds of work. Most of all they were an example and one our children will never forget.

Your encouraging and facilitating this involvement was a wonderful act of leadership that tipped the scales and gave this school new life. As you know the board of education formally acted to keep the school open and it is now, thanks to you and your personnel, one of the finest schools in Santa Rosa County.

My personal thanks and my very best wishes to your new assignment.

Sincerely yours,

John Dunworth, Principal
c.c.: Captain C.D. Hale, USN

Munson Elementary School
11550 Munson Hwy.
Milton, Florida 32570

June 2, 1998

The Board of Examiners
National Council for the Accreditation of Teacher Education
2110 Massachusetts Ave., NW
Washington, D.C. 20036-1023

I am writing briefly to share with you the exceptional relationship Munson Elementary School enjoyed this past year (1997–1998) with the College of Education at the University of West Florida. It is an unusual success story which should include the fact that 80% of the faculty at Munson are graduates of the UWF's College of Education.

Munson is a little school that was on the verge of closing—with the lowest test scores in Santa Rosa County, the highest costs, and declining enrollment. The Board of Education gave the school one year to change or be closed permanently.

College of Education students and faculty volunteered hundreds of hours of time to work with teachers as well as individual pupils. They were professional, competent, dedicated and exceptionally knowledgeable. COE faculty and graduate students volunteered their time in a host of ways from staff development to individual pupil assessment. *Munson Elementary School became in effect a professional development school of the COE.* The only major difference was the fact that the school's very survival depended on whether we could all produce. What we were about was deadly serious in the lives of these chindren and the future of this community.

To put it briefly, it worked! Headlines such as "Munson Makes the Grade" and "Students Catapult Munson Test Scores" were common. The Board of Education voted unanimously and with much praise to keep Munson open for the forseeable future. Awards were made and in recognition of the unusual and exceptional collaborative relationship that developed between the COE and Munson School, the State of Florida awarded the University and the College the state's highest honor for such service. I would urge that the model be replicated in other Colleges of Education across the country.

It is clear that the COE is committed to reality based professional programs of the highest quality and is to be commended for facilitating the marriage of top practitioners with top faculty and with the students of the University preparing to be professionals in education. This relationship will continue to the great benefit of both institutions, their students and programs, and ultimately all children who will be touched by the graduates of this outstanding and exceptional College of Education. They risked everything to help children, which is what I believe the teaching profession is all about.

Respectfully,

Jonh Dunworth, Principal

cc: Dr. Morris Marx, President, UWF
    Dr. Wesley Little, Dean, COE
    Dr. William H. Evans, Chair, Division of Teacher Education

Munson Elementary School
11550 Munson Hwy.
Milton, Florida 32570

June 2, 1998

Parents and Families:

As it is the end of school and my last day as principal I wanted to say a personal "thank you" for letting me be apart of your lives and sharing your sons and daughters for this past year.

You have reminded me of some very important lessons for which I will always be deeply grateful. One is that family, hard work, independence, resourcefulness, and determination even in the face of hardship, is what makes America great. You all have these qualities in abundance. You also reminded me that faith and caring come in many forms.

Sometimes when the complications of life press hard we do not have too much love and caring left over to share. Yet, most of you find it for your children. I often feel that the child who seeks a moment of caring for a little finger that seems to hurt, is really seeking a touch of tenderness for a little heart that hurts so much. I know you will continue to let your children know how much you love them. They love you deeply.

Thank you for your faith and support and also for your gracious wishes for the future. They have meant more than you can know. I leave Munson in the very capable hands of Mr. Johnson and the absolutely wonderful team of teachers and staff that will serve you and your children. If you give them the same support in the future you gave this year, your children will be the beneficiaries and Munson will be the finest school in Santa Rosa County.

I wish you the very best.

Respectfully yours,

John Dunworth, Principal

United States Department of Education

The Secretary

July 31, 1998

Dr. John Dunworth
Former Principal
Munson Elementary School
4300 W. Francisco Road, #18
Pensacola, Florida 32504

Dear Dr. Dunworth,

This is just a note to express my thanks and congratulations on the success of Munson Elementary School during the 1997–98 year. You should be very, very proud of all that you accomplished there in just one short year!

Thank you, too, for your offer to be of help to the Department. We'll certainly keep that in mind for future undertakings.

Yours sincerely,

Richard W. Riley

Ode to a Honda

Every day for 200 grueling days this faithful friend braved floods, fog, blistering heat and savage storms to reach children in need in the little school so far away.

Many days were beautiful but many were not.

Never once did it falter.

Never once did it let down those who depended on it to serve the children in that little school.

May it always be blessed. And may all that travel in it share that blessing—especially children—for it is their friend.

Dr. John Dunworth
The Dollar-A-Year Principal
Pensacola, Florida
Vehicle Number 1HGCD5656TA060995

Honor Roll

Munson Community Volunteers

Joe & Fiona Adams

Willie Armstrong

Kenneth Baxley

Jon & Theresa Brown

Teena Buchanan

Tim Burnham

Anthony & Kathy Cabaniss

Ricky & Sharon Cabaniss

Westel & Becky Cabaniss

Beth Cadenhead

Cynthia Campbell

Claudine Caylor

Nadja Chandler

Rakko Christie

Keith & Melody Church

Donna Cleghorn

Tony Coogle

Doris Crain

Andy Davis

A.C. & Nina Diamond

Danny Dixon

Michele Dozier

James & Sharilyn Drewry

Eddie & Karen English

Mike & Nell Ennis

Derryl & Sandy Foster

Cindy Garrett

Rhonda Gilmore

Donna Gomez

Wade & Kathy Hatten

Alice Hobbs

Doris Hoffman

Rhonda Holmes

Foy Holt

Howard & Shirley Lail

Randy & Carol Lawhorn

Robert & Doreen Lewis

Andrea & Lisa Lips

Jackie & Kathy Long

Janet McCurdy

Pat & Karen Morris

Stephen & Sandra Motsco

Tonya Nelson

Trina Odom

Rae Parrish

Marliah Pitman & Janice Pitman

Vanessa Pittman

Jamie Sanders

Kim Scott

Danny & Jinks Sexton

April Sharit

Janice Shultz

Al & Rebecca Slater

Linda Spears

Rene Temple

Pat Turner

Jennifer Watson

Sheila Watts

Michael & Susie Wolfe

Tammy Wolfe

Epilogue

The school year 1998–99 had been underway for some time when the press responded to the questions that were in the minds of many, "How is Munson Elementary School doing? Has it lost the momentum of the dramatic 1997–98 turn-around year or is it the wonderful little school everyone has come to respect and love?"

On November 9, 1998, the *Pensacola News Journal* headlines told the story in large print, "MUNSON REVELS IN SUCCESS. Enrollment, energy soar…"

Enrollment is indeed up 15% to 94 pupils—a far cry from the dismal projections for that fateful fall over one year ago. The dynamic dream team has returned in full. Mr. David Johnson is now principal. Two new teachers have been added to the team—one to replace Mr. Johnson (when he moved from the classroom to the principalship) and one to accommodate the increase in enrollment which continues to inch up weekly. Before long it will reach the magic 100 mark, a figure not seen for 15 years. With one exception the critical support team is back in force too. It is like a fine orchestra that makes beautiful music.

Of course, as in all of life, there are some sad moments too. Former school secretary Mrs. Judy Lindsey, "Mrs. Judy" to students, lost her courageous battle with cancer. Literally hundreds of former Munson students, in addition to family and personal friends, paid their last respects to this wonderful lady who befriended boys and girls at this place for over a quarter of a century. She is greatly missed.

Mr. Benny Russell, Santa Rosa County School District's superintendent and ardent supporter of Munson Elementary School, has been diagnosed with the serious blood condition myelodysplastic syndrome. He is on leave undergoing intense chemotherapy and faces a critical uphill struggle. He is in everyone's prayers.

Mrs. Debbie Marmont, the superb teacher assistant with the background in finance, was wooed back to the world of business. A great loss for Munson. To add to the distress, the position itself is now funded by the Federal government at only 50%. Flexible Ms. Cadenhead, P.E., pitched in and serves as half-time Teacher Assistant and half-time Physical Education teacher. Again, Munson survives another critical situation with grace.

New teachers were selected with great care. Mr. Johnson was thorough and knowledgeable. After 50 applications, the candidate pool was closed. It could easily have doubled, so many teachers now wanted to be part of Munson Elementary School. Not always the case in past years. Mrs. Ronja Ashworth is teaching first grade and Mrs. Tracy Dixon the fourth/fifth combination class. Both are great people and superb, dedicated teachers. And why not? For I know that Mrs. Dixon was Mr. Johnson's fourth-grade *student* more years ago than either wish to admit! Not only that, but Mrs. Ashworth and Mrs. Dixon are protégés of two of the finest principals in the entire system. Thanks to the addition of these fine teachers there are fewer combination classes, groups are relatively small and emphasis on meeting the needs of individual children is clearly in evidence.

It is obvious that Mr. Johnson has some good connections! Of course, all good principals have good connections. They work hard at it. At Christmas break the school was entirely recarpeted. New roofing, paint, instructional television and additional Internet cabling is everywhere. The old surplus room, which was hoped to become a Pre-K, has now been completely refurbished and furnished and is now a beautiful "new" kindergarten—with windows no less! Mr. Johnson says it is just a matter of time and the Pre-K will become a reality. An additional classroom, salvaged from the old storage building, is now a fine "new" resource room for special classes and for projected growth. All very impressive.

The use of volunteers at the little school continues to be a strong program. Young aviators from the U.S. Naval Air Station, Whiting Field, come on a regular basis to tutor individual children, work on landscaping projects and assist with various special P.E. activities. Parents may be seen in the hallways and workrooms working on bulletin boards, assisting with instructional materials, or listening to one child read who needs that very special encouragement and help. The College of Education at the University of West Florida donates hundreds of volunteer hours as Dr. Schmid and his students give almost every Munson child individual diagnostic tests to help teachers pinpoint areas of strengths and weaknesses.

Donated computers from the U.S. Air Force and Navy are everywhere. They will surely prove to be a pivotal link in the establishment of a computer-in-the-home program dreamed of last year. The idea was the brain child of Mrs. Rogaliner and Mr. Johnson, who are prone to say, "We can put more educational tools on the hard drive of a computer than we can ever send home in a book." I believe them!

When the 1998–99 test scores were announced in early spring it was no surprise that Munson's composite scores were higher than the preceding year. How much higher was the intriguing question. Last year they went from 44 to 59 on the Competency Test of Basic Skills (CTBS), a remarkable increase. This year they did it again, going from 59 to 70. Double digit gains two years in a row. In addition, Munson's first grade scored at the 92nd percentile, the highest school in the system for grade one. This is the second year that Munson's first grade scored highest. On the Florida Comprehensive Achievement Test (FCAT) which is administered to fourth and fifth grade pupils at the elementary level (and in other grades at the secondary level), Munson's fourth graders posted the highest gain in reading in the system ranking them next to the top of all fourth graders in the county.

The euphoria surrounding these accomplishments must always be balanced by the reality that academic malnutrition is not overcome easily or quickly. It is rooted in the child's total environment and can begin even before birth. Some Munson children continue to struggle with their lessons but they also continue to progress, even if slowly. If these children are judged by some arbitrary criteria they may still fall short of the mark. However, their perseverance is both admirable and reassuring. They do not give up and neither do their teachers.

Clearly, children are happy, are learning, are challenged and continue to show steady progress. Parents know Munson is a good school—parents always know. Every day and especially on an occasional visit, I am so very proud to be a part of this beautiful place. You see, my portrait hangs in the hallway. For a year, I went to school here.

As Munson Elementary principal David Johnson emphasizes, "One important lesson of Munson shouldn't be lost on any reader. Much has been written and said in recent years about the condition of public education in America. Munson stands today as an example of what can occur in any school when people care. It took much hard work on the part of many people but it took one person to take the lead in giving of himself to make it occur.

"There's a school, just down the road from where you live, that needs your help. You may not be a Dr. John Dunworth. You may be a parent, or a grandparent. You may be a community member with no children enrolled, or you may be a college student, or perhaps a school board member. Frankly, it does not matter who you are. It matters what you do.

"What impact would it have if tomorrow you walked into the principal's office and asked what could you do to help? Maybe you could give an hour every once in a while to listen to a child read, or check some papers for a tired teacher. Perhaps you could assist the custodial staff with some landscaping project or paint some bookcases for the library. What would it say to the teachers, to the community, and especially to the youngsters if they saw you actively involved, helping out, being a part of the solution?

"It can happen. You can make it happen. Your community can have one of the best schools in America. Munson, Florida, already does. All it takes is one person who really cares and believes it is possible."

In Memoriam

Benny Russell

1944–1999